MISSILE AND ARTILLERY ENGAGEMENTS PRE 1914

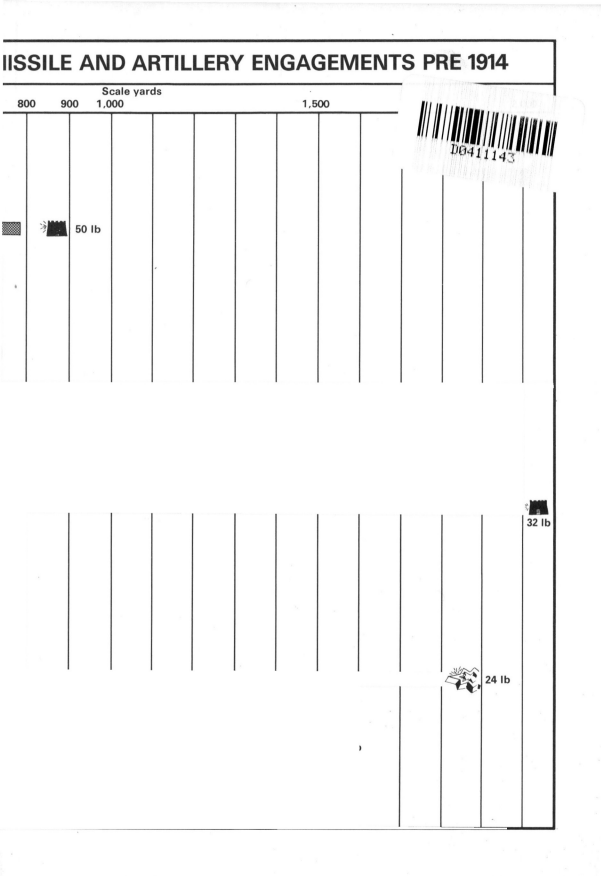

Scale yards

800   900   1,000   1,500

50 lb

32 lb

24 lb

THE **GUINNESS** HISTORY OF
Land Warfare

THE **GUINNESS** HISTORY OF
Land Warfare

by Kenneth Macksey

with special maps and diagrams drawn by Michael Haine

GUINNESS SUPERLATIVES LIMITED

2 CECIL COURT, LONDON ROAD, ENFIELD, MIDDLESEX

© 1973 Guinness Superlatives Limited

Published in Great Britain by
Guinness Superlatives Limited, 2 Cecil Court,
London Road, Enfield, Middlesex

SBN 900424 20 6

Set in Monophoto Baskerville Series 169,
printed and bound in Great Britain by
Jarrold and Sons Limited, Norwich

Contents

Introduction

For biological as well as topographical and technical reasons **the first outbreaks of fighting** had to take place on land, generations before men constructed the first rudimentary boats and long before they learnt to fly. War, whatever conscience teaches, is a fundamental of life, representing the ultimate expression of man's interminable struggle for food and space in addition to his yearning for security, power and self-justification. Because war is a dynamic, extremist activity it lends itself to description by means of the dramatic—by the eulogisation of superlative feats; by the creation of an heroic image. The essence of victory in battle is the commitment of whole-hearted endeavour, the winner he who throws predominant force into the struggle and, by superior numbers, weapon power or prowess, overcomes a weaker or inept opponent. Yet although feats are readily propagated and frequently exaggerated into legend, hard facts are more difficult to ascertain. The temptation to extol deeds of gallantry, which enhance or guard national or personal prestige, is liable to earn precedence over the historian's requirements for objective definition. The justification of war, for political or personal purposes, is frequently the glorification of a lie, the purveying of distortions carried forward in the guise of historic fact. A victor's tale of battle is unlikely to coincide with that of the defeated. The unravelling of the facts about war is a feat in itself.

Historic events are the outcome of new ideas impinging upon existing circumstances. The genesis of ideas may be discovered either in surviving documents, memories of conversations or in pictorial form. However, whereas there is often a chance that political archives have been generated in fairly cool surroundings, fighting is rarely accurately recorded since frightened men in the heat of combat only occasionally recall their experiences with accuracy. The historian has to arrive close to the facts by sifting the conflicting evidence, removing the chaff of hearsay and then evaluating the seed of truth that remains. There comes a point, however, from which he can go no further and, with the story incomplete, he reverts to the study of what Alfred Burne used to call Inherent Military Probability (I.M.P.)— an assessment of the common-sense courses of action. Even so, in the final analysis, it is possible only to present a simplified compression of events which, had they been described in full, would be so verbose as to be indigestible.

Compression is achieved in this book by concentrating upon those events which demonstrate the crucial factors and phases that conditioned the art of land warfare throughout the ages. Secondary consideration is given to those battles which changed political history. This, therefore, is not a definitive history of war but a tabulation of its quintessence.

Let it be assumed that an important reason for embarking upon war is to take advantage over an opponent: let us accept, too, the maxim that war is the implementation of political means by force. Of course the aim of combatants worthy of survival has always been the development of methods which are superior to those of their enemies. The methods themselves, however, are by no means dependent upon what a fighting man may desire but upon the resources provided. Throughout the measureless years of prehistory, for example, man must have wished often for weapons that were superior to those made of flint. Yet it was not until immensely late in time—a mere 3,400 years ago, approximately in the year 1400 BC—that **bronze was first discovered**, and used for weapons with a marked upgrading of man's ability to attack and defend. Though the development of bronze manufacture was by no means at the beginning of man's intensive search for knowledge (**the first cuneiform writing** dates from about 3200 BC and marks a turning-point in the systematic recording and transmission of information) it heralds the beginning of significantly faster improvements in his technical expertise by the creation and adaptation of new materials. Iron-making was known to the Egyptians somewhere about 3000 BC, but seems not to have been adapted to general weapons use until 800 BC, though there may have been a few such instruments available not long after the advent of bronze. The fact of the matter is that the subsequent pace of improvement was continuous and accelerating. The accidental manufacture of steel as a by-product of iron-making may have occurred in the fourteenth century AD—perhaps even earlier—but in small quantities only. Nevertheless, all manner of alloys were being produced by the experimental search to improve metallic strength in relation to savings in weight. Thus, when Henry Bessemer introduced the mass-production of steel in 1856, there already existed a store of knowledge from previous research and development which could be adapted to exploit the avalanche of new materials that revolutionised, within a few generations, all manner of manufacturing processes associated with weapon technology.

At the root of this rapid advance in knowledge and technology, of course, lay the burgeoning art of mass communication—the increase in the numbers of men who could read, write and reason from the proliferation of books produced by the intellectual minority. The invention of mechanical printing in the fifteenth century vastly expanded dissemination—yet Gutenberg's development of the **first engraving process** was dependent upon **the discovery** of a new alloy comprising lead, tin and antimony. However it is not to be suggested that man's sudden desire for knowledge lay waiting only for the metallurgist to find new materials to improve upon stone, wood and hide. Man was for ever trying to burst beyond the constrictions imposed by natural barriers—endeavouring to move into new territory, both intellectual and geographical, across mountains and desert, through forests and down rivers, and then across the seas—dreaming always of his greatest ambition—to fly. Each outward surge was, inevitably, a venture in conquest which almost invariably caused friction with neighbours that led to war. Whatever the outcome of each surge or migration, land communications were being developed, waterways cleared, roads constructed and transport systems rationalised.

It was in the eighteenth century that the brakes upon advancement were most suddenly released, and produced both the wish and freedom to make changes in society, technology and war-making. It was then that gunpowder weapons reached a significant level of reliable performance; then that machinery, driven by steam, gave impetus to the Industrial Revolution which made possible a proliferation of all manner of war material; then that the fall in death-rate, due to better health precautions, created a growing reservoir of manpower. In keeping with this vast output in manpower and material it became imperative to make radical changes in basic organisations so that politicians and soldiers could retain control of swarming individuals. Telegraphic and, later, radio communication offered the means to centralise command, but this divorced leaders from the led and if, in this separation, the ethics of freedom and humanity did not suffer undefended, it can hardly be claimed that they emerged unscathed. The fact remains that whereas, prior to the Industrial Revolution, military organisation tended to concentrate, in the main, upon enhancing the combat value of small bands and armies who 'lived off' the country in which they fought, in the age of the *levée en masse* the emphasis fell upon improvement of arrangements for supply and movement to and from battles. Thus emerged the technique now known as "logistics". Battles, though justifiably, because of their drama and instant effect, attracting the brilliant glare of publicity, became minute "factors of effort" by comparison with the basic administrative effort designed to support pre-combat, strategic manoeuvres.

The meteoric expansion of war's scope in the late nineteenth and early twentieth centuries, in the course of two gigantic world-wide conflicts, in no way completes the tale. It can be claimed that land warfare, though to this day it absorbs the highest proportion of military manpower in actual physical combat, no longer predominates. In incidence of decision it may be subordinated to what takes place at sea and, of vital significance, in the air. This is as debatable as the suggestion that, though technology made its first contribution to land weapons, its greatest outpourings have since been given, in order of time and quantity, to naval and air warfare. Within the past three decades the grapple of armies has been conditioned, or even delayed, by essential preliminary action on the sea and, most of all, in the air. Indeed the air weapon has intervened so effectively in the land battle, not only against the regular armies but against their sources of support in the homelands which supply them, that major land campaigns are difficult to contemplate in the absence of air superiority.

Nevertheless, generals persist, by insidious ways of their own, to steer an independent course. Since 1945, of course, they have been limited in scope by political inhibitions under threat of the nuclear holocaust. Nobody dares risk total war. As a result the forces of total war, which naval and air weapons chiefly represent, have been neutralised. There has arrived a de-escalation in destructive force by weapons of massed destruction in favour of limited, basic weapons—the sophisticated, modern equivalent of the axes, spears, bows and arrows of prehistoric man which selectively kill only a few individuals. The essential techniques of combat instinctively adopted by the earliest fighting men persist. For the most part the process of war-making has returned to the land, the art of war reduced to combat between men and licensed by the most advanced weapons of technology which are kept threateningly in reserve. This interminable so-called "limited land warfare", which infests our fundamental environment, remains the expression of man's hereditary habit of physical combat. The alternative is total destruction.

Acknowledgements

The author and publisher wish to thank the many individuals and organisations who gave generous assistance during the preparation of this book and also to those who gave permission to reproduce material in their copyright. The undermentioned are the major contributors:

Archaeological Museum, Istanbul
Armor, Washington, D.C., U.S.A.
H.Q. Army Aviation Centre,
   Middle Wallop
Bildsarchiv der Österreichischen
   Nationalbibliothek, Vienna
British Museum, London
Department of the Army, Washington, D.C.,
   U.S.A.
Das Deutsche Soldatenbuch
Encyclopedia Britannica
Her Majesty's Stationery Office, London
Kriegsarchiv, Vienna
Imperial War Museum, London
Mansell Collection, London
Ministry of Defence (Army), London
   (in particular the Library Staff)

Museum of Archaeology, Ankara
National Archives and Records Service,
   Washington, D.C., U.S.A.
National Army Museum, London
National Museum, Stockholm
Dr. K. Peball
Radio Times Hulton Library, London
Royal School of Artillery, Larkhill
Royal Armoured Corps Centre,
   Bovington Camp
Royal Armoured Corps Tank Museum,
   Bovington Camp
Soldier, London
Turkish Military Museum, Istanbul
Vardali Co., Istanbul
Victoria and Albert Museum, London
Major S. J. Williams

Paintings by Gerald Embleton

SECTION I
The Roots of Strife
—from primitive man to the dawn of civilisation

Nobody can date, with accuracy, the emergence of man as the dominant creature upon earth. Cave drawings depict him in pursuit of beasts, though it can be said with confidence that it was not an entirely one-sided contest. From early drawings and archaeological discoveries it has been shown that Palaeolithic man was armed with weapons constructed almost entirely of primary materials—of stone and wood. It is also known that he used animal by-products as means of protection, by taking hide, for example, as body armour or for shields. In other words, no matter how primitive the equipment may have been, fighting men from the outset developed combat techniques which remain basic to the art of war today.

Man is practically unique among the animal species in that he alone has a disposition towards self-destruction. A few rodents possess this habit but it is doubtful if they make such a virtue of the practice as man does, and certain that they cannot so lavishly publicise their fascination with the subject.

The emotive factor in fighting is that of a persuasive and, if possible, valid cause—those reasons which seem strong enough to urge one person to injure or kill another. The origins of aggression were almost certainly those of pure survival. In time of famine one man might try to steal from another and provoke a scuffle which would enlarge into a skirmish between bands or tribes whose people had learnt to live in groups for self-protection or reasons of economy. The struggle for survival engendered pugnacity and promoted acquisitive urges that sought not only feeding-grounds but also terrain suitable to defence. For example, one can imagine conflict between gangs for some highly desirable cave which contained a spring and which happened to be situated in a readily defensible position adjacent to a prolific hunting- or grazing-ground. Struggles such as these would require collaboration between individuals and, therefore, a demand for leaders. There would be further internal competition for the power that leadership conferred and thus additional conflict. Women would become involved—perhaps in defence of their young and almost certainly as slave or prize for the victor. This is not the place to explore the deep psycho-analytical reasons for man engaging in combat. The facts remain that he is much more addicted to struggle than peace, and that battle is most commonly provoked by acquisitive motives rather than those of ideology. But one acquisitive motive cannot be ignored—the acquisition of glory stemming from the sheer love of a fight that is inherent in people whether for tribal or personal reasons. It is a motive still present in civilised people, readily observed in primitive tribes as well as in football crowds and the like.

The primary aim of a fighter is to give blows either for an aggressive purpose or as an integral part of a defensive gesture. Violence in its earliest form must have been actuated by striking with the arms, legs or head or by crushing or strangulation.

Axe-heads and arrow-tips

A variety of Stone Age weapons

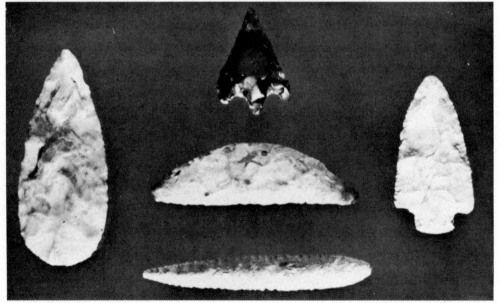

The first weapons would have been lumps of stone either hand held or thrown—introducing a preference to fight at the longest range possible to evade enemy retribution. Eventually pieces of sharpened stone would be attached to wooden shafts by means of leather thongs to make axes that allowed greater force to be exerted. But with such feeble weapons it would be preferable to catch an enemy unawares, attacking him by surprise from the side or from behind.

The instinctive reaction to a blow is evasion. A combatant may perhaps try to avoid combat altogether, either by flight or hiding. If compelled to fight he may resort to ducking and dodging his enemies' blows, either in the hope of exhausting the opponent or creating an opportunity to land some decisive blows of his own. In effect he practises the basic arts of mobility by employing agility and guile.

The first material attempt to nullify blows was the creation of armour as a means of deflection. Primitive man wore skins both as protection against cold as well as hostile blows. In due course he took to attaching the skins to wooden frames and carrying them as a shield, turning himself into an armoured fighting animal capable of giving as well as receiving blows while yet retaining a measure of mobility. The presence of such a combination itself instigated the next advances in combat technique—redoubled efforts to catch the enemy by surprise, from flank, rear or above, and the motivation to combine superior numbers of poorer more cheaply equipped men in concerted action against the expensively equipped, stronger individual. Thus was created, at the latest in the fourth millennium (though probably much earlier), the eternal contest between giant and dwarf, and the quest to produce a universal fighting man or machine.

The first pictorial evidence of a military organisation and its armament is to be found on the celebrated Standard of Ur, dating from 3500 BC, where warriors are shown armed with clubs, axes and spears. Dress appears to be fairly uniform and of a protective nature, perhaps of leather. For the first time in history fighting vehicles are on display—carts with leather panels fitted like shields to a wooden frame, each transported on four wheels made of two segments and drawn by four onagers. A semblance of organisation can be detected as well as an indication that humanitarianism was practised. Prisoners are held under escort, most uncommon then and for centuries to come since rules of war based on mercy were practically unconsidered. Yet if these prisoners had been taken only for ransom or hostage, that at least was in mitigation of massacre.

The first weapon designed to engage an enemy beyond arm's length was the sling to fling a stone (with quite considerable accuracy and velocity in the hands of an expert) much further than a simple hand throw. Slings remained an individual's weapon for centuries. Only later were they developed into far larger, missile-throwing devices that demanded a crew to operate them. **The most famous shot from a sling** is that thrown by David to slay Goliath—a Biblical story which, like so many of the kind, remains apocryphal.

The most important long-range weapon to appear concurrent with the Late Stone Age was the bow. Made of wood (often yew) its arrows were tipped by stone (bronze and iron, in due course). **The first drawings of bows** appear in cave-paintings in Spain and are probably Neolithic. **The best contemporary illustrations of early bows** are to be found in bas-reliefs depicting the Assyrian armies which flourished prior to 1000 BC. The archers are shown on foot, on horseback or mounted in chariots. The bow is drawn to the full stretch of the arm. Range, commensurate with tolerable accuracy and penetration, was probably in the region of 50 yd (45 m). Used in mass, with a fast rate of delivery in the hands of trained men, archery fire could saturate part of the battlefield killing or incapacitating individuals and breaking up enemy formations as they grouped closely for combined action.

The first attempts to obtain military advantage by the use of natural terrain will have been the occasion when a man in action sought advantage by climbing on to a piece of ground slightly above that occupied by his opponent or took post at a defile—such as a log crossing a swiftly flowing stream—in order to reduce the number of enemy actually opposed to him. From this beginning man began to make hilltop camps clear of forest, to strengthen them with ditches so that the enemy was compelled to make his assault under the disadvantage of climbing from below where he was most vulnerable to missiles hurled from above. Where hilltops were not to be found fortified camps would be built in, for example, the bend of a river, on a peninsula or upon an island surrounded by a wooden stockade. These, in due course, might be extended and strengthened by earthworks and finally by high stone walls.

The earliest known example of a fortified city is Ur of the Chaldees, the walls of which date from somewhere about 2500 BC—although that is not to claim that they were first of their kind. The earliest ruins of Troy may be somewhat older, for example. Ur's walls were about 23 ft (7 m) thick at the base and had towers at intervals of 140 ft (42 m), often as additional protection at vulnerable points such as gateways. There was a moat, but there is no positive evidence of its depth or of the wall's height.

Formidable improvements upon the Ur pattern were constructed by the Assyrians after 1000 BC—edifices of immense height and thickness (80 ft (25 m) in some cases) defended by complex overlooking towers and interconnected parapets so that reinforcements could be moved swiftly from one threatened point to another. Inner and outer walls also were introduced so that enemy penetrations might be localised and key points afforded double protection. These extra precautions were devised as counter to the greatly improved siege-engines which threatened the earlier forts—mobile fighting towers with shielded sides to carry warriors close to the wall's top level to engage defenders with equality; covered battering-rams to beat down gates and loosen stones while giving a measure of protection to the crews.

The first prehistoric occasion in which an element was used as a weapon would have been when a fire was lit to burn people out of their abode; or thick smoke generated to fill a cave and compel the occupants to leave; or a river's course diverted across land occupied by a community. These were the forerunners of boiling oil poured from battlements on to assailants milling about below, and of chemical weapons which were to appear at a much later date in history.

The first occasion upon which someone tried to frighten an opponent into surrender was the first example of psychological warfare. There was much to be said in favour of this method if the outcome was a guaranteed reduction in slaying by a lowering of tempers. That this was not always the case is made plain by a famous Biblical example of psychological warfare. When the walls of Jericho fell down, after seven days' trumpet playing round the city's perimeter and a single great shout by the people, it states: "And they utterly destroyed all that was in the city . . . with the edge of the sword. . . . And they burnt the city with fire, and all that was therein: only the silver and the gold and the vessels of brass and of iron, they put into the treasury of the house of the Lord." This extract from Joshua presents the epitome of war-making of the period about 1451 BC. Accepting that the Old Testament is of doubtful historic truth, the action at Jericho is authentic, emphasising an understanding of terror as an important factor in the winning of battles and of plunder as the goal.

The first recorded examples of major population migrations and conquest date from about the year 2000 BC when a vast outward movement of tribes took place from central Asia. These tribes were what is known as Indo-Europeans, impelled upon their journeys, it seems likely, by a pressing need to find fresh grazing for their herds and horses. Over a period of several hundred years they moved westward into Europe to become the forebears of today's population; south-west and southward into the Middle East, to project dominance over the indigenous tribes (such as the Assyrians) and, most important of all, somewhere about 1700 BC, into Egypt. They also moved south-eastward into the Indian subcontinent to inject an Aryan content and perhaps eastward into China along the Yellow River Valley. The tribes were variously named and of different origin, but their technology and military techniques were very similar. Armed with bronze-tipped

Hittite war chariot of 900 BC

weapons, mounted on horses or fast chariots of lightweight construction, they overcame less well-armed peoples, it seems, by the imposition in war of a warrior élite. Permanently established regular armies were probably unknown. Each populace provided a militia surrounding and led by a small aristocracy who rose to prominence because of their prowess and wealth. Only a strong man could win and retain wealth in days when violence was unchecked by humanitarian diplomacy. Only a wealthy man could afford the essential weapons to maintain his predominance in combat—that is, the most expensive bronze or iron weapons, the highly prized chariots and the horses upon which his vastly superior mobility was founded.

The best established records of the progress of invasion are to be found in the Middle East. Asia Minor fell to the Hittites after 2000 BC, and the Hurrians moved into Mesopotamia between 1700 and 1600 BC. At about the same time the outward surge rolled into Palestine which was ruled, at that time, by Egypt.

The first known example of a campaign waged by chariots took place when a tribe called the Hyksos (a Semitic people sometimes known as "the Shepherd Kings") invaded Egypt in 1680 BC. The Hyksos were formidable warriors whose organisation and methods were far superior to those of the Egyptian militia led by the Pharaohs whose power was then approaching its nadir, after a prolonged (but typical) succession of internal disorders, and whose pursuits tended to be peaceful rather than warlike. The Hyksos utterly defeated and proceeded to suppress a disunited, passive race. At the same time they introduced their horses, chariots and war techniques to Egypt. At once the Egyptians copied what they saw—the perfectly normal defensive reaction of a baffled people whose short-term needs cannot be supplied quickly enough by genuine innovation.

The first identified example of a regular army comes to notice as a result of the Egyptian counter-attack against the Hyksos in 1600 BC. The key to complete Egyptian success was the establishment of strong central government under Amosis and his insistence upon creating a fighting force of integrated weapons—an all-arms combination. He merged his mobile chariot arm with foot-soldiers supported by archers—the whole organisation trained to act in concert and in support of each other in battle. Thus **he was among the first to begin the systematic suppression of individuality as an essential part of war.** There are no records of specific battles fought by Amosis. All that is known is that he created the forces which later expanded Egyptian conquest to the banks of the Euphrates somewhere about 1500 BC—a great feat of conquest in itself against warrior opponents, but confirmation, above all, that unity is might and disunity a fatal attraction for predatory men.

The first battle known in detail to history took place at Megiddo in 1479 BC as part of the reconquest of Palestine by the Egyptians whose army at this time numbered 10,000 and was under the command of Thutmose III. The campaign was itself a classic, a model in form despite its detailed imperfections. For a start the Hyksos leader, the King of Kadesh, who had raised a revolt in Syria and north Palestine, seems to have underrated his young Egyptian opponent. He was strategically surprised when the Egyptian Army, supplied by the fleet on its coastal flank, concentrated rapidly near Gaza, made a swift march northward to Yemma, and put itself within striking distance

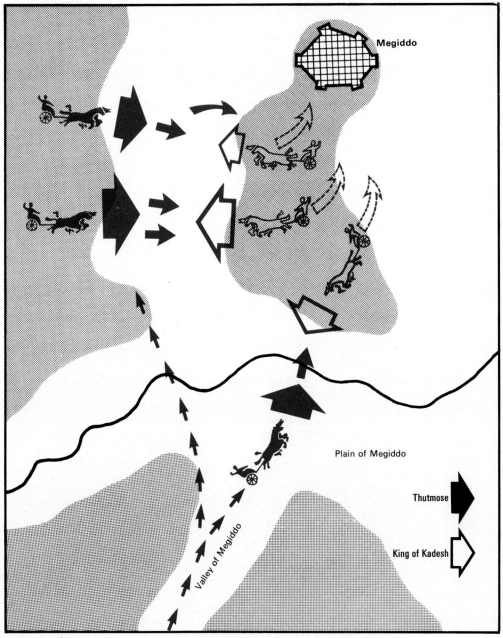

Megiddo—the first recorded battle

of the fortified town of Megiddo which was the Hyksos centre of administration and resistance. Both sides were equipped with numerous chariots —some 1,000 with the Hyksos alone—but it would seem that the Egyptians were not only better armed but also of superior morale. At any rate, their desire to attack was immense. The Hyksos held high ground to the south and west of Megiddo. The Egyptians approached from the south,

seeking to engage every Hyksos formation head-on, but also side-stepping
to the north in order to overlap the Hyksos right flank and thus threaten
Megiddo and the retreat to its gates. It was against this weaker flank that
Thutmose threw his greatest strength, to open a breach, spread confusion
to the left and engulf the Kadesh King's army in panic—driving them in a
race for safety to Megiddo where the garrison had also taken fright and
prematurely locked the gates in their face. Those who escaped by being
pulled up the walls were already partly disarmed and wholly immobilised
without their chariots. Indeed, had the Egyptians immediately exploited
their initial triumph they might well have entered the city on the crest of
success and subdued it without siege. However, an army without an internal communication system once launched into battle is almost powerless
to change its line of advance without a prolonged halt for reorganisation.
Moreover the Egyptians found themselves deep in pillage—some 924
abandoned enemy chariots, good weapons, 2,238 fine horses, treasure and
the rich trappings of an army which yielded 200 suits of bronze scaled
armour. That the ensuing siege was of short duration (bringing to an end
this phase of operations which heralded the zenith of Egyptian influence)
owed nothing to a fragile discipline which broke under the temptation of
plunder.

   Though Thutmose achieved victory at Megiddo by direct assault (as
was the normal practice of his day) he did not overlook the effects of flank
pressure. It cannot have been entirely by accident that he directed his
attack against the enemy's weakest point. This indicates, however, that he
was well supplied with information about the ground and his enemy's
disposition. How else could he have directed his advance and attack with
such accuracy?

**The first army state was that of Assyria, its rise and fall the best early example of military
cyclics**, linked to the evolution of an advanced civilisation and technical
prowess. Assyria, in conjunction with, but finally absorbing Babylonia,
battled for survival in the front line against the invasions from inner Asia,
and strove after the year 2000 BC, to balance her allocation of manpower
between food production and frontier protection. From the purely military aspect she was for ever at disadvantage since there was nowhere upon
which to base a strong, natural fortification—no pronounced area of high
ground and no readily defensible waterways, even though the Tigris and
Euphrates intersected or adjoined her territory. Hence artificial fortifications were mandatory and it was usually a case of fight or die with everything to win and nothing to lose—the education of a people in violence.
The prowess of the Assyrian armies can be gauged from the fact that they
managed enormously to expand their territory and survive virtually
intact (though with many crises and set-backs) for nearly 1,500 years
before being overcome by the Medes—the next powerful group to
emerge from the north-east in 612 BC.

The overwhelming technical advantage enjoyed by the Assyrians was the more extensive (and
practically exclusive) availability of iron to them. The Assyrians were **the
first military power to use iron-tipped weapons and armour** on a
large scale.

   The greatest Assyrian asset was the gift of strong leadership at critical
moments. From Tiglath-pileser I, who led the most extensive expansion
between 1116 and 1093 BC, to Tiglath-pileser III, who established firm
control between the Tigris and Egypt, there ruled a succession of men who
combined autocratic power with military genius.

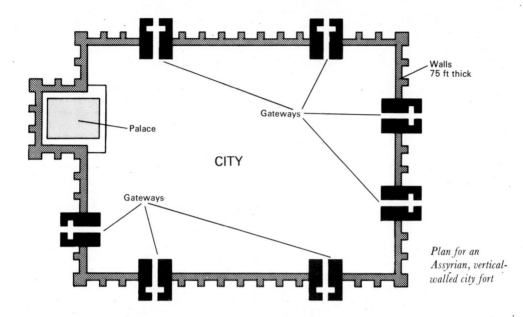

Walls
75 ft thick

Gateways

Palace

CITY

Gateways

*Plan for an
Assyrian, vertical-
walled city fort*

The first well-organised siege train was to be found in the Assyrian Army. It comprised fighting towers (their first use is recorded at Jerusalem in 600 BC) as well as missile-throwing devices (probably based on the sling) and hand-propelled, armoured vehicles to move close beneath enemy walls. Fire was frequently employed—projected by flaming arrows over the walls of a beleaguered city or directed against enemy fighting towers and machines, whose wicker-work and wooden components were vulnerable to this kind of attack. For crossing rivers, inflated goat-skins (possibly stuffed with chaff) would be attached to chariots and used for flotation. Yet by no means all these devices, with their apparent modern character, were purely Assyrian inventions. Ideas and methods were collected throughout their Empire, exploited and improved as the fruits of conquest.

The key to Assyrian success may well have been a **superior system of communication** in that they used a well-developed writing—which is one reason why so much is known about them today. Ink was often being used on leather, for example, in addition to the older methods of inscription on stone or wood. Thus orders could be transmitted with reasonable reliability and ease while systems and methods could be recorded in perpetuity.

The first recorded example of a drilled integration of fighting elements comes from the Assyrians. The Royal bodyguard, usually mounted on horses or chariots, formed an élite core bracing the massed militia and conscripts (many of whom were prisoners of war) who mounted guard and were pawns in battle. But since the horsemen rode bareback they as often as not had to dismount to fire their arrows with accuracy or use their swords. The charioteers, on the other hand, could fire their weapons from a stable platform which provided the basic vehicle for a two-man team of archer and shield-bearer—the latter given the task of driver and escort to the archer who was, after all, the vital, long-range 'striker' in the army. Fundamentally, therefore, the Assyrian Army consisted of mounted infantry who fought in relatively loose formations which depended upon individual prowess rather than tight, corporate discipline to achieve its main hitting power. Hence it was relatively easy for chariots to charge in and about an enemy formation of similar composition without being brought to a halt and thus losing the protection afforded by mobility.

The most significant attribute of the Assyrian reign of supremacy was a basic high civilisation thriving alongside the unrivalled brutality of its war-making methods. After the Egyptians the Assyrians acquired the finest culture, though by contrast, the Egyptians were not so conspicuously martial. Yet the Assyrians encouraged many distinguished art forms in conjunction with their military technology—sculpture, wall-paintings, architecture, rich clothing and ornamentation, music and literature—even cosmetics. They imported and looted much of this, but they were, at least, highly appreciative and discriminatory of the best things in life besides being connoisseurs of death. The phenomenon is by no means unique in history. A strong culture prospered alongside a military hierarchy which perpetrated large-scale genocide and destruction. Ideas and the integration of methods into systems were the dividends of a vital, cohesive leadership which flourished under the spur of dire necessity. Armed force created wealth which simplified the accumulation of more wealth. The priorities were judged firmly in the Army's favour: they were the last to suffer from shortages in manpower or material. Nearly all the scarce iron supply went to them.

The rapid decline of the Assyrian Empire was the product of its own opulence, sprawling size and internal divisions. The rot may well have begun about 684 BC, when the Army suffered a succession of defeats as well as a severe depletion in strength of Palestine—possibly as a result of malaria and thus becoming **one of the first recorded examples of collapse through a breakdown in health**. Revolt followed as innumerable deities raised their standards in far-flung parts of the Empire, though sometimes close to home. Each uprising was put down by vigorous and pitiless force, but sapped the strength of the Army and compelled it to dilute its strength with numerous garrisons of foreign troops spread throughout a vast terrain. Contraction towards the centre began somewhere about 630, internecine struggles abounded among the ruling hierarchy and split the leadership. In 626 came a Babylonian revolt led by Nabopolassar who received assistance from the neighbouring Medes. In 612 an alliance of dissident forces conquered the Assyrian capital of Nineveh, finally destroying the Army—with the exception of those elements which continued desultory guerilla warfare for a couple more years in outlying districts. The end of this great Empire merely announced the entrance of its successor—that of the Medes and Persians whose battle techniques were not so very different to those of the Assyrians they had deposed— the point being that the development of land warfare does not change rapidly overnight but gradually in response to changes in technology which, contrary to journalistic impression, do not proceed from breakthrough to breakthrough but by a progressive acquisition of knowledge confirmed by trial and experiment.

One of the most important events in connection with future warfare took place in 621 BC as the Assyrian Empire moved towards its close. An Athenian called Draco passed a series of repressive laws which, above all else in their drastic (or Draconian) repression, placed the people in slavery, depriving them of justice and individual freedom. Athens was but a city state within Greece, the populace of which, it will be remembered, was formed very largely out of earlier migrations from the East. Thus Greece, as a nation, did not then exist but comprised a loose collection of warring tribes ensconced in mountainous hideouts, pursuing interminable guerilla and civil warfare in isolation from the mainstream of Middle East development. The nature of the terrain militated against the sweep of great equine armies such as drove across the undulations of the Middle East. Mountainous country was better suited to foot soldiers supported by horsemen and chariots. Yet since the infantry had sometimes to enter the plains and join in battle with the omnipotent mobile armies, they perforce, developed special tactics, formations and weapons. The Grecian armies, however, were of little importance at the time of Draco's laws. Even **the most powerful Grecian military state**, Sparta, had only local influence within the peninsula. The initial importance of the Draconian laws, therefore, was as an agent of discontent and a spur to a fight for so-called "liberty" which was won when Solon succeeded in repealing the laws, creating a much more liberal code and forming a Council of Four Hundred drawn from the four tribes of Attica. From this moment onward Greece tended towards loose homogeneity and began to look outward as a nation, making wider and close contact with the outside world through maritime trade. Thus their travellers acquired news and knowledge of other peoples and methods which they adapted, where appropriate, to their own conditions.

The most militaristic of all the Greek city states—and definitive of the type—was Sparta. Each man was from birth a recruit to the Army—and destroyed in childhood if reckoned a weakling: each woman was dedicated to breeding warriors. The Spartans were devoted to fighting—the terms of the Peloponnesian League, of which they were founders, stating that, though each member was bound to come to the others assistance in case of external attack, they were perfectly free to carry on wars against each other. The Spartans contributed the best land forces to Greece when the other tribes were turning towards naval war as protection of their maritime trade. Thus, when the time came for landward operations, the Spartans were expected to take the lead. They actually resented intrusion in the art by those they considered their inferiors. Sparta, in fact, provided the élite, while the remaining Grecian city states contributed the mass—but a mass that used its intellect in the spirit of freedom was not nearly so inflexible as the one employed by the Assyrians and their conquerors.

(above) The first recorded picture of an army—the Standard of Ur from 3500 BC

(below) Early siege warfare—Assyrian assault team of a mobile battering-ram and fighting tower supported by archers
River-crossing in the Assyrian style—men with flotation bags, surrounded by archers

SECTION II
The Millennium of Organisation
600 BC–AD 400

Between 600 BC and AD 400 occurred the crystallisation of organised warfare, a turbulent period distinguished by the gradual but accelerating incorporation of individualists into standard military formations commanded by leaders imbued with a code of strategic and tactical doctrine. Empires rose and fell with cyclic inevitability, though their periods of bloom and decay were of ever shorter duration in accord with the swifter march of progress. Weapon systems were improved though the balance between striking power, protection and mobility swayed only marginally to and fro, the alternating reaction of conflicting techniques and technologies competing, one against another, with each upgrading of materials—but, again, within an ever closer time frame as the pace of technical development increased. This is known because historians began to keep records and from their publications could come a systematic analysis of the art of war. Indeed, at the beginning of the millennium appeared **the first great treatise on war**—by a Chinaman, Sun Tzu—and at the end one of the most influential —*De Re Militari* by the Roman Vegetius.

The oldest known work on military philosophy—the *Art of War*—was written by Sun Tzu somewhere about 500 BC. It is rated among the greatest military classics of all though its influence was first felt only in the Far East—in the lands now known as China and Japan. China, in all its vastness, was at this time in a state of fractionalisation in the aftermath of the great days of unification under the first Shan (1523–1027 BC) and Chou (1027–600 BC) Dynasties. Chinese methods and weapon systems were comparable with those of the

Middle East and therefore tactics were also alike. It is possible that command and control in battle was better implemented in China because signals were passed by drums, though it is certain that some arrangements of instant communication was also employed by Middle Eastern armies. Sun Tzu defined the elements of war with original precision, pointing to an essential need for accord between ruler and people, the binding rules of strategy, the vital necessity for unified command under a strong and wise commander and the demands of method and discipline—that is, the marshalling of any army into functional subdivisions, the gradations of rank among the officers, the maintenance of roads by which supplies may reach the army, and the control of military expenditure.

The first great captain in the sense of being both diplomat, soldier and administrator, was Cyrus of Persia. Under his leadership Median influence was demolished in less than a decade and that of Persia substituted. He instituted a benevolent dictatorship, carrying the people with him. In parallel he rationalised the Army by making sound training of his archers and infantry take precedence over development of the mounted arm. The fighting troops he **reorganised into divisions—first of their kind**—of 10,000 men, each of ten battalions with ten companies, each of which contained ten sections. A well-established commissariat supplied them in the field and communication was maintained from one end of the Empire to the other by messages carried on horseback between post-houses spaced 14 miles (23 km) apart. This unique dispatch service enabled a message to travel 1,600 miles (2,600 km) in seven days. Cyrus built what was probably the **first all-purpose Army of all arms**, capable of being controlled from the nation's administrative centre and of adapting itself rapidly to a wide range of different conditions and terrain. Thus the Army was able to expand the Empire beyond the open plains of the Middle East to which the Assyrians had been confined by the predominantly chariot composition of their Army and by lack of compact infantry formations able to repel a cavalry or chariot attack.

The essential feature of Persian expansion was its concentration upon land warfare. Maritime ventures were restricted to support of the Army and exploration beyond the seaward frontiers. After absorbing the Medes and taking over all that Assyria had possessed, including Egypt, Persia stretched eastward and reached the banks of the Indus. The most remarkable feature of this expansion was its accomplishment by generals who obeyed their King. This loyalty was the key to their superiority over the Assyrians and Medes. Battles were won by a small élite against grossly inferior opponents. Central control was through trusted military governors appointed to the various conquered territories whose inhabitants were given a share in government and who filled the ranks of the Army and police grouped round a Persian nucleus. Inevitably, therefore, the Persian military system was composed of a multitude who had not the slightest knowledge of Persia itself. The Indian race, in particular, assimilated these new methods, adapting chariots but adding war elephants to their order of battle as a shock weapon. The seeds of eventual Persian disruption were therefore sown by the Persians themselves.

The most important Persian move, in the light of subsequent events, was the invasion of Europe in 511 BC. Darius I, second in succession to Cyrus, consolidated the work of Cyrus by crushing the local revolts which flared up after 522 BC. Thereupon he was posed with a familiar problem—the difficulty of maintaining a rich empire's frontiers against jealous neighbours. When Darius built a bridge of boats across the Bosporus and invaded Thrace and Macedonia, penetrating northward as far as the River Danube, he initially projected a mere punitive expedition designed to create a buffer zone north of the colonised area of Asia Minor. Yet to do even this, he had to call up Phoenician as well as Grecian seaman to man the ships which protected his left flank.

Darius I of Persia—faced with frontier rebellions he was the first to lead a Persian army into Europe

The first Persian invasion of Europe was the first of the amphibious kind in modern history and brought Darius into collision with the Greeks as well as the Scythians who, at that time, operated mobile bands far to the south-west of the Russian steppes from which they sprang.

Persians against Greeks. A relief from what is claimed to be Alexander's tomb in the Istanbul Museum of Archaeology

The first densely packed infantry formation seems to have appeared in Assyria before 3000 BC, but fell into disuse when equine armies proved more effective in open country. It was for the Greeks to rekindle the idea with a well-disciplined formation called the "phalanx" whose members (the hoplites) were dressed in helmet, breastplate, shield and greaves (shin-guards) and armed with an 8 ft (2·3 m) spear and short sword. Surrounding this élite formation (which was recruited from the upper and middle classes) were lightly clad, less well-armed skirmishers called "psiloi", recruited from the poor. In support might be found a few slingsmen, but usually at this time the Greeks forsook long-range weapons. The essence of Greek tactics was to close with the enemy and defeat him by a combination of armoured momentum and combat virtuosity. The fundamental design of their equipment was a compromise between heavy hitting power allied to protection that was sufficient to deflect, though not stop, blows without so overweighting the fighting man as to deprive him of nimbleness.

The first battle of Greek phalanx against Persian archers took place at Marathon in 491 BC as the culmination of the first major amphibious invasion of Europe by Persia, and at a moment when the Greek states were in the midst of the sort of political turmoil and civil war which is sometimes extolled as the "battle for freedom". The Persians landed to the north-east of Athens in the Bay of Marathon in the hope of decoying the Athenian Army away from the city to allow pro-Persian elements to stage a revolt. The Persians were about 15,000 strong and somewhat low in morale, perhaps because they had their backs to the sea and feared for their retreat. The Greeks, deprived of Spartan aid because the Spartans were celebrating a religious festival, had about 11,000. Command among the Greeks was by committee, the leader for an aggressive policy being Miltiades. In the final debate it was left to the commander, Callimachus, to give the casting vote to attack, when his generals were equally divided on strategy. The tactics were simple. The Greeks merely charged in close formation in order to close with the Persians before archery fire could take effect. Had they been too heavily armoured this would have been impossible. Remarkably they retained their cohesion, arriving at the point of impact in crescent formation, those on the flanks overlapping the Persians on either side, while the centre thinned out. In the centre, therefore, the Persians were able to rather more than hold their own and press the Greeks back, while on the flanks they began to give way as pressure built up against men who, from the side, were caught semi-defenceless. In effect there was a race in which the Greek centre held firm just long enough for the flank pressure to do its work and induce an over-all Persian collapse which turned into rout as they ran for their ships. It is claimed that 6,400 Persians fell and only 192 Greeks. By all standards it was a complete victory in that it repulsed the enemy, gave the Athenians time to return and crush the internal rebellion, and dissuaded the Persians from continuing the campaign.

The zenith of Grecian power was reached suddenly due to the genius of one man—Alexander the Great—when he ascended the Macedonian throne at the age of twenty in 336 BC. In the intervening years the power of the Greek fleet and the phalanx had neutralised the supremacy of Persian military prestige. At Platae in 480, after a campaign of manœuvre, the Greeks under Pausanias routed a numerically superior force of Persian cavalry and archers under Mardonius. At Salamis, in 450, the Greek Navy defeated the Persian fleet and brought the Greco-Persian War to an end for the time being—allowing the Greeks to revert to that internecine struggle which constantly boiled above and below the surface. Feuding also disturbed the Persian Empire, quarrels in which Greeks became involved on the insurgent side as mercenaries. These quarrels caused land warfare on a large scale and led, for example, to:

The best-documented battle between chariots—at Cunaxa in 401 BC near Babylon between a rebel army, under Cyrus the Younger, and the Persian Army under Artaxerxes II. The two armies stumbled across one another, foot and horse mixed up with chariots in a cauldron of attack of charge followed by counter-charge. But the greatest feat of the battle was the triumph of a Greek phalanx which so withstood every attack that it was enabled afterwards to retreat intact to Trebizond (a distance of nearly 600 miles (960 km))—one of **the most famous withdrawals in history** and of such emotive value as to inspire the Greeks with notions of world conquest.

The greatest Greek Army of all appeared in 336 BC as a direct result of persistent practise and imaginative development by Philip of Macedon. Philip was able to take the lead in Greek politics because the other factions had neutralised themselves by deceit and struggle. He was well served, too, by men of inquiring minds of whom Aristotle was pre-eminent. Under Philip the phalanx was raised to new heights of excellence and armament: its depth was increased to sixteen men, its density increased and the spear (sarissa) lengthened to 13 ft (4 m). Armour was also improved and made weightier, though strict training taught the men to carry this burden without loss of efficiency. But under Philip, and to an even greater extent, his son, Alexander, the mobile and missile-throwing arms were given far greater emphasis than with previous Grecian formations. Light infantry was formed to forge a link between the heavy phalanx and the cavalry, and the latter was improved to become an arm of decision, to exploit the central victory won by the phalanx. Archers and light catapults were carried by mule to support the field army. A corps of engineers was trained to make larger siege-engines at the site of a siege or for a river-crossing. Immense versatility was acquired by what was **the most sophisticated army so far conceived**. It was provided with a useful tactical signalling system by means of smoke and trumpet signals (in addition to carriage of messages by liaison officers) and it was given a rudimentary medical service to enhance the men's morale. The ambition behind Philip's design was a projected invasion of Persia with an army that could engage the Persians on ground which, previously, had been dominated by mobile troops alone. After the assassination of Philip the task fell to Alexander who was to spend the first two years of his reign putting down Greek insurrections which were stirred at the inspiration of Persia.

The first move by Alexander into the Persian Empire began in 334 BC when he crossed into Asia at Gallipoli. Until his death in 323 BC there was to be an almost constant turmoil of marches, sieges, political intrigues and battles.

The military conquests of Alexander are among the greatest in history, though less, in actual dimensions, than those of Genghis Khan were to be. As the crow flies they took his army—a mere 33,000 at the outset but expanding with its conquests—a distance of 3,000 miles (4,800 km) from Salonika to the River Sutlej. However, there were innumerable deflections from this course —the invasion and subjection of Egypt, the journey through Parthia to the shores of the Caspian Sea and the penetration to Kabul being the most considerable among them. His longest single campaign was of 1,700 miles

(2,720 km) to the River Sutlej in India at which point his army at last refused to go further. There were numerous expeditions on the side and, in addition to interminable skirmishing and many sieges, four major land battles.

The first major battle fought by Alexander against the Persians was at the River Granicus in May 334 BC. This was to be followed in 333 by the Battle of Issus, in 331 by the Battle of Arbela and in 326 by the Battle of Hydaspes on the banks of the Jhelum River in present-day Pakistan.

The relative strengths of the opposing forces and their losses at these battles were as follows:

	Alexander	Losses	Opponents	Losses
Granicus	35,000	115	40,000	30,000 (?)
Issus	30,000	450	100,000	50,000
Arbela	47,000	300	200,000 (?)	90,000 (?)
Hydaspes	11,000	300	34,000	23,000

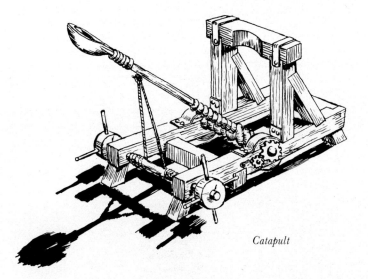

Catapult

The finest example of Alexander's strategic and tactical genius is the Battle of Hydaspes. When the battle took place he was at the extremity of his advance with an army that was sickened of travel. The enemy—a mixed force of Indians, commanded by Porus, of chariots, cavalry, elephants and infantry—took up a strong defensive position behind the River Jhelum which was wide and fast flowing. Alexander brought forward boats which had been used to cross the Indus and took to nightly simulations of a river-crossing by noisy demonstrations up and down the river-banks. Eventually Porus tired of policing these diversions. Then came the time when Alexander suddenly threw a force of 5,000 cavalry and 6,000 infantry over the river at an unguarded landing-place, some 18 miles (29 km) upstream from the main position, leaving the remainder of his army under Craterus opposite Porus' camp. The crossing was made in a storm and nearly came to grief because it

landed on a large island which previous reconnaissance had suggested
was the far bank. At dawn the bridgehead was struck by a light Indian
chariot raid but this was brushed aside. Once he had gathered his force on
the enemy bank Alexander set off downstream to attack Porus as he drew
up in order of battle. At the same time Craterus began crossing the river
to threaten Porus' flank. Porus adopted a conventional order of battle—
infantry in the centre with elephants to the fore; cavalry and chariots
on the flanks. Alexander, however, deployed the bulk of his cavalry on the
right so that it was nearest to the river and Craterus, throwing only a light
cavalry raiding force round the left to harry the Indians if they reacted to
his main assault. He intended to disrupt the enemy with cavalry and
archers before the infantry became engaged, the archers bombarding the
Indians at extreme range. The Indian cavalry was ordered into the attack,
but no sooner did it begin to deploy than the Greek cavalry detachment
was detected coming in from the right. Now came Porus' counter-order
to create disorder. Part of the Indian cavalry was instructed to meet the
new threat but, at this very moment, Alexander launched his main
stroke, driving the Indian cavalry back upon the elephants who, mad-
dened by the archery, turned tail and fled among their own infantry mass,
trampling men and causing frightful confusion.

The action became general, phalanx against infantry and elephants,
cavalry wheeling and charging each other or any other shaken crowd
which hove in sight. The general effect was of a merciless compression of
the Indians into a confined space as Craterus began to appear on their left
flank to threaten total envelopment. Yet a complete encirclement was
beyond the scope of Alexander's weary men. The Indians began to slip
away—those who were not already slain or made prisoner. Then Craterus

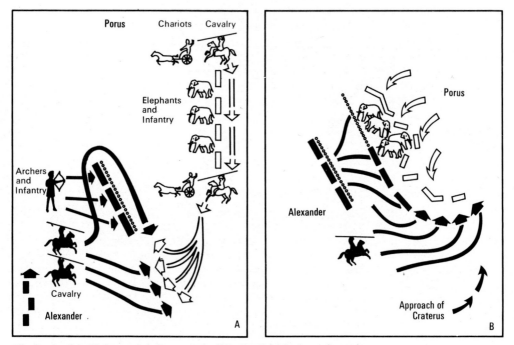

The Battle of the Hydaspes. (a) Contact and mêlée. (b) Exploitation and pursuit

arrived in force and, with his fresh troops, exploited Alexander's initial advantage with a ruthless pursuit. It was a classic victory, complete in that Porus was taken on the field of battle along with the total destruction of all his chariots. Alexander had employed every skill—deception, strategic and tactical manœuvre—to catch his opponent at all possible disadvantages. So complete was his foresight and planning that his subordinates knew previously what to do in every situation, from the use of long-range weapons, to unsettle the enemy before coming to the clinch, to ruthless pursuit at the end. Alexander is also on record for taking care of his wounded, visiting them after the battle and conferring honour upon his heroes— not a commonplace thing in those days.

The death of Alexander in 323 BC reduced the development of the art of war to a much more even rate. Alexander's Empire immediately began to crumble amid the warring of his successors when its major parts reverted to localised government. In India the *Arthasatra*—a treatise on politics and war, produced about 300 BC—laid down a philosophy of conventional organised government and military subdivision. Regular armies of the sort defeated by Alexander assumed a standard composition that was rarely varied. Indeed the Mauryan Empire, which rose under Chandragupta (who had once met Alexander) was to absorb practically the whole of present-day India and Pakistan by the employment of military methods which had failed at the Hydaspes. But like Alexander's, Chandragupta's Empire, and that of his successors, depended upon personalities, waning when strong leadership was missing.

The Great Wall of China

The longest and most durable piece of military construction ever built was the Great Wall of China— 1,684 miles (2,694·4 km) long from Chiayukuan to the Gulf of Pokai. It was the creation of the Emperor Shih Huang Ti, the founder of the Ch'in Dynasty and, in effect, of China as it is known today. Its purpose was twofold: to act as a high barrier, 15 to 39 ft (4·5 to 12 m) high, against invasion by those northern tribes he had pacified; and to do duty as a fortified roadway along which to move troops swiftly from one threatened spot to another—it is up to 32 ft (9·75 m) thick in places. Between 222 and 210 BC Shih Huang Ti suppressed feudalism and established a system of military government not unlike that devised by Cyrus the Great, controlling his regions through a network of roads, built to standard dimensions for chariots so that their wheels could easily follow the ruts like a railway. Like Alexander's successors, those who followed Shih Huang Ti were too weak. Power was seized by Kao Tzu who founded the Han Dynasty. Technically the Ch'in armies owed their supremacy (like the Assyrians) to the exclusive possession of iron. Militarily the most important feature of the Han system was the rise of cavalry. So it can fairly be claimed (as will be seen) that the Chinese were ahead of the West in the development of both combat techniques and fortification, though probably lagging in weaponry.

The greatest immediate rivals to the Greeks in the Mediterranean were the Romans and Carthaginians—neither of whom, in 323 BC, had anything original to offer in the art of war-making. With them, as with the Indians, the evolution of war depended on individuals rather than methods.

The most celebrated of great captains to appear after Alexander was the Carthaginian Hannibal. The Carthaginians had expanded in the western Mediterranean while the Greeks tried to keep control in the east. Between them Rome struggled to hold her own and then expand. It need hardly be added, of course, that concurrent with their imperialistic ventures each nation prosecuted minor wars on their frontiers and spent immense energy on the game of internal rebellion and counter-rebellion. Fighting was virtually ceaseless. Of major importance however was the Second Punic War between Carthage and Rome from 218 to 202 BC, in which Hannibal rose and fell and Carthage was humbled; the First Macedonian War from 215 to 205 BC, in which Hannibal formed a military alliance with Philip V of Macedon against the Greek states, and then the series of Macedonian wars after 200 BC until the power of Greece was crushed by Rome. Two military facts dominate all others in this epoch—the strategic and tactical genius of Hannibal and the sophistication of the Roman legion.

The most famous of Hannibal's strategic movements was the crossing of the Alps from France into Italy in October 218 BC when the passes were already blocked by snow and held by local tribesmen. Not only was it a masterly feat of logistics to transport 30,000 men with horses and elephants under such conditions, but it also threw the Romans completely off balance as they had sent their main force to Spain to attack Hannibal's base—believing he must conform to their strategy and little thinking that he would ignore them and attack their capital at Rome.

The most famous of Hannibal's victories was the Battle of Cannae in 216 BC. Here he relied upon the Romans repeating their standard manœuvre by attacking his weakened centre. Deliberately he gave way before their charge and then carried out a double envelopment from either flank until their mass was totally surrounded and destroyed with a loss of 62,000 men out of 65,000. Hannibal's losses were only 6,000 out of 32,000. Eventually Hannibal was to fight no less than fourteen major battles in seventeen years, losing only three.

Hannibal's elephant Arm being rafted across the River Rhône during the approach to Rome

The greatest of Hannibal's many opponents was Scipio the Younger who inflicted a series of defeats on Hannibal's lieutenants and demonstrated the power of the Roman legion at the height of its early development. In its formative days the Roman infantry formation was but a phalanx. Experience with its tactical inflexibility, however, gradually led to changes—the substitution of the long spear by a throwing-spear (pilum); the subdivision of the mass into "maniples" (small companies of between 60 and 120 men) spaced out to allow greater freedom of movement; and a slight improvement in armour protection by enlarging the shield. By the introduction of regular pay a first step was taken towards changing from a force of feudal nobles and their followers, supported by a militia of citizens, into a permanent army. The Roman system of command, however, remained archaic—a hotchpotch of elected consuls and the like taking turn and turn about to distort strategic and tactical policies. As a rule, the Romans won their victories by a reliance upon attack over defence. Yet quite frequently after an aggressive general was victorious in battle it was taken as good reason to remove him from command in case he grew too politically powerful.

The superior flexibility of the "maniple" legion was well shown at Zama. Here Hannibal drew up his army, some 45,000 infantry, 3,000 cavalry and a corps of 80 elephants in a conventional formation covering the approaches to Carthage itself. He placed the elephants in front with orders to break down Scipio's legion, the cavalry on the wings and his infantry in three rows—the best troops in rear, second-best in front, along with Balearic slingers, and the least reliable in the middle. The Romans also put their cavalry, 9,000 strong, on the wings, but the legion, deployed in three lines, was so spaced out by maniples that lanes were created through which the Carthaginian elephants could expend their charge.

Once the elephants had charged and lumbered away into the distance, and the Roman cavalry had driven the Carthaginian cavalry from the field, the infantry formations converged and clashed. Finesse was thrown to the winds in a grim mêlée of interlocked, hand-to-hand combat, the ground piled high with the dead and wounded. When the first lines were exhausted they drew apart, removed the wounded, and made way for the Roman reserves to climb across a barrier of dead to reach their opponents. The best troops of both sides began a stern grapple which might have brought stalemate had not the Roman cavalry, returning from pursuit of the Carthaginian horse, charged the Carthaginian infantry in rear and brought about their utter rout. Carthaginian losses were more than 35,000 dead and prisoners; those of the Romans more than 1,500 dead and perhaps 4,500 wounded. Hannibal escaped, but this defeat destroyed his power. He committed suicide in 183 BC.

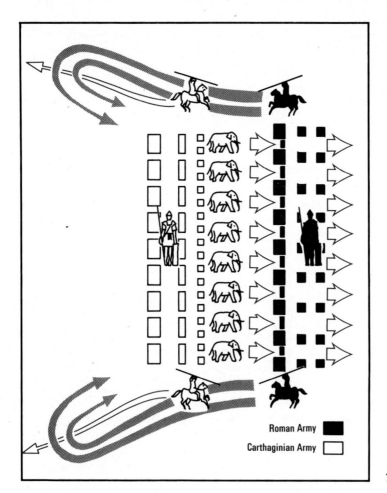

Roman Army ■

Carthaginian Army □

The Battle of Zama

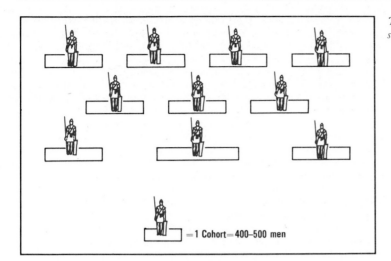

The Cohort Legion in its standard deployment

= 1 Cohort = 400–500 men

The most important change to the Roman legion took place under pressure of a great disaster. By 109 BC Rome's Empire was expanding and her wealth increasing. However, the maniple legion, which had destroyed the power of Greece, was now seriously weakened by internal dissent and inept leadership just as Rome was coming into almost constant collision with the warlike tribes bordering her new territories in both the eastern and western Mediterranean. After 113 BC several consular armies were roughly handled by the Cimbri, a teutonic tribe, and in 105 BC a Roman army some 80,000 strong was annihilated at the Battle of Arausio. Reform was essential to keep pace with a new situation.

The driving force behind the Roman Army reforms was the Consul Marius. He scrapped the maniple legion composed, officially, of rich, part-time soldiers (who armed themselves at their own expense and fought with the motive of personal gain), replacing it with a professional army recruited from the entire population instead of an élite supplemented by the poor. Under Marius a man signed on for twenty years and was paid and equipped by the State. The legion remained the principal fighting formation and was given a standard—an eagle—and later a numbered identity upon which to centre its loyalty. Each legion consisted of ten units (cohorts) of between 400 and 500 men; each cohort was divided into six centuries whose leader (the centurion) was both commander and sergeant-major—a most formidable professional soldier who frequently, by sheer personal prowess, made up for the deficiences of the higher command. A century handled with the sensitivity of a maniple, bunching to add power to its javelin-throwers, expanding to give space for each soldier to use his sword freely in close combat.

A cohort usually deployed three centuries in the front rank and three to the rear, while the legion adopted still greater depth with three rows of cohorts. With its capability of well-drilled marching the legion could open and close its frontage (usually about 1·5 miles (2·4 km)), form square or circle, or attack in columns and, above all, leap-frog cohort through cohort to sustain a particular movement with fresh reserves. A special scout section of ten men sought information and was aided by the cavalry. Missile support came from a train of catapults and ballistae, not only during sieges but also for bombardment prior to the assault. Thus the legion, while attaining a very high standard of practice in the mass, tended to simplify training by eschewing specialists, dispensing with archers by making the ordinary infantryman carry out the dual role of missile-thrower and close-combat soldier, and compensating for the archer's absence by missiles from war-engines.

Of vital importance in every phase of Roman war was the fortress. Despite the legion's main role as a decisive offensive formation, its soldiers spent most of their time resting from mobile campaigns behind walls, defending key localities. Roman forts were hardly more sophisticated in general design than those which had, for so long, dominated the Middle East. However, in detailed construction—the techniques of bonding stone with wood, in precautions to reduce the risk of fire and the mounting of iron sheets as armour for towers—they were distinctly tougher. The incentive for this strengthening was, of course, the steady increase in the ingenuity and power of siege-engines.

In addition to conventional catapults there is mention in various Roman records of a boring machine; a compressed-air throwing-machine, invented by Cresbius; of a movable siege-tower 150 ft (45·5 m) high used by Julius Caesar; of an engine which could throw 1 cwt (50·8 kg) stones a distance of 400 yd (364 m); and of "Greek fire" (made of a mixture of naptha, sulphur and quicklime) to be flung into cities or flung back by the defenders themselves. There is even a report of a siphon-type of flame-thrower used by the Byzantines. Every strong city, as part of its standard defensive equipment, kept pots for flaming tar ready to decant on to those clambering up from below. It was also the Romans who developed **the most famous "clambering device" of all**, the *Tortoise* in which members of a legion's maniple bent under their shields to act as a human platform for their comrades scaling a wall in the assault.

It is one of the cohort legion's detractive distinctions that it won fame from triumphs against less well-organised and trained opponents—fighting as an army of conquest against fanatical tribesmen who, though usually superior in number, were inferior in prowess at arms. The most revealing battles were those when legion fought legion during civil wars, notably in the final period of Julius Caesar's rule and in the aftermath of his assassination.

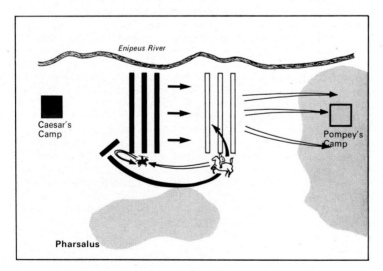

The Battle of Pharsalus

Caesar's legion and British tribesmen fight it out on the beaches. The artist had an interesting insight into the Roman technique of fire and movement

The most important of Caesar's civil war victories was that of Pharsalus in Thessaly in 48 BC over an army of 60,000 infantry and 7,000 cavalry under Pompey. Though Caesar possessed only half the infantry of Pompey and but a seventh the cavalry, his force was vastly superior in training, morale and qualities of leadership. Each with a flank resting securely on the Enipeus River, the legions faced each other in the conventional three lines of cohorts, with cavalry on the open flank. Only Caesar's deployment possessed originality, a grouping of six cohorts on the open right flank, echeloned back in support of his outnumbered cavalry. The battle began with the advance of Caesar's legions for a head-on collision with their opposite number, but with the third line under strict orders to refrain from getting committed. As the battle lines collided, Pompey threw his cavalry, supported by missiles, into action against Caesar's cavalry. A horsed melée broke out on Caesar's right and was going against him when he signalled the six reserve cohorts into the fray. Much more than stabilise the threat to Caesar's flank, they completely overthrew Pompey's horsemen, flung them back on their archers who gave way and then scythed ahead to crash against the left flank and rear of Pompey's legion. At this moment Caesar released his third line which, filtering through the combat-weary ranks of the first and second, struck the shaken enemy and won.

Pompey fled, leaving his men to their fate. Caesar, meantime, demanding no pause for looting, pressed the pursuit to the limit of his men's endurance, surrounding and cutting down the enemy until, twenty-four hours later, surrounded and deprived of water, they were compelled to surrender; Pompey lost about 6,000 men, though many more changed sides to Caesar, whose losses may have been less than 1,000.

One of the fiercest tribal movements into Europe began as the result of war by the Chinese Han Dynasty against the Hsiung-nu, a war-like Mongoloid race. Throughout their existence the Hans had been severely bothered by this tribe and between AD 89 and 91 sent an expedition which meted out awful punishment and finally drove the Hsiung-nu westward. From this began a shunting of fresh violence into Europe until the first appearance of a belligerent people, who became known as the Huns, took place in

AD 372. Driven by them or in their train came more tribes—Goths, Alans, Franks, Vandals—all at the throats of any who stood in the way.

The vital military importance of the Huns lies not so much in their conquering ways as in the fact that they carried into Europe those elements of military art which they had acquired by war against the Chinese. Hence the strong cavalry instincts of the Ch'in and Han Dynasties were imported to the West as part of the growing tribal violence then being generated against Rome.

The greatest Roman work on military affairs was written in AD 390 by Flavius Vegetius Renatus as a synthesis of the military customs of Rome, and a plea for the failing Empire to revert to the practices which had made the city great. But *De Re Militari* is really only a memorial to past greatness.

By AD 400 when the frontiers of Rome stretched furthest and widest of all, her power had passed its zenith. The rich culture and trade which grew out of the Empire had created soft attitudes. The hard core of Romans who had once fettled the Army into shape and dominated the increasing number of foreigners within the legions's ranks, was emaciated as able-bodied men turned aside from strife in search of wealth and pleasure. The tribes of Europe and the Middle East which had been subjugated by the prowess of the legions began to score successes and could no longer be kept at bay by linear defences, such as Hadrian's Wall, which divided tribal Scotland from colonised England.

A crucial tribal victory over the Romans took place in AD 9 when German auxiliaries under Arminius instigated an insurrection against the Roman commander, Varus, in the Teutoberger Wald. Guerilla warfare blossomed into a formal campaign when Arminius deserted Varus and put himself at the head of a popular uprising. Caught on the march in autumn rains in afforested and hilly terrain, the Romans were worn down by persistent raids from highly mobile (and often mounted) guerilla bands which sapped their morale. Eventually the legions disintegrated and they, with all their camp-followers, were massacred. Never again would Rome have dominion over central Germany, launch punitive raids though they might to avenge Varus. Arminius wrote the message of doom which said that it was possible for secondary forces to destroy a first-class legion.

The death-grapple between the German tribes and Roman legions in the Teutoberger Wald

SECTION III
The Equine Millennium
378–1415

The most important military development of the first millennium AD was the appearance out of China of the horse's saddle and, a little later, stirrups. Nobody knows who invented these vital items of equipment which allowed a man to fight mounted on the move, nor from whence or exactly when they came. Saddles appeared in Gaul about AD 100 and thereafter saddled cavalry began to assert dominance over chariots as the better, mobile weapon platform. Clearly two horsemen in lieu of one two-horsed chariot produced a much more economical weapon system, both in number and mobility, when horses were relatively scarce, expensive, sometimes hard to feed and mostly, as yet, of inferior quality due to low breeding.

The turning-point in the struggle between infantry and cavalry formations occurred at the Battle of Adrianople in AD 378. Prior to this the Roman Empire had suffered the fatal civil war which had resulted in Constantine transferring the capital of his more virile government to what is now Istanbul in AD 330. From Constantinople he and his successors directed the struggle to preserve the frontiers of Rome, employing an army which rapidly became more mercenary (and some say "effeminate") in manpower, and gradually acquiring a stronger horsed element at the expense of the legion whose organisation, because it was no longer possible to enforce the outstanding level of training which made the cohort legion viable, began to drift towards that of the old phalanx. At Adrianople the Roman Army, commanded by the Emperor Valens, was 40,000 strong in infantry and 20,000 in cavalry. The enemy were mixed tribes—Goths, Sarmatians, Huns and Alans who had erupted from the northern flank of the Empire. They were commanded by Fridigern and are variously estimated at between 100,000 and 200,000 strong. Essentially they were a highly mobile cavalry force firmly based upon something new to European experience—a defensive circle of waggons parked on high ground. Within this circle—or laager as it is now more generally known—supplies were held, the women and children stayed, and infantry acted as a garrison while the cavalry raided, pivoting on the laager.

Valens had tired his men by extensive marching and so he tried to delay their committal to battle by a bogus parley with Fridigern. Simultaneously the Roman cavalry advanced towards the laager and were themselves attacked by Fridigern's horse who had, but moments before, returned post-haste from foraging. There was a mêlée in which weight of numbers and the sheer *élan* of the Gothic horse assured the destruction of the Roman horse. Now it was the turn of the legion, caught on low ground and in the confusion of an inept deployment. Bombarded by arrows, delivered by an opponent who was constantly on the move and whose exact location never could be pinned, the legion began to wilt. At this the Gothic infantry arrived and completed the massacre.

The Battle of Adrianople is usually rated as beginning the cavalry era even though infantry played an important part. In point of fact this battle demonstrated Roman generalship at its nadir and the fighting qualities of the men in a steep decline at the end of an epoch. The real lesson of Adrianople was stated by General J. F. C. Fuller: "That valour remained the first requisite in shock warfare, and that a return to barbaric vigour was inevitable unless a new moral inspiration could be discovered." Try though they would to create new combinations of men, beasts, weapons and techniques, the Romans were to discover that, in the reality of close combat, none of these things quite compensated for high morale and excellent generalship.

The outstanding leader among the anti-Roman forces and the epitome of ruthlessness was Attila the Hun. He was that most dangerous kind of man who ruled by fear and coveted power without riches, preferring only the simplest of things in life. One can gain a vivid picture of Attila as a vain, superstitious, cunning, arrogant and cruel man. He commanded a swarm of mounted archers whose semi-mobile base was a great waggon laager. The swarm was nomadic, setting forth from its source in search of forage and plunder, fighting a guerilla-type war of hit and run at the periphery of its ambit. Yet quite capable, should the occasion demand, of returning to concentrate rapidly for a battle of position close to the waggon laager—as was the case at the Battle of Chalons in 451 against a combined Roman-Frankish-Gothish army. Attila's army certainly possessed the inherent frailty of an irregular guerilla army, performing at its worst in a formal battle and always tending to disperse when threatened by superior force. When its leader died it broke apart almost immediately and for ever.

An army which depended almost entirely upon horse mobility was also at the mercy of Nature. In winter the difficulty of shifting the waggon-train to new pastures became almost insuperable in mud. Hence, as forage for the horses became hard to obtain, the beasts lost condition. So long as the horse was considered indispensable, campaigns tended to close with the onset of winter—a proclivity which persisted into the age of mechanisation. The Huns were far from unique in martial tradition— merely the latest wave of desperate people striving to escape the brutalised conditions of the inner Asiatic wastes in search of an easier livelihood. As such they contributed next to nothing of significance either to the art of war or culture.

Attila and his Huns on the march

Bayeux tapestry is one of the earliest, complete pictorial records of a campaign, recording the moves leading up to the conquest of Britain by the Norman Army of Duke William. Here Norman cavalry is attacking King Harold's infantry at Hastings. Allowing for the fact that Queen Matilda and the ladies who made the tapestry were not too precise as to the soldiers' dress, it is clear that both sides wore chain mail—though that of the Normans was better. The Normans, however, also possessed in quantity what the English lacked—efficient archers, the effect of whose fire on the close packed English is already noticeable. All the elements of fire and movement by the Normans against the defended English locality are apparent. This is the crucial moment when neither side has yet won an advantage.

The most important force to appear as counter to the latest swarm from Asia was the modified Roman military system which grew up within the Byzantine Empire. **It is one of the profoundest facts of military history** that the relocation of the Roman capital at the Greek city of Constantinople almost coincided with the first growth of the two greatest religious forces ever—Christianity and Mohammedanism—and also gave birth to cultures which exceeded any which had gone before. It is a fact of military organisation and tactics that the Byzantine Army was the first fully effective, disciplined international force of closely combined all-arms. Yet this army did not appear phoenix-like from out of the ashes of defeat at Adrianople, but was the product of slow forging under the hammer of events—as are all sound military organisations.

The first great Byzantine General was Belisarius who served the Emperor Justinian from 529. His first major appointment to command came in 533 for the reconquest of North Africa from the Vandals with the parsimonious allocation of a mere 10,000 infantry and 5,000 cavalry, an army of multiracial mercenaries most of whom were barbarians though highly trained fighting men withal. The allegiance of such a force could only be assured by bribery, victory and plunder. The high proportion of cavalry to infantry was justified by knowledge of the enemy's composition, an opponent who fought in loose formations such as cavalry might readily penetrate with a disciplined charge.

The first decisive battle fought by Belisarius was at Tricameron to the west of Carthage. His 15,000 were opposed by 50,000 Vandals (though this might well be over-estimated). Numbers, however, were of scant consequence. Vandal generalship under Gelimer was vacillating and typified by complex, impractical plans. Presented with an opportunity to charge the Byzantine cavalry by surprise, Gelimer stood back and awaited attack, despite earlier bombastic exhortations. Charged by a smaller cavalry force, the Vandals stood firm, but fled when Tazazon (their only leader of merit) was killed. Yet they might easily have held out, but the mere advance of Belisarius' infantry put such fear into Gelimer that he deserted, followed with alacrity by the rest of his army. Then came the second and, to some combatants, most vital phase—the orgy of plunder for which members of the Byzantine Army were in business. It would have been the same had the Vandals been the victors, but, as the Duke of Wellington was one day to say, referring to the British soldier of his time, "No reliance can be placed on the conduct of troops in action with the enemy who have been accustomed to plunder."

Belisarius

The most remarkable feats by Belisarius in sustaining forty important victories against Persians and Vandals over a period of thirty years was that he usually won them by ingenuity as compensation for a desperate inequality in numbers. Perhaps his final triumph was the greatest, in 559, when he drove off a horde of Bulgarians from Constantinople employing a mere 300 well-trained cavalry as nucleus to a scratch force of local untrained conscripts. Nevertheless, although the military influence of Byzantium was established firmly by the genius of Belisarius, and also that of his colleague, Narses, it has to be admitted that they won not so much because of their armies' prowess as from superior personal command matched against inferior generals. As the art of war entered the doldrums the subtlety of Byzantium alone shone forth.

Infantrymen of Byzantium

The elements of the Byzantine Army at the peak of its development, circa 650, were:

● *Heavy infantry* carrying a large shield and wearing helmet, mail shirts and greaves, armed with lance and either a sword or an axe. Known as Scutati, they formed a firm base for the rest of the army to pivot upon— standing sixteen deep in two lines of battle.

● *Light infantry* whose principal armour may only have been leather jerkins but whose weapon was usually the bow. They provided missile power and were to be found on the flanks of the heavy infantry.

● *Cavalry*, lightly armoured in mail and carrying a small shield, their principal armament might be bow, lance, axe or sword. In battle they would be found either in small parties as a screen to front and flank of the heavy infantry; as strong flank protection to the light infantry, thus extending the line of battle; or as a reserve in rear, ready to check a breakthrough or exploit victory. Their vitality was founded upon well-bred horses—a type that could carry an armoured man with endurance and yet was relatively nimble.

● *The conventional siege-train* to which may have been added an early flame-thrower rather like a siphon.

● *Manpower* drawn, in later centuries, from the indigenous people of the Empire to the exclusion of mercenaries, above all, if possible, the Greeks. Training was strict, command and staff most carefully selected and given wide experience. Indeed something similar to a general staff corps was formed—**perhaps the first recorded example of this sort of professional élite.**

The greatest threat to the Byzantine Empire came not so much from the northern peoples as from fanatical Moslem Arab tribes to the southward whose crusading armies formed up in the wake of the religious revival of Mohammed and began to drive northward out of Arabia in 629—three years prior to the Prophet's death. There was nothing original about the weapons or fighting methods of these Arab tribesmen. Mounted or dismounted, they were armed with simple spears and swords and delivered furious charges to the heart of an enemy formation. The rapid spread of Mohammedanism is only partly to be accounted for by their fervour at arms overcoming enemies weakened by interminable conflict. It was missionary zeal which rapidly extended their Empire to Spain and southern France in the West, moving along the entire North African shores to the south and to the Indus to the east, sweeping back the boundaries of Byzantium to Asia Minor in the north—reaching the very walls of Constantinople itself, in 717.

One of the longest sieges up to that point in history took place when the Moslems invested Constantinople in June 717. For the next fourteen months, by assault from land and sea besides the deprivation of supplies (which reduced the besieged to eating human flesh) the Moslems tried and failed to capture the city. Defeated in battle and suffering enormous losses from an extremely cold winter, the Moslems could but hope to starve out the Byzantines under Leo III. But they neither possessed a siege-train worthy of a properly prepared assault on the defences, nor could their fleet, defeated in the Bosporus, penetrate the entrance to the harbour in a battle in which Greek fire was used with particularly impressive results. In June 718 came Leo's turn to counter-attack. At sea he utterly destroyed the Moslem fleet (whose crews, mostly enslaved Christians, turned on their masters). Then his army landed on the Asiatic shore to win a decisive land battle. Within a matter of days, too, the Bulgars, descending from the north, routed the Moslem Army covering the northern flank of the siege. At this the Moslems took flight, a mere 30,000 out of the original force of 200,000 returning home, the survivors fighting among themselves as tribal jealousies overcame religious discipline.

The greatest defender against Moslem penetration in the West was the army of Charles Martel—whose Frankish antecedents were as barbarous as the Huns and no more indigenous to present-day France than had been the Romans. Their methods of mounted fighting were like those of all Asian tribes, the difference between them and the Moslems being simply a matter of weight and the fact that the Franks had a higher proportion of infantry. Immense fervour in attack, and emotional unsteadiness in defence were typical of both sides. To the art of war they contributed nothing. The Battle of Tours in 732, for example, was merely a sustained sequence of charges in which the Frankish Army fought dismounted, in a compact mass, grappling with successive head-on Moslem advances until the latter were exhausted and deprived of their leader, Abd-ar-Rahman.

The rock to which Western Europe was anchored was the Carolingian Empire founded by Martel's grandson, Charles, who became known as the Emperor Charlemagne. Charlemagne, an illiterate genius, gave distinction and durability to the wild Frank warriors by devising a military system based on regulations, sound administration and tactical methods which, like those of Byzantium, combined the principal fighting arms into a single cohesive body. Infantry provided a base for heavy and light cavalry offensive action; a siege-train was built and a sound logistic system devised so that the armies could make long advances without plundering the countryside. Thereby they partly avoided committing sins, like those of their Moslem opponents who systematically antagonised the population. Like the Byzantine Empire, too, that of Charlemagne gained strength from culture and a disciplined faith. If at times the armies of the Franks have been gilded with an exaggerated aura of Christian humanity, it is also fair to say that these principles gave commanders the excuse to enforce their will with hard measures upon soldiers who broke martial laws.

A distinctive feature of Charlemagne's reign (768 to 814) was the land campaigning that was constantly in progress. Sometimes there were two or three going on at a time—to put down rebellion, to expand the Empire and to spread the Christian faith by compulsion. Against the Saxons, for example, there were thirty-three years of consecutive struggle with fearful atrocities committed by both sides, terminating in the mass dispersion of the Saxon race throughout the Empire. In about 98 per cent of cases Charlemagne's arms prevailed, and when failure occurred it was converted for propaganda purposes into legend.

The most famous failure was at Roncevaux in 778 when a carelessly straggling column of the Frank rearguard was ambushed in a Pyrenean pass by Basque guerillas. Attacking suddenly from the hilltops above, the Basques penned the Franks in a valley and utterly destroyed them. The chronicler Einhard describes the guerilla technique to perfection: "They then snatched up the baggage and, protected as they were by darkness which was just beginning to fall, scattered in all directions without losing a moment."

Probably the most important military trend of Carolingian times was the emergence of the cult of Chivalry which, even in its early, rough-hewn form, provided a code of conduct during combat, and a substitute, through a crude type of central government, for tribal systems and their inherent jealousies. Because cavalry was an expensive fighting arm to maintain it became populated by the rich aristocracy and their sycophants. In the Frankish Army a knight was a military tenant to a noble person, given the name *caballariis*. A privileged class, they devised rules which were elaborated throughout the centuries in the interests of their own self-preservation. Clemency in battle became a point of honour; one knight, brought to his knees, could surrender to another and his life would usually be spared and redeemed by ransom. Thus the rules of chivalry were **among the first to introduce a legalised limitation of the act of combat**—though only in a narrow sense. The practice of slaying the underprivileged classes went on as though nothing had changed at all—as, in fact, it had not. For the rules of chivalry, which were closely allied to feudalism and most strongly identifiable among the Christian knights (such as the Knights Templar in later years), subsisted on a system of slave labour devised for the benefit only of the strongest. Even chivalry's highly romanticised courtesy to women is grossly exaggerated by legend: the facts are that women were kept firmly in their place for breeding and, chiefly, as chattels.

The dominant strain in warfare round (and often cutting into) the periphery of the Carolingian Empire emanated from the interaction of raiding tribes who operated freely on land, but who obtained their principal strategic mobility on the sea. Throughout the terminal stages of the Roman occupation of Britain and Gaul, the Saxons, Angles and Jutes began raiding the coasts. Once Roman rule was withdrawn the number of raids increased until wholesale occupation of the coastal belts and, finally, complete occupation of all but the western and northern extremities of Britain was accomplished. The waves of Norsemen from Scandinavia who began to harry the Saxon successors and Franks, were amphibious soldiers—lightly armoured infantry who carried wooden or leather shields and swung mighty battle-axes, and who were protected by bronze or iron helmets fitted with nose-pieces. Coincident with the first fading of Carolingian power in 800, as the result of internecine struggle among Charlemagne's successors, the Vikings entered Western Europe in strength.

Viking warrior—carved in elk horn

The first sustained Viking incursions hit Scotland and eastern England in 802. By 807 they had penetrated to Ireland; in 811 into Holland and from then onward ever deeper into France until Paris was raided in 845. In 862 the Vikings were pushing into Russia too—though by this time they were beginning to settle down among their conquests and were loosing their impetus. Needless to say the fighting was chiefly maritime. King Alfred the Great of England, though he raised a comparatively efficient counter-Viking army in Britain, concentrated upon the fleet, harbouring it in fortified ports round the coast from which he, in turn, raided the Vikings. Infantry fighting was the essence of this warfare since footmen alone could be carried in sufficient number by ships. However, as the Vikings gained a foothold, they began to acquire horses and expand their mounted arm, first for reconnaissance and then as an armoured, mounted force closely resembling that of the Franks. Indeed, the gradual subjection of the Frankish defenders in Normandy permitted the installation of the most efficient Viking land-based army of the day—the Norman Army which absorbed the better part of northern France by 911.

The chief civil and military product of the Viking settlement in Western Europe was a strengthening of the feudal system as a means both of government, defence and offence. Alfred fostered it as a cheap way to recruit strong men for his key fortresses. He bought men and power by offering land at little or no charge to himself! There was nothing cultural about this movement.· Fortifications which began as earthworks and stockades lacked ornamentation. Nor was combat looked on as an idealistic fight for freedom against oppression. To reiterate from Section I: men fought for survival, glory and acquisition, often from sheer delight of a fight. Though let it be remembered that combat was rather more welcome to the best-armed and armoured members of the community whose chances of survival were commensurately higher than the rest.

The best antidote to the armoured man—bearing in mind that, until the fourteenth century, armour was rarely more elaborate than a linked mail shirt—was a missile-throwing weapon of such power and accuracy that it could penetrate armour and enable the unarmoured man to kill at long range. Archers acquired renewed importance as armoured knights became more numerous. Yet the Orders of Chivalry resisted the introduction of improved archery weapons, grimly recognising a mortal threat to their own occupation, while regretting that it was a difficult weapon to fire while mounted. Thus the mounted knights compelled themselves to fight at a disadvantage against anybody who rejected their "rules". For the first time, perhaps, appeared the sort of fundamental contradiction which invariably dogs attempts at limitation of war's violence—an attempt by the strong to make the weak weaker yet in order to preserve a bogus *status quo*.

The most important advance in weapon technology prior to the year AD 1000 was the advent of the cross-bow—**the first mechanical infantry weapon.** Originally the Chinese may have practised with them—as far back as 2598 BC it is sometimes suggested—but this is hard to verify. Certainly the technique of mounting a bow on a stock to enable more careful aim to be taken, consonant with holding the stock to the shoulder and releasing the bolt through a trigger device instead of by hand, was known to the Romans. Vegetius mentions it as a weapon for specialised troops. Nevertheless its general use was delayed for many centuries. There is no evidence to substantiate the claim that it was used at the Battle of Hastings by Norman invaders of Britain, but undoubtedly the device was, by then, proliferating. In 1139 the Second Lateran Conference banned it as an unfair weapon of war because its powers of penetrating mail armour had been devastatingly demonstrated in battle. But there was a legal reservation—the cross-bow might be used against the Moslems though not fellow Christians.

The chief tactical disadvantages of the cross-bow was its relatively low rate of fire and range. Whereas a Welsh long-bowman might get off six aimed shots per minute at 200 yd (180 m), the cross-bowman would be lucky to shoot one and a half per minute over 130 yd (118·3 m). Hence the long-bow which, in British hands from the twelfth century onwards was to be a dominant weapon on the European battlefield, took precedence as a weapon of rapid fire while the cross-bow was used more deliberately by less highly skilled (and muscular) men at the shorter ranges.

The most carefully prepared seaborne invasion by Norsemen was the one launched by the Normans under Duke William against the English under King Harold in 1066. The Army of Normandy was a great improvement upon that of their forebears a little more than 100 years ago. In common with the English they had been almost perpetually at war, engaged in a struggle between north and south. Yet whereas the English had contained the Norse invaders by the employment of basic infantry tactics, the Normans had fostered the cavalry cult in their tussle with Carolingian chivalry, adopting the bow and retaining their affinity with the sea.

The first decisive cavalry battle on English soil took place at Hastings. Yet the struggle was prefaced by the very antithesis of mobile warfare. Both sides first sought to secure a fortified position—William constructing a wooden fort to protect his logistical organisation as it was brought ashore, Harold holding a hilltop with both flanks secured by difficult ground. Harold had but recently fought a hard battle against the Norwegians near York and his men were exhausted by a forced march to the south: he desired only to rest and therefore chose a topographically constricted locality on high ground. William, who had to advance in order to give momentum to his invasion, wished most to exploit the superior mobility of his 400 mounted knights. The initial Norman advance, led by infantry and supported by archers, was a complete failure. They were held in a grapple and swept back by a counter-attack. Nor was the cavalry more successful when it, too, charged up the slope. The "wall of English shields" and its axe-swinging defenders would not give way. A decision could only be obtained by persuading the "wall" to shift into the open, thereby loosening its cohesion and exposing its flanks. This William induced by feigning a retreat and tempting Harold into pursuit. Then the English infantry, caught in the open under high-angle archery fire, were charged by the Norman cavalry. Broken in a few places they at last fell apart and were cut to ribbons by an enemy who excelled in pace and whose blows in man-to-man combat were struck from above.

The Battle of Hastings was the last opposed invasion of England to succeed. It introduced a new ruling class whose military and civil methods remoulded the nation in a myriad ways. English guerilla bands who operated from fenlands and forests could not long hope to prevail against a thoroughly disciplined opponent who established a comprehensive system of feudal government—which effectively controlled the very source of existence— agricultural produce.

The most advanced military systems in the world at the time of Hastings, however, continued to be that of Byzantium and those in the Moslem world which, through contact with Byzantine power, had copied their ideas. Moreover the art of the military engineer was more dominant than ever—a fact which is all too frequently lost to sight in the cloud of euphoria whipped up by the drama of infrequent major battles.

The most expensive items of military power were fortifications. Simple entrenchments thrown up by armies in the field, as had been the practice for years, were cheap, of course. The Romans had, of routine, constructed simple earth mounds as a base for tactical operations, often using half their men in the fighting while the other half dug. This method was a normal charge against campaigning. It was not to be confused with permanent, elaborate fortifications erected with stone to protect points of strategic importance or even entire cities—the sort of enormous edifices dating further back than Assyrian times which had become common in the Middle East and

The weapons of medieval
siege warfare

(A) Covered battering-ram

(B) Launching winches

(C) Trebuchet

(D) Mobile shields

(E) Fighting tower

southern Europe (including Spain) and to which had been added greater
depth of defence by constructing higher towers, surrounding them with
thicker walls, which themselves sprouted more towers at strategic points,
and incorporating deeper ditches. In effect, fortifications acquired
greater complexity even when incorporated in some naturally strong
topographical feature—the bend in a river, the top of a hill or the sur-
rounds of an existing communication centre or port. They thus protected
the core of burgeoning urban communities.

Evolution of fortress design was in response to the familiar threat of better siege devices and methods, and commensurate with whatever sums were available for materials and labour. For example, walls had to be built yet higher, to combat taller fighting towers, and thicker to defeat missiles hurled by somewhat more powerful siege-engines, such as the trebuchet. Ditches dug close alongside walls also deterred battering-rams and hampered collapsing of the walls by burning away the pit props holding up an underground mine shaft. The defence of forts remained supreme to the methods of attack. Their construction, therefore, provided a good return on high capital expenditure. In fact the most economic way to compel their surrender was by starvation which was itself an unattractive system since, as often as not, the besiegers starved first due to the paucity of their logistic system. Bearing this in mind Richard I of England decided not to besiege Jerusalem in 1192.

The most restrictive element of feudal practice in relation to land warfare was the agreement between overlord and tenant in connection with military service. Since a tenant's essential occupation was tilling the land his period of military service had to be severely curtailed. Hence it was almost impossible, unless very special terms were arranged, to make a man serve far from home. This reduced the range to which military expeditions could be projected.

Another crucially restrictive factor was that of cost. The entire resources of a poor, small village community might be needed over several years to equip a knight with all his accoutrements. Of course, excellent dividends might be received if the knight happened to be successful at war but, in the event of his dying or, worse, being taken prisoner and held to ransom, the penalties against the exchequer might well be crippling. The best-known example of release by ransom is that of King Richard I of England when he was held prisoner by the Duke of Austria. England, already mortgaged by the price of sending an army to the Third Crusade, was further impoverished by the need to pay for her King's release.

The first Crusade of all took place in 1096, and represented the first major attempt by the Christian nations of the West to fight at the side of the ailing Byzantine nation in its struggle against the Moslems. Annihilation of the Byzantines at the Battle of Manzikert in Armenia, in 1071, emphasised to the rest of Christendom the peril in which they stood. The emotive cry to retake Jerusalem was a rallying call to feudal forces, the identification of substance with a cause to enhance morale and help overcome the barriers to recruitment erected by short-term feudal levies. The Crusades did little to advance the art of war. Familiar weapons and repetitive cavalry tactics were exported from the West to meet Moslems whose armament and tactics also had only slightly improved with experience. While it is probable that the Westerners learnt more from the Moslems than the other way about, there can be no doubt that soldiers had most to learn from Byzantine.

The first Crusaders, started out but 25,000 strong to challenge a people in arms whose religious fanaticism in battle was the equal of their own. City after city had to be reduced at great sacrifice in life, or left intact. Gradually the Crusaders' strength waned and so it is something of a miracle that, in 1099, a mere 10,000 strong, they took Jerusalem. And it was typical of a religious war that, in the aftermath, the Christians proceeded to slaughter the Moslem and Jewish population. In the siege of Jerusalem the Crusaders used both fighting towers, battering-rams and scaling-ladders in the assault. Their success was impressive in that they had learnt fast. Their experience, when they returned home, was converted into an almost universal programme of castle strengthening modelled on those of the Middle East. The remains of these piles and those of their successors are to be found everywhere throughout Europe today. Yet, in terms of past achievement, the castles of pre-Crusader time were rarely as advanced in technology as those of the Romans, and it was years before the art of Roman construction was surpassed.

The Storming of Jerusalem from a fighting tower

The revival of élite fighting forces grew out of the Crusades and brought chivalry to the zenith of its power. The Christian armies which garrisoned the conquests in Palestine after 1100 were composed of highly trained fighting men who equipped themselves with the best armour, arms and horses available. Governed by strict discipline they formed a formidable fighting force which, by degrees, migrated back into Europe. The Teutonic Knights, for example, shifted home to Eastern Europe as bearers by the sword of Christianity against the "heathen".

*The crusaders assault
Constantinople in 1204*

The first successful assault upon Constantinople—capital be it remembered of the Christian Eastern Church—was made, paradoxically, by a Christian army as part of the Fourth Crusade. Christian rivalries allied to mistrust of Byzantine's rulers in their anxiety to avoid a clash with their Moslem neighbours, provoked followers of the Roman Church to route the Fourth Crusade via Constantinople instead of direct to Palestine by sea. In December 1203 the city agreed to terms after a preliminary attack had achieved small gains. But a month later, when the Byzantines rebelled against the Crusaders, a final, combined naval and land assault was made and in two days' fighting overwhelmed the garrison. At that, to the shame of the Crusaders, there ensued wholesale looting, burning, rape and murder. In the final analysis, bearing in mind that nothing was done to reconquer Jerusalem from the Moslems and that Byzantium was so weakened as no longer to be a serious factor in resisting the spread of Mohamedanism into Asia Minor, the Christian cause had been undermined by its own most enthusiastic militants.

*King Richard I of England
in action at Jaffa*

The first stirrings of one of the greatest outward surges from Asia ever to take place was to be found among a small group of ironworkers who supplied the Chinese Wei rulers with weapons. They were called T'u Kue or Turks—a race who thrived on the profits of other people's wars in the barbaric regions of north-west China and who gradually acquired power for themselves by becoming indispensable to their erstwhile masters. By local war and gradual expansion into an empire that, by 600, stretched from north-east China to the Aral Sea, the Turks brought gain though nothing original to the art of war. They won their successes by the oldest of methods—a single-minded devotion to battle against opponents who were divided among themselves. A Turk took it as an act of divinity to win a battle, of great glory to fall in combat and a shame to die by any other means. But once combined, neighbouring states moved against the Turks they began to fail. They were defeated by Persians and Chinese and, by 840, had lost almost everything they once possessed. But they had created a strong civilisation of their own—a system of writing, a measurement of time, communication systems and diplomatic contacts with strong neighbours such as Byzantium. In the eleventh century they began a migration to the West.

The most volatile expansion of all time by an invading people began in 1190 when the Mongols, under their great, if ruthless, leader Genghis Khan, began to acquire territory, followers and power as by-products of a series of dynastic disputes. Their domains centred upon the Gobi Desert, where some of the toughest, most self-reliant warriors in the world had predominated until the middle of the ninth century. The subsequent invasions by the Mongolian horde thereafter took either racial, nationalistic or religious motivation. The result was the almost total conquest of present-day China, India, Persia, Russia and part of Eastern Europe.

Genghis Khan

The most remarkable feat attributable to the Mongols is not so much the immensity of their total conquests but the fact that they accomplished them with small forces. It seems likely that the largest Mongol Army ever deployed was the 240,000 men used by Genghis to conquer Persia.

The unhappiest memory of the Mongols is their record for destruction to the exclusion of replacing old civilisations with cultural improvements. The history of Mongol militarism is of foundling dynasties and militant feats overlain by standards of barbarity and genocide excelling those of the Assyrians.

The dominating features of the Mongol armies was the sheer ability and zeal of their commanders. But they also displayed important military skills:

● *Organisation.* The basic formation was the *touman* of 10,000 men subdivided into ten battalions of 1,000 men, each battalion having ten squadrons of ten troops of ten men each.

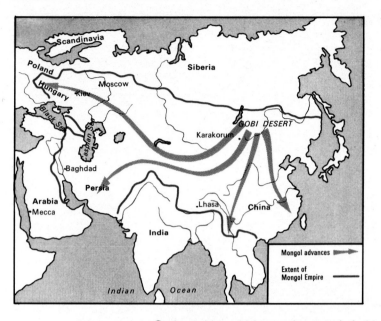

The Mongolian expansion

● *Composition*, which was almost entirely horsed—60 per cent of them "light", protected only by a helmet and armed with bows, the remaining 40 per cent "heavy" with mail armour or leather clothing in addition to the helmet. The "heavies" were usually armed with a lance. In addition there was a siege-train of conventional type and dimensions which, in 1113, breached the Great Wall of China—no great feat, as it happens, because it was easily outflanked as well.

● *Special weapons*. There is no proof that the Mongols used guns, though there is a suspicion that they had weapons employing some sort of explosive propellant—a bamboo tube containing gunpowder that was used to shower pellets to a distance of 250 yd (227·5 m), it is said. Flame was frequently used, but in siege warfare slings, along with trebuchets, were the commonest way of dispensing fiery and stone missiles. In open battle there is a suggestion that toxic gas was once used against Polish troops, but one has to remember that the Mongols were merchants in terror warfare who went to extremes to propagate that reputation. Much that is claimed for them may only have been the products of typical wartime rumours, sedulously spread by agents.

● *Communications*. Since the Mongols did not possess accurate time-measuring instruments and because few among them could read, the transmission of orders had to be by sound or visible signal. They improved upon existing methods by signal flags (black and white), drum beat and shouted commands. Serviceable route maps were carefully drawn on information from a network of spies. The Mongol armies always had an acute navigational sense.

● *Administration*. The Mongols lived systematically off the country, but the task was eased because their armies were relatively so small and campaigned on the move. The men lived hard, drinking horses' milk—a supply of which was assured by mounting the army chiefly on mares. Occupied territories were governed by nominated indigenous officials under Mongol supervision with strict implementation of fiscal and judiciary policy.

● *Tactical practice.* Ingenuity and surprise stimulated every campaign and battle plan. The unusual was commonplace by comparison with the methods of their foes. Attack was mandatory with thrust lines aimed at enemy flank and rear rather than by frontal assault. The enemy would be harassed by a wide-fronted advance and charged where confusion in the ranks appeared. The main assault would be by the heavy cavalry after preparation by the light which would seek enemy weak spots, give archery support in the initial stages and then exploit the victory once the enemy formations began to break and dissolve.

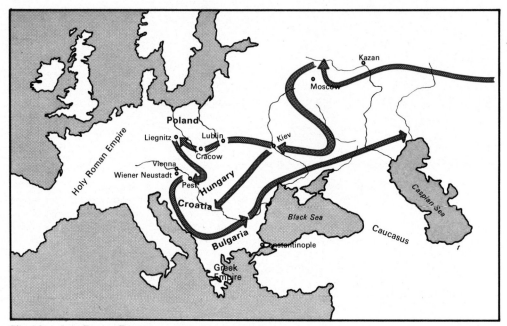

The Mongols in Eastern Europe

The first major Mongolian invasion of Europe began in 1237 when fifteen *toumen* (150,000 men) under the command of Sabutai, crossed the River Volga in winter, poured into Russia, took Moscow and reached the River Dnieper. In 1240, once the conquered Russian territories had been digested, Sabutai moved west, again in winter, besieging and destroying Kiev and subjugating every minor opponent between there and the Carpathian Mountains. The only element, so far, which had held up the Mongols was the condition of the ground, swollen rivers and administrative problems. In the meantime European factions, fearing the coming onslaught, tried to unite in defence of their continent. Although Christianity was in direct peril, the Christians, for all their so-called unity of faith, were unable to present a solid battle-front to the heathens. Indeed the Europeans continued with all manner of war among themselves throughout the period of the Mongol threat. For example, the Hundred Years War between England and France began in 1337, as the Mongols first struck Russia, and remained in full spate throughout the worst days of the invasion in the East.

The first great battle between Europeans and Mongols took place at Liegnitz on 9th April 1241. Sabutai took twelve *toumen* to invade Poland, Hungary, Bohemia and

Croatia, and divided them to make a three-pronged advance upon Pest in Hungary. The northern prong, working with habitual co-ordinated strategy, met and defeated a series of small unco-ordinated European detachments—armies which, had they withdrawn from their feudal territories and combined with others would have outnumbered the invaders and, indeed, might have outfought them since their armament and experience were far from inconsiderable. As it was the Europeans countenanced wild rumours that the pair of *toumen*, 20,000 strong, approaching Silesia, were an army of 200,000. Near Liegnitz Henry of Silesia and the Grand Master of the Teutonic Knights, with some 20,000 men, were brought to battle and crushed before they could be joined by 50,000 Bohemians under King Wenceslas. Henry took flight and was slain on the run, his head displayed to the defenders of besieged Liegnitz as a sign of Mongol intent. Perhaps it was this which determined the people of Liegnitz to successfully hold out even though Wenceslas withdrew. For Mongol treatment of the besieged was well known—clemency and servitude for those who surrendered at once and massacre for all who resisted to the slightest degree and who failed to persevere.

Mongol cavalry

The decisive Mongol success against the Europeans came on 11th April at the Sajo River where three concentrated *toumen*, after defeating three separate Hungarian detachments, came face to face with the main Hungarian Army of 100,000 under King Bela. Bela was safe at Pest—the Mongol's main objective. But he marched out to give battle and drove off the Mongol advanced detachments of light cavalry on the 10th. Then Sabutai attacked with all his strength, employing every device of smoke and noise that he could manufacture, pummelling the Hungarians with arrows and stones to such effect that an army nearly twice the size of the Mongolian force began to panic and, quite unnecessarily, seek ways of escape. As Mongolian horsemen appeared on all sides and in rear a general débâcle ensued. Bela escaped, but of his army some 65,000 paid with their lives.

The last defences of central Europe had been destroyed and the Mongols were free to go where they pleased. And then, apart from local exploitation and the destruction of Pest, the Mongols stood still and, as was their practice, spent the summer compelling the local people to till the fields for the benefit of their horses and in building stocks in readiness for the next winter's campaign. It is, of course, possible that this pause in the Mongol advance was intentional, that they never intended to penetrate any further into Europe. Be that as it may, the necessity for long pauses by horsed armies that lived off the country was underlined, and with it the advantage enjoyed by defenders who had depth of territory available in which to absorb an opponent's advance.

The crucial factor determining the Mongol strategy may have been dynastic. There were quarrels among the hierarchy. Ogedie, third son of Genghis, and now Great Khan, died. There arose problems of succession. Whatever the cause, the Mongols contented themselves with crossing the frozen River Danube on Christmas Day 1241, lunging at Wiener Neustadt and threatening Vienna; then setting off southward in pursuit of Bela through Croatia and thence, by a circuitous route, through Bulgaria on a return journey home via the Ukraine. It should be noted that:

● The vast distances were covered almost with impunity.

● The utter incapability of any existing army to stand against the Mongols.

This was one of the greatest military campaigns ever launched and completed, undefeated, yet without plucking the immense prizes which were to be taken for the asking.

In contrast with the Mongol campaigns, both in Europe and throughout Asia, the battles of the Hundred Years War were insignificant except for one vital factor—a dramatic demonstration of increases in fire-power.

The most deadly archery weapon ever introduced to the battlefield was the long, elm or yew bow in the hands of Welshmen. With a rate of accurate fire at six shots per minute at 200 yd (182 m), an iron-tipped shaft is recorded as penetrating a door 4 in thick. Mail armour was not proof against it and plate armour could also be penetrated. Its first use in battle may have been in 1120 near Powys when Welsh archers ambushed the English under Henry II, whose breastplate deflected one arrow. By 1250 the bow was standard equipment for English infantry under Edward I and archery practice made compulsory on Sundays to the exclusion of other games. Edward knew that, in battle, dismounted knights, well supported by archery, could defeat a charge by armoured horsemen, but that the archers, to survive, had to be trained to the highest pitch and strongly disciplined. This the English archers certainly were in 1337 when Edward III, provoked by Philip VI of France, raided the French coastline.

An expensive tactical lesson had been learnt, however, by his father, Edward II, in combat against the Scots under Robert Bruce at Bannockburn in 1314. Here the English, 23,000 strong, gave their archers only a secondary role, preferring to bludgeon the 19,000 Scots with a charge by 3,000 armoured knights. Thrown into confusion on soft ground the English were themselves charged by Scottish infantry who got to close quarters because the English archers were in a poorly sited firing position. In a mêlée the Scottish pikemen were superior to knights in disarray. The English were routed—but the memory of their mistakes lingered on.

*The most deadly soldier of his day—
the long-bowman*

The cross-bowman

The first major battle of the Hundred Years War was at sea off Sluys in 1340 when English archers and stone-throwing catapults laid such heavy fire upon the French fleet that entire crews were wiped out. The French fleet was eventually annihilated.

King Edward III of England.
The victor at Crécy

The Trebuchet

The decisive land battle of this first phase of the Hundred Years War was in 1346 at Crécy. The English had been busy supporting local dissidents against the French Crown in Brittany when the French invaded England's ally, Gascony. Edward III, with an army about 16,000 strong, composed, perhaps, of some 9,000 archers, 4,000 Welsh spearmen and 3,000 heavy cavalry, moved to the indirect support of the Gascons in the south by invading northern France, thus compelling the French to turn on him. The French Army's real strength was in its 12,000 aristocratic, heavy cavalry and 17,000 light cavalry. No reliance was placed on the 25,000 levies, while the 6,000 professional, mercenary Genoese were treated with ill-placed disdain.

The first definitely recorded use of artillery in open warfare was at the battle of Crécy—though there is reason to believe that primitive cannon were used in siege warfare at Metz in 1324 or Algeciras in 1342. Gunpowder—a mixture of saltpetre, sulphur and charcoal—may have been invented by the Chinese but there is no corroboration of this. It was found in Europe in the early fourteenth century and may have been invented by a German monk called Berthold Schwarz or the Englishman Roger Bacon. The first artillery pieces were nothing less than iron pots stuffed with gunpowder which, when detonated, threw a shower of stones or iron balls. Edward had at least three at Crécy, each almost as dangerous to friend as to foe. They were no substitute for archers whose weapon Edward employed in much the same way as artillery was to be used in the future—as a long-range missile-throwing device in support of infantry and cavalry.

The first contact at Crécy occurred in the late afternoon of 25th August 1346 when the French Army, advancing in column, came across the English who were in a defensive position upon a hill, with flanks secured by the village of Crécy on the right and Wadicourt on the left. The English front line, 2,000 yd (1·8 km) long, was held by men-at-arms supported on flanks and in centre by archers and cannon which could fire across the front as well as straight into the bottom of the valley some 550 yd (500 m) distant. In the rear stood the King with his reserve. All were dismounted except for a small counter-penetration force. The French were furiously determined to punish the English for plundering northern France and, filled with confidence in the knowledge of the preponderance, their mounted knights chose to attack direct from the line of march without careful reconnaissance or deployment.

Amid growing confusion the Genoese cross-bowmen, who were marching at the head of the French columns, were pushed into a ragged attack across low ground that was overlooked by the English and which had been made soft by a heavy thunderstorm. Behind came the cavalry, arrogantly elbowing its way into action. Desultory fire at long range was opened by the Genoese, but the English maintained a disciplined silence, fighting as they were to a strict plan and concise orders. Then, with the range at 150 yd (136 m) and well within killing distance, the English opened fire both with archery and artillery. The air darkened with arrows humming with rhythmic fall. The Genoese staggered, halted and ran—straight among the oncoming cavalry who added to their discomfort by riding and

The Secret weapon introduced at Crécy— early cannon

hacking them down, in the belief that they were deserters. Some of the Genoese retaliated by firing back. Meantime the French chivalry breasted the slope, falling in handfuls but eventually, in broken array, reaching the English men-at-arms. Hand-to-hand fighting ensued, with no attempt at a flank attack—which, it has been suggested, would have dishonoured the rules of Chivalry. The plain fact of the matter was that the French were too eager to bother with such refinements.

There never was much hope of the French penetrating the English line, not even when the English right flank, under the command of the Black Prince, came near to breaking. Here a counter-attack from the left relieved the position. Indeed, not once was Edward compelled to commit his main reserve except for twenty knights sent to strengthen the Black Prince at the height of the struggle. Into the dusk the French kept arriving in waves, and like waves recoiled at the shore of the English line. Only black darkness brought an end to the barrage and allowed the French to retire with losses of about 10,000 against some 200 English dead and wounded.

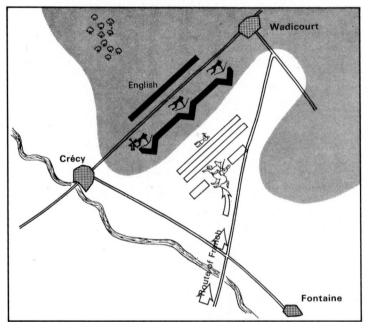

The Battle of Crécy

Crécy taught one of the profoundest lessons in the art of war—the inadvisability of assailing an entrenched, unshaken and well-armed opponent without resort to manœuvre, surprise or carefully prepared supporting action. The lesson was lost on the French for they were to repeat their mistakes at Poitiers in 1356 and at Agincourt in 1415 against those deadly archers who invariably proved that the well-aimed missile must overcome the armoured man no matter how much additional protection he tried to carry upon his person or horse.

The dominant impression of Crécy is ingrained in the strategy of Edward III and the way he forced the French to abandon their attack upon Gascony and in the battlefield tactics which enabled dismounted men—above all archers—to engage and defeat a mounted enemy with such economy.

SECTION IV

The Gunpowder Revolution
1416–1760

Although it was but a short step from the discovery of gunpowder to its employment as a missile propellant, the development of firearms and artillery was largely dependent upon parallel discoveries in chemistry and metallurgy before they became significant in battle. It is a measure of the increasing pace of technological progress that it took 200 years of gunpowder weapons to establish their essential characteristics.

The first steel was accidentally produced prior to the fourteenth century, but thereafter, as much larger furnaces for the production of pig-iron came into use, steel was made in greater quantities by prolonged heating of the raw material over charcoal in clay boxes or jars.

The first successful casting of iron took place in the fifteenth century. While the earliest guns were usually made from cast bronze or brass, or by welding together a circle of wrought-iron bars, it was cast-iron cannon which became universal towards the end of the fourteenth century. These guns took all manner of names, were of an enormous range of calibre and either loaded through the breech or muzzle.

The biggest artillery piece of the era—and the largest ever produced—was the Russian "King of Cannons" with a calibre of 915 mm in 1502. It fired a 1 ton (1,017 kg) stone down a barrel that was 17 ft (5·2 m) in length.

The Moscow "King of Cannons"—the largest gun ever

The first attempts at rifling gun-barrels to improve ballistic properties were made and failed in the fifteenth century. Therefore for many years the smooth bore only was used.

The primary hazard of the artillerist was the gunpowder itself which was unstable, did not travel well and therefore had to be mixed on site amid the flame of battle. Gunners, in consequence, became specialists in the art of mixing and judging the correct charge to use. Nevertheless, ignition of the slow-burning powder chains was of such a random and incalculable nature that uniform accuracy of aim was impossible and, therefore, each gun had to be manhandled and aimed individually.

The first positive step to converting gunnery from an art into a science dates from the publications of an Italian, Nicolo Tartaglia who, in 1537, 1546 and 1551, wrote books defining the science of ballistics. And in 1550 Charles of Spain was first to actually rationalise calibre size by standardising the artillery of his army into seven types:

40-pdr	cannon
34-pdr	cannon moyen
17-pdr	culverin (two types)
6-pdr	(two types)
3-pdr	falcon

The earliest cannon were usually emplaced either in an earthen mound or upon wooden platforms. Not until the early fifteenth century were mobile carriages produced and later yet that gun trunnions (the supporting projections on either side of the barrel that act as the pivot for elevation) were devised by the French.

The most important battlefield development in the use of firearms and artillery came at the direction of John Zizka, the leader of the Hussites (early Protestant Republicans) who, in 1419, fervidly opposed the conventionally armed and armoured Bohemian Roman Catholic, Monarchist armies. Zizka founded his army upon wooden waggons, that mounted cannon (called "snakes") to fire through loopholes. By driving the waggons into defensive circles to occupy dominating vital ground, he tried to compel the enemy to attack at a disadvantage. The stationary waggons were linked by heavy boards and protected by thick timbers which were virtually proof against missiles. The Bohemian knights, on the other hand, though enjoying protection from the greatly improved plate and steel armour of the day (personal armour attained its zenith in quality and thickness in the fifteenth century) were vulnerable to firearms. Chiefly, however, their casualties increased because **Zizka was the first commander to train his men to aim firearms from the shoulder** in addition to teaching his artillerists to shoot more precisely than their predecessors. With Zizka artillery became a death-dealing weapon instead of a noise-making, secondary device.

The first "handguns" date from 1388 and a primitive system of almost "instant ignition", by means of touching the powder with a match, appeared near the end of the century. By 1411 a mechanical device to apply the match to the powder via a touchhole in the cannon's barrel was in existence.

The blind John Zizka at the head of his Hussite Army. Note the agricultural nature of his followers' weapons, in particular the flails

The true genius of Zizka's army, however, lay in its tactical methods and burning zeal. Basically a peasant army whose weapons, in addition to the artillery, were agricultural flails (hardened by iron projections), cross-bows and swords, it possessed, in addition to the waggon fortress, an élite, cavalry arm. Zizka began his military career as a mercenary guerilla fighter, in support of Polish and Lithuanian forces fighting against the arrogant Teutonic Knights in the campaign of Tannenberg in 1410. Like most guerilla armies Zizka's was forced to do its training in battle. His thrived on success and grew from a score to many hundred waggons strong. In fourteen years (before at last they were overborne by sheer numbers and divisions within their ranks after Zizka died) they won fifty battles.

The most significant of Zizka's battles was fought in December 1421. By that time the Hussites had fixed a firm grip upon Bohemia amid religious warfare of the vilest kind. King Sigismund of Luxembourg was determined to restore the old order in what amounted to a "crusade" and, throughout 1421 had assembled a numerically superior force of about 40,000 men composed of Hungarians, Rumanians and Slavs commanded by an Italian called Philip de Scolari (Pipo Spano). Yet Sigismund's approach to Bohemia was tardy while his inept political initiatives strengthened Hussite resolve instead of tapping the potential of their factional divisions. Early in December, Zizka (who by now was totally blind) concentrated his forces at Kutna Hora, 40 miles to the east of Prague, thus barring the slow approach of Sigismund from the south-east. On 21st December Sigismund swung westward and wheeled to approach Kutna Hora from the west, seeking battle with some 30,000 men against the 12,000 Hussites Zizka could muster. Zizka was taken by surprise. Leaving the town under a small garrison, he was only just in time to position the waggon fort atop a ridge almost at the moment the attack developed. All day it was pressed, but easily beat off a series of cavalry charges, its artillery making an indelible impression by its noise even if the casualties it inflicted were much lower than claimed. At dusk, however, Pipo by-passed the waggons and appeared at the walls of the city where the German citizens opened the gates and permitted the slaughter of the Hussite inhabitants. Meantime Zizka was almost surrounded as well as cut off from his supplies at Kutna Hora. He was compelled, therefore, to break out and risk battle in the open, choosing to do so by night—a reflection of his confidence in his men's sound discipline and training—launching the waggons northwards against the Royalist positions, stopping only to fire his guns and burst through to reach a fresh tactical sanctuary on the road to Kolin whence he eventually shifted to revictual.

Sigismund now concluded that the campaign was over, and, since it was deep winter and extremely cold, did the conventional thing by retiring into Kutna Hora. But Zizka was master of the counter-attack and counter-offensive. Just as sometimes he would launch his cavalry from the midst of a waggon fort once the enemy appeared exhausted and disorganised, so now he made a surprise advance with his whole army against Sigismund. On 6th January he caught the main body at Nebovidy and rolled it back with heavy losses towards Kutna Hora. Dispersed as he was in winter quarters, Sigismund had no option but to abandon Kutna Hora and begin a disorderly retreat, hotly pursued by the Hussites who were thirsting for vengeance. When he attempted to give battle at Nemecky Brod on the 8th it proved but a gesture. The Hussites charged and the Hungarians bolted. There was a wild pursuit that drove a terrified mass of heavily armoured knights pell-mell towards a narrow bridge across an ice-covered river. Many tried to ride on the ice which broke under their weight. The bodies of over 500 knights were fished out in due course and Sigismund's survivors driven from sight. At this the waggon artillery was turned upon the walls of Nemecky Brod which was finally taken amid an orgy of slaughter by the Hussites.

The most bestial wars are those with a religious bias and religious wars were on the increase in the fifteenth century. At the Siege of Carolstein in 1422, to give an example of bacteriological attack, the bodies of the slain along with 2,000 cartloads of manure were catapulted into the city. Prior to the Siege of Constantinople in 1453, sulphur fumes were employed by the Turks to gas Byzantine defenders.

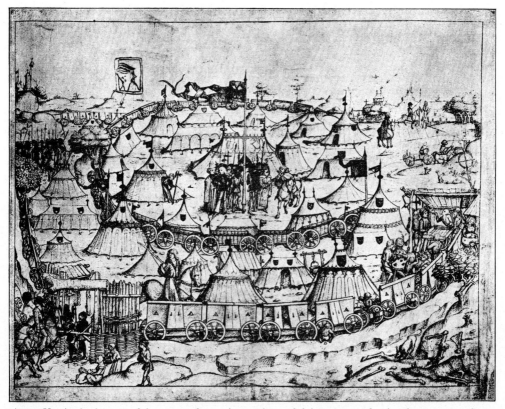

A post-Hussite development of the waggon fortress in two rings—fighting waggons forming the outer one and baggage waggons the inner

One of the most powerful military organisations of this period was that of the Osmanli or Ottoman Turks. Emerging out of Mesopotamia in the mid thirteenth century they lodged in Asia Minor and began to share in the erosion of the failing Byzantine Empire with Bulgarian, Genoese and Venetian mercenaries as well as itinerant Christian Crusaders. The Ottoman Army waxed strongly, forming an élite corps of enslaved Christians called Janissaries, whose discipline was based on total military discipline to the exclusion of lesser worldly pleasures. By 1320 the Turks occupied the bulk of Asia Minor and were beginning to enter Europe. Eventually they were to reach the walls of Vienna and encompass the Crimea and great stretches of the Middle East, including the entire Mediterranean coast from the northern Adriatic eastward to Palestine and thence westward along the southern shores beyond Oran. The Ottoman Navy contributed much to these conquests, of course, but the Army, undeniably among the best of its day, was predominant.

There were three vital elements that made the Ottoman Army strong:

● *The fighting ability of the foot and mounted soldiers* who were armed with swords or bows and, usually, armoured from head to foot in chain mail, sometimes carrying a shield. By 1450 the regular element was about 15,000 strong described by J. F. C. Fuller as ". . . the most formidable soldiers of the fifteenth century". Their love of a fight was immense, their self-sacrifice boundless.

● *The artillery* which was equipped with some of the best pieces then in existence. The largest in 1453, for example, was a 19-tonner made in Hungary, capable of firing a 1,500 lb (675 kg) missile a distance of 1,100 yd (1 km). Its rate of fire, however, was very low since it took more than three hours to replace the gun in its mounting after displacement by the recoil of firing.

● *The art of fortification* which reached its height of excellence both in design and construction coincident with heavy artillery's announcement of the doom of stonework fortresses of the old type. For example, the Rumeli Hisari, which was built by 10,000 men, so it is said, in four and a half months in 1452 to dominate the Bosporus from the northern shore, is a superb example of well-bonded stonework up to 24 ft (7·3 m) thick. Yet this fort's effectiveness was entirely dependent upon its artillery reaching across the Bosporus at this, its narrowest point (where Darius once crossed), to deal with ships attempting the passage.

The last Crusade moved against the Turks in 1444 in an effort to save the surviving fragments of the Byzantine Empire from destruction. The Turks had deeply invaded the Empire on many occasions prior to 1443, but had at last been held in check by successive defeats at the hands of the Hungarian forces of King Ladislas, commanded by John Hunyadi—whose techniques were learnt from Zizka. A truce was signed, as a result of which Murad II, the Turkish Sultan, was forced to abdicate. Buoyed up with success, Ladislas almost at once broke the truce and launched the Crusade, asking the Venetian Navy to lift his army by sea from Varna on the Black Sea coast to Constantinople. The Venetians, however, failed to arrive at Varna. Murad, restored to power, raced with an army that was 50,000 strong to attack the Crusaders, who could but muster only 15,000, including 4,000 Polish mercenaries, where they lay marooned at the port. Hunyadi deployed his predominantly cavalry force outside Varna and emplaced a waggon fort on the right flank, adjacent to the coast. The battle on 11th November was a swirling encounter between horsemen. The first lunge by the Turks against Hunyadi's left was thrown back by a fierce Hungarian counter-charge which dispersed the Turks and drove them back upon the Janissary infantry who were backing up. Once Hunyadi's cavalry was fully committed still more Turkish cavalry appeared and attacked the waggon fortress, to be held at bay by the cannon and cross-bowmen. Successive Hungarian charges got weaker as Hunyadi switched his cavalry from flank to flank in attempts to spoil each Turkish formation's cohesion. When at last his cavalry was destroyed (though he himself survived), the waggon fortress fought on, spitting artillery defiance and acting as shelter to the infantry and survivors from the main battle. Eventually sheer weight of numbers had to tell and break among the waggons to complete their destruction along with most of the defenders. Lives to the Turks meant nothing, but the guns in the waggon fort were invaluable for by this time **pieces of artillery were the most precious of war material**.

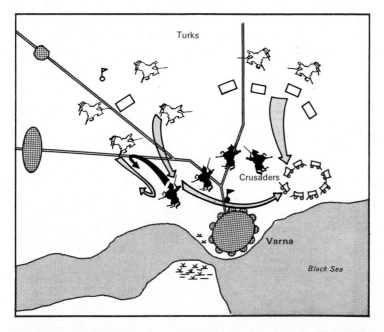

The Battle of Varna, 1444

The final collapse of the Byzantine Empire dates from the Siege of Constantinople in 1453 and was the culmination of the Turkish Sultan, Mahomet's, burning ambition to possess the city. Mahomet, a dynamically cruel and unstable character who was also endowed with innate political cunning, could raise an army of about 80,000 men supported by a fleet and some seventy pieces of artillery, including the monster described above. The Emperor Constantine XI had less than 10,000 men who were divided in loyalty, entrenched behind ancient walls which were much in need of repair. However, his Genoese commander, Giustiniani, was a superb soldier of experience and guile, who might have fared even better had not Hunyadi advised the Turks upon artillery tactics, telling them to concentrate fire against specific weak spots in the walls instead of scattering their shot in the pre-Zizka pyrotechnic manner.

The first massed artillery bombardment in history began on 12th April and was to continue without let until 29th May. Yet when the Turkish infantry made their first assault on 18th April it was premature: the breach had not been made, the defenders were uncowed and the assailants swept away by fire from massed Byzantine guns, bows and catapults.

The first recorded example of a fleet taking to the land occurred when Mahomet transported seventy warships along a greased runway behind Galata to enter the upper waters of the Golden Horn and thus threaten the garrison from within. The manœuvre led to no conclusion, though as a formidable feat it seriously lowered the garrison's morale. Nevertheless, renewed assaults against the western walls of the city were beaten back in response to the example of Constantine bracing his people to the struggle. Each fresh breach in the walls was held by Giustiniani and repaired after combat. When the Turks rolled up a wooden fighting tower to dominate a breach, Giustiniani had it demolished by gunpowder barrels rolled down from the flanks. Attempts to undermine the walls were repulsed by counter-mining, inundation or sulphurous smoke. All this time the Turks were getting weaker instead of stronger because their logistic system was beginning to break down and they faced starvation quite as much as the garrison.

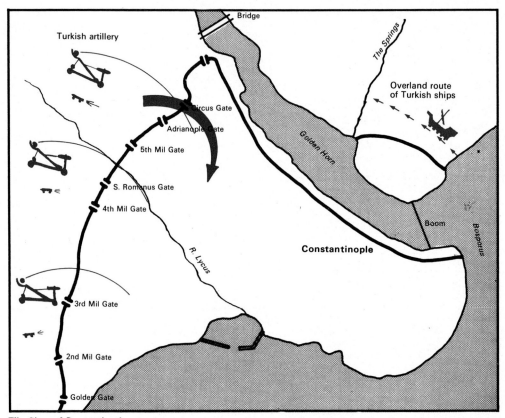

The Siege of Constantinople, 1453

The last desperate assault was made on Constantinople on 29th May by the entire Turkish Army, supported by a naval bombardment to pin some of the 4,000 surviving defenders to the walls and prevent them reinforcing the selected point of land assault. Yet both Turkish troops and Janissaries were held and might have been utterly defeated had not Giustiniani been wounded. With his departure from the front confusion set in. Penetrations were made by the Turks, the garrison began to lose hope and collapsed when Constantine was killed in action. Though Mahomet introduced measures that respected the existence of the Greek Orthodox Church he was quite unable (and probably unwilling) to prevent his men looting the city and doing immense damage—though with smaller loss of life than during the assault by Crusaders in 1204.

The two most paradoxical military phenomena of the fifteenth century were the English and Swiss armies which managed to retain a measure of supremacy against the armies of the day despite an almost invariable inferiority in numbers as well as in outmoded weapons. Trusting in the long-bow, which, for the next century, possessed far greater accuracy and range than field artillery and hand firearms, the English persisted in using them against France. It was not until 1487 that the English, who had been among the first to use cannons, turned to adopt them in earnest. But by then they had lost a series of battles in which artillery, bombarding the archers from beyond long-bow range, had proved crucial in inflicting decisive defeats— above all at Formigny in 1450 and at Castillon in 1453. Thus Crécy, Poitiers and Agincourt were avenged by the French and for very similar, fundamental reasons—the by-products of the victors' superior technology linked to sane tactical plans which abstained from the temptation to close for hand-to-hand combat until complete moral and physical ascendancy was assured. It was not until 1595 that the English officially abolished the long-bow, though many years later before it finally disappeared from their armament. In the meantime sheer weight of numbers had ejected them from the Continent, their last bastion, Calais, falling in 1558.

Rated among the best infantry in Europe throughout the fifteenth century, the Swiss, like the English, rejected artillery in preference for a disciplined phalanx armed with a 21 ft (6·4 m) spear, supported by a select band of arquebusiers (predecessors of riflemen) and such cavalry as would join them from allied nations. The Swiss adopted the phalanx for the same reason as had the Greeks—as a mountain race who fought guerilla-type campaigns in hilly terrain they were frequently forced to descend into the plains in order to achieve a decision in formal battle. The Swiss phalanx was unique in that it usually manœuvred at exceptional speed and with drilled precision in columns that were a mere 30 men wide but 100 deep. The Swiss acquired a reputation as the fiercest of European soldiers in their struggles to eject foreigners—notably the French and Austrians—from their soil. They survived against cavalry, however, for the technical reason that their spears held horsemen at the fringes of effective pistol range.

The most complete of all Swiss victories were those won at Morat in 1476, when their 25,000 surprised twice that number of French under Charles the Bold and killed about 10,000 with scant loss to themselves; and at Nancy in 1477 when they again shattered the French, this time killing Charles himself in the course of pursuit. The Swiss now came into acute demand as mercenaries, as had the Genoese and Venetians before them. They fought for the highest bidder, won a reputation for implacable cupidity ("When the money runs out so do the Swiss") and independence in that they were invariably reluctant to fight except, rather sensibly, under tactical directions that suited their own concepts. They were professional fighting men *par excellence*, the product of a country which was under almost perpetual external pressure as well as internal dissent (so like the Assyrians) who made their mark on the eve of the sequence of religious wars which were to ravage Europe for the next two centuries or more. Swiss ferocity made an awful impact; but they, in their turn, would be forced to compromise when stronger artillery decimated their packed ranks.

The gunpowder revolution, which inevitably altered the tactics of open battle, also changed the nature of siege warfare in the aftermath of the fall of Constantinople. The Turks, rid of danger from Byzantine, struck out to east and west both

The Turkish Army at the walls of Vienna, 1529. This print admirably depicts not only the lines of battle but also the weapons and administrative resources of the besiegers

by sea and land. Everywhere their siege-train followed, to batter holes in the walls of cities which, for generations, had withstood the ancient engines of war. In May 1529, under Suleiman I, they invaded Hungary with 80,000 men, supported in their advance up the River Danube by warships carrying the siege-train. The advance was slow but, upon reaching Buda on 3rd September, the siege was conducted with such vigour that the place fell within five days. The garrison was massacred. Austria was next invaded and ravaged, the Turks reaching Vienna on the 23rd. But here they found defenders who, scared by the uncomprising savagery of the Turks, had every incentive to resist and who, strengthened by clear insight into the artillery war, had emplaced guns close to the walls with fields of fire opened up by demolishing houses so that the Turkish batteries and infantry could not deploy, unopposed, within range. The Viennese also dug trenches close outside the walls to give additional protection to gunners and defenders and to act as a counter-mining device. By 23rd September, the Turkish flotilla had unloaded the artillery and sailed upriver to complete the investment. Here they were confronted by a system of defence which set a pattern for the future.

The Viennese were well supplied with munitions and dynamically led by Marshal William von Roggendorf. They indulged in heavy counter-bombardment, repeated sorties and raids upon the Turkish outposts and batteries as well as a counter-mining programme which was as ambitious as that of the Turks. The Turkish assaults lacked the power to penetrate the walls and were disrupted in their forming-up places. On 14th October, Suleiman had the good sense to realise that he could not succeed and that, if he stayed, his army would be destroyed by the winter's cold. However, his withdrawal soon turned into a disaster. Early snow and mud-bound roads caused a fearful movement problem which was deranged by fierce harrying from the Austrian land forces and a destructive bombardment of their ships as they ran the gauntlet of Austrian guns located at Pressburg.

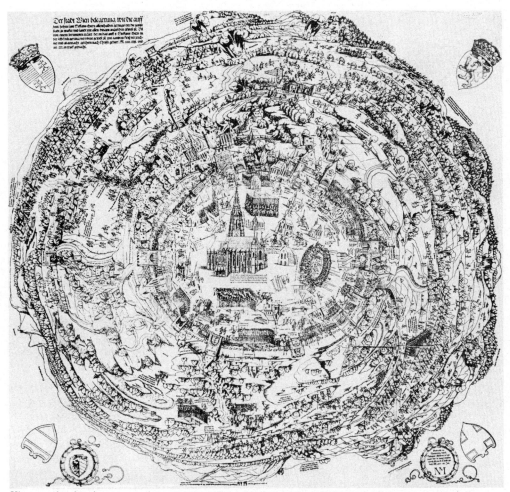

Vienna under siege in 1529

The fundamental medium for a sudden prolific dissemination of knowledge was the invention of mechanical printing, usually credited to John Gutenberg somewhere about 1450. The invention owes much to the science of metallurgy being dependent upon the development of engraving upon a new alloy of lead, tin and antimony. Before the end of the century printing-presses had sprung up all over Europe, ushering a new age of inquiry and analysis which revolutionised sociological, religious and economic, as well as military thought and practice, by a cross-fertilisation of ideas and a tendency towards industrial standardisation.

Most influential among the military philosophers of the early sixteenth century was Niccolo Machiavelli whose *The Prince*, completed in 1514, and the *Art of War*, were aimed at restoring the prestige and power of Florence and the Italian States. Machiavelli studied the rapidly evolving art of war as practised by France and Spain who were at that time in fierce competition. He claimed that "The main foundations of every state . . . are good laws and good arms" and "A Prince should have no other object or thought . . . except war, its organisation and its discipline." Machiavelli was very much a man of his own day, as the main tenets of his principles show:

● Creation of an infantry-based militia and condemnation of mercenaries and auxiliaries since they were ungovernable.
● Rejection of fortresses because they caused enmity.
● The implication that wars of aggression could be conducted with unbalanced forces that were somewhat light in the striking power of artillery and cavalry.

Niccolo Machiavelli

Machiavelli was right when he inferred that the day of the armoured horseman was over. Come the sixteenth century and all serious attempts at achieving complete personal protection on the battlefield had been abandoned. Armour had been reduced in weight and was designed only to guard a man's most vulnerable parts in the hope of deflecting rather than defeating a blow or missile. Emphasis was placed upon increased striking power with superior weapons: protection was relegated to the art of agility and evasion. Yet fortresses did not of a sudden disappear, for Europe was entering a phase of 200 years' interminable war.

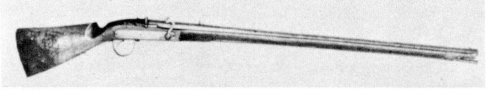

A matchlock musket

The most important step forward towards increasing firepower was the invention of a satisfactory matchlock hand-gun which could be aimed from the shoulder, if necessary with the aid of a rest to support a weapon which could weigh as much as 25 lb (11·3 kg). A glowing match was applied to the charge by means of a finger-actuated lever—the precursor of the trigger. Throughout more than two centuries, matchlock small-arms (given a variety of names which included arquebus and musket) evolved into quite reliable weapons with a mechanism that, under tension, released the flame, against the charge enabling the gunner to select an almost exact moment to fire when his aim was correct. These weapons had a slow rate of fire due to the time needed to reload (two rounds a minute was good in battle) and a low standard of accuracy due to the difficulty of measuring the correct amount of powder. In addition, since the discomfort of absorbing the musket's kick on recoil got worse because each succeeding shot fouled the barrel, aim declined as a battle progressed.

The earliest exponents of massed small-arms fire in battle were the Spaniards under Gonzalo de Cordoba, to whom may be accorded the title "Father of Trench Warfare" in the gunpowder age. He sought to emplace arquebusiers behind barricades or in trenches, siting them so as to cover a wide frontage while relying upon pikemen, halberdiers and swordsmen, interspersed among the arquebusiers, to repel a charge to close quarters. However, although Cordoba, who organised his infantry units into columns of between 1,000 and 1,250 men, succeeded in creating, in 1505, one of the first fully integrated formations of all arms, he was forced to abandon the type of universal infantrymen the archer represented with consequential loss of flexibility in action.

The best demonstration of Cordoba's system was the action against Swiss infantry and French cavalry at the Battle of Cerignola in 1503 when his arquebusiers, supported by artillery, swept the enemy away. It was a lesson which, apparently, was lost on Machiavelli but not the French who, along with other nations, hastened to copy the Spanish method and also develop ways of defeating it.

The first confrontation between two truly modern field armies was the Battle of Ravenna in 1512. The French, under Gaston de Foix, had about 32,000 men, including 8,500 German *Landsknechte* (mercenaries of the Swiss kind) and 54 guns. The Spanish were about 18,000 strong with 30 guns, but well entrenched with their flanks and rear secured by the River Ronco. After a formal challenge from Gaston and its acceptance by Raymond de Cardona, the Spanish commander, a prolonged duel took place between the opposing artillery, a duel which left, virtually untouched, the Spanish infantry but decimated every unit above ground, particularly the cavalry. Indeed the Spanish cavalry were so galled that they launched a premature attack and were eliminated from the contest. When at last the French and Germans assailed the Spanish lines a grim struggle took place within the entrenchments, neither side gaining much advantage. However, Gaston now demonstrated the superior virtues inherent in mobile artillery, ferrying a pair of cannon across the river to shoot against the Spaniards from the rear and so undermining their morale that they broke and fled. Then, caught on open ground, when trying to break out of the ring, the Spanish infantry were exposed in full vulnerability. Their losses rose to 9,500 killed against 4,500 French—which included Gaston, killed at the moment of victory.

The first steps in the creation of what, one day, would be the largest army in the world began in the mid-sixteenth century during the reign of Ivan IV (the Terrible) of Russia. From 1547 until 1584 Ivan's Russia was almost continually at war to suppress internal revolt, to quell the Tartars, and win from the Swedes and Poles an outlet to the Baltic Sea. Inevitably, too, he came into collision with the Ottoman Turks. In the process he reshaped Russia by replacing the old aristocracy with a new breed of landowners and a feudal bureaucracy. Upon this he based **the first regular Russian Army** of infantry supported by a siege-train of somewhat limited equipment and scope. Ivan's army, and particularly the Oprichniki (its 6,000-strong praetorian guard) imbibed the philosophy of the Mongols. In victory or defeat, deeds of the utmost cruelty were perpetrated by soldiers who took Ivan as their example. And defeat occurred rather more frequently than victory in parallel with the execution by Ivan of military advisers, with whom he disagreed, and massacres which led to wholesale depopulation. Ivan could have learnt from Western Europe, with which he had diplomatic contacts, that brute force was no panacea. Skill and the more powerful armaments of a burgeoning technology could, in due course, take their toll.

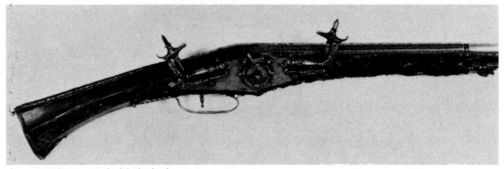

A seventeenth-century wheel-lock pistol

The first battleworthy pistol was, by obligation, the first practical firearm that could be handled by a mounted horseman. For the matchlock system was incompatible with a genuine one-handed weapon, above all in use by a mounted man on the move. There are many claimants to the invention—Leonardo da Vinci in 1500, Martin Löffelholz in 1505 and so on. In simple terms a wheel-lock is a kind of cigarette lighter in which a spark, generated by releasing a spring-loaded wheel against iron pyrite, ignites the powder in the weapon's flash-pan. In combat this enabled a cavalryman, armed with two or three of these relatively expensive weapons, to ride within range of the enemy, discharge them at close quarters and either retire to reload or return them to their saddle holsters and set to with sword in close combat. Tactically, therefore, the pistol acted in dissuasion of the headlong charge and reverted the horse to the role of a mobile fire platform such as once the chariot had been.

The first battleworthy flintlock firearm was produced by the Frenchman Marin Le Bourgeoys in 1615—although there are references to this method dating back as far as 1547 in Italy and also in Sweden. The flintlock was a much-improved adaptation of the wheel-lock except that the complex spring mechanism was discarded in favour of an arm held in the "cocked" position under tension, by a sear attached to the trigger. When the trigger was pulled the arm struck flint against a steel plate and projected sparks on to the powder.

The relatively sudden appearance of so many new inventions in the sixteenth century did more than test the ingenuity of soldiers. It overtaxed exchequers in their attempts to re-equip armies to a modern scale. Suitable materials were in short supply and, like the skilled armourers who manufactured weapons, commanded a high price. For economic reasons re-equipment had to be extremely slow and so it was many years before armies were universally equipped with matchlocks. Therefore, having once completed a re-equipment programme, the infantry were unlikely to be allowed almost at once to scrap new matchlocks in exchange for the superior flintlock, particularly when the aristocratic cavalry were demanding the yet more costly wheel-lock pistols, and the artillery was clamouring for bigger and better guns of increased size, range, reliability and mobility. Throughout the sixteenth and, to a large extent, the following century, armies made do with a polyglot hotchpotch of weapons— some that were of ancient derivation, some modern and slowly being introduced into élite units, and a mass which had been captured or bought cheap in an emergency from abroad. Standardisation was almost unknown: improvisation the order of the day; formal military education was acquired mainly by practice at war.

An example of sixteenth-century field artillery. Note the gun-shield, which was unusual

The first military college in "modern style" was founded in Holland by John of Nassau in 1617 to study the demand for better organisation forced upon the larger armies by complex logistic requirements. It was nearly two centuries before this example was seriously copied by other nations.

The military genius of one man synthesised the vast range of separate elements among the changing aspects of land warfare and harnessed modern technology to a practical military philosophy. It then required an inflammable political situation to set that man on course to demonstrate his brilliance. The man was **King Gustavus Adolphus of Sweden**, the situation those fanatical collisions between religious factions in the struggle between the Protestant successors of Martin Luther and old-world Roman Catholicism—the confrontation known as the **Thirty Years War** which began in 1618. Political and dynastic matters intervened, but religious intemperance supervened throughout.

Gustavus Adolphus succeeded to the Swedish Throne in 1611 at the age of sixteen and was at once involved in battle against the Danes. An

A Janissary

(above) The Rumeli Hisari—built by 10,000 men in four and a half months (below) Murad II defeats the Hungarian cavalry under John Hunyadi at Varna in 1444

intellectual of cultured imagination, drive and courage he revelled in war. Addicted to well-ordered administration and disciplined military systems he enhanced his flair for leadership and command with an extraordinary clemency by comparison with the standards of the day. There is hardly an assessment of Gustavus which does not portray him as a paragon of political and military virtue, the epitome of Machiavelli's Prince. But Gustavus was a realist who never doubted that well-controlled small-arms fire was the key to battlefield success. With French financial backing he reorganised and re-equipped the entire Swedish Army, endeavouring to economise in manpower while at the same time increasing—redoubling— combat effectiveness:

● *The infantry* he formed into brigades of two or four regiments, each of which had eight battalions of four companies that were composed of seventy-two musketeers and fifty-four pikemen. The weight of the musket was reduced from 25 to 11 lb (4·8 kg), so that it could be aimed without a rest, the wheel-lock was slowly introduced and the **first practical fixed cartridge** issued to enable each musketeer to load the charge and the bullet in a single operation, thus eliminating inequalities of performance caused by measuring powder for each discharge as well as greatly increasing the rate of fire. This permitted a reduction in mass concomitant with extensions to the flanks in a longer line of battle than hitherto considered safe. The infantry fought in ranks six deep, instead of the conventional Spanish system of ten men deep. Firing was by volley of three ranks at a time—the first kneeling, the second stooping and the third standing. Flanking musketeers were taught to aim across the front to apply angled converging fire rather than the direct kind.

● *The cavalry* was also formated in ranks but reduced from the ten ranks of the Spanish system to only three. Some were partially clad in armour but some were simply mounted infantry. All were trained to charge, however, knee to knee instead of executing the *caracole*, which was the standard manœuvre of the day—trotting forward to discharge pistols and then retiring. Gustavus's cavalry was not treated as a bunch of prima donnas but carefully integrated with specific phases of the battle—to reconnoitre and drive in enemy skirmishers, to attack the enemy flank and rear, to pursue in victory or act as rearguard in a withdrawal. Infantry could be mixed with them, but it was upon artillery that they chiefly depended for support.

● *The artillery* was severely rationalised into three classes—siege, field and regimental. The first two copied the traditional functions of artillery in that they were taught to mass their fire. But they acquired extra mobility because Gustavus ruthlessly reduced the weapon's weight by lightening carriages and cutting down barrel length. Charges were standardised and rates of fire increased above that of the musket by the introduction of "fixed" ammunition. Yet at one leap Gustavus went beyond technical practicality. The copper-tubed 4-pdr gun, covered by leather, at a weight of only 90 lb (40·7 kg)—(the invention of Colonel Wurmbrant)—became too hot during periods of rapid fire with the result that charges ignited spontaneously during loading—to the detriment of both gun and gunners. A heavier material had thus to be substituted. With a modified weapon of 1631 Gustavus achieved the distinction of being **first to closely integrate light artillery with infantry and cavalry organisations**. Each regiment was given one or two of the new light 3-pounder guns which could be drawn by a single horse or by three men. (Contrast this with the standard 33-pounder of the day which might need twenty-five horses.) The artillery (like the cavalry) of the new Swedish Army was almost wholly manned by Swedes, Gustavus abolishing the tradition whereby specialist gunners served guns which were towed into battle by hired civilian contractors. Nevertheless this army did not just rise phoenix-like from the fire of Gustavus's imagination and genius but empirically throughout two decades of almost ceaseless experiment in battle.

Light Swedish quick firing regimental gun

The initiation into major action for the reorganising Swedish Army occurred in Sweden's wars against Poland between 1617 and 1629. Gustavus attempted to seize the eastern Baltic States at a time when the Poles were engaged already in war against the Turks and Greater Russians. In a drawn-out series of campaigns the Swedish Army both grew in strength and evolved, yet it never quite mastered the Poles who fought to a policy of mobile harassment, and managed eventually in 1629 to negotiate peace on satisfactory terms. Gustavus, too, wanted peace with Poland, for at the request of Cardinal Richelieu of France and in return for substantial foreign money to supplement Sweden's penurious treasury he was about to intervene in the Thirty Years War.

Before the Swedish intervention in the Great War, in 1630, numerous small confrontations between belligerent Catholics and Protestants had merged into one gigantic struggle engulfing the whole of central and large parts of Western Europe—a struggle, be it remembered, which raged in parallel with an almost ceaseless series of independent battles involving Turks in Eastern Europe. The forces of the Catholic League were mostly organised upon the Spanish model and commanded by men of military distinction such as:

● *Count Johan Tilly* who won a succession of victories in Bohemia and southern Germany at the beginning of the war and had progressively pushed northward, overcoming his opponents in a remorseless advance towards Denmark and the North German Plain. In 1626 he severely defeated the Danes at Lutter and repeated the process next year in collaboration with Count Albrecht von Wallenstein. In 1630 he failed, however, to reduce the garrison of Magdeburg, when his army suffered worse

Albrecht von Wallenstein

privations than those of the defenders. Indeed Tilly's commissariat was not nearly as efficient as Gustavus's. Nevertheless he persevered throughout a dreadful winter and at last took the city in May 1631, permitting his men to run riot and perpetrate an unwarranted but celebrated (though perhaps exaggerated) massacre of 25,000 people. In September he took Leipzig.

● *Count Albrecht von Wallenstein*, who was a convert from Lutheranism and all the more dangerous for that. He came late to soldiering in 1618 at the age of thirty-five as commander of the levies of Moravia. As a rich landowner and industrialist he hired himself, in 1623, with 20,000 men to the Catholic cause as defender of the Habsburg lands against the Bourbons. In 1625 he joined in offensive operations with Tilly against the Danes. At no time, however, was he popular with his own side. He viewed the Turkish threat with as much fear as the Protestant one. Even though he won victories there was constant pressure upon the Elected Emperor Ferdinand to remove him, the Electors expressing their concern that Wallenstein was becoming too powerful in Germany. As the Swedes entered the war and landed with 13,000 men at Usedom in Pomerania, Wallenstein was asked to resign, as a sop to waverers among the Catholic Electors and in an attempt to ensure German unity. It was therefore to Tilly that the Catholic League looked as its military commander against the reviving Protestant armies under Gustavus.

The first act of the Swedish King was to establish a logistic bridgehead in Pomerania and attract some 27,000 north German people to his standard. In April 1631 he struck south at great speed for Frankfurt on Oder and captured it by storm off the line of march. He hoped this would force Tilly to abandon the Siege of Magdeburg, but the city fell and Tilly riposted by invading and laying waste to Saxony, intending thereby to detach the Saxons from Gustavus. In the outcome it did the opposite, persuading their prince, John George, to place his army under Gustavus's command.

The main clash came at Breitenfeld on 17th September 1631, when Tilly, with 36,000 men, met Gustavus with 26,000 Swedes and 16,000 Saxons. Gustavus deployed his infantry in the centre, his cavalry on the right and the Saxons on the left. Tilly placed cavalry on both flanks of his infantry who were packed in the conventional squares. To the sound of trumpets and drums the artillery exchanged fire for over two hours—to the advantage of the Swedes, not only in damage inflicted (they fired three times faster than Tilly's) but for the psychological effect upon Tilly's left-wing cavalry under Count zu Pappenheim who, unable to restrain his men or himself, launched a premature attack upon the Swedish right and rear. Seven times the *caracole* was executed and beaten back by the Swedish volleys. When counterattacked Pappenheim's survivors bolted from the field. It was the turn of Tilly's right-wing cavalry to attack, also without orders, but charging among the Saxons who scattered. Against the exposed Swedish left Tilly now advanced his strength—his first tactical foray which was not involuntary. However, Gustavus detected the start of this movement and, exploiting the greater speed of his army's reactions, strengthened the exposed flank with infantry and light artillery, meeting the advancing enemy with a blaze of fire and a charge which shattered them. At this Gustavus ordered his right-flank cavalry to charge Tilly's left, thus achieving a double envelopment, running among the Catholic artillery and crumpling all resistance. Lost Saxon guns were recaptured and combined with captured Catholic guns to blast their previous owners. Briefly Tilly's men stood, but he himself was wounded and then the rout began. His army lost 13,000 men and all its guns to a vigorous pursuit. Swedish losses were slightly more than 2,000, nearly all of whom fell to artillery fire.

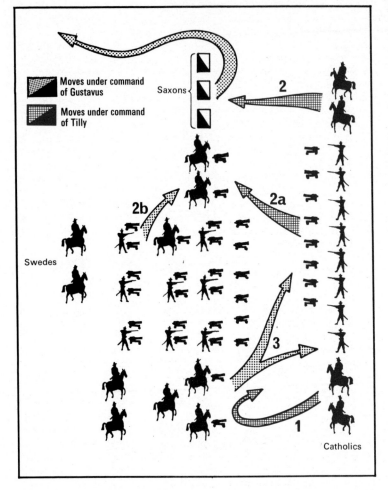
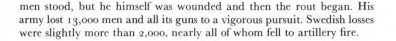

The Battle of Breitenfeld

The immediate results of Gustavus's victory at Breitenfeld amounted to conquest of the North German Plain and the Rhineland while thousands flocked to his side in a resurgence of Protestant confidence. In April 1632 he invaded Bavaria and defeated Tilly at the Battle of the Lech. Tilly died from wounds and Wallenstein was recalled to command with dictatorial powers. Manœuvre and counter-manœuvre filled the summer and autumn until Wallenstein inflicting defeat upon Gustavus at Alte Veste in September. As winter encroached Wallenstein entered quarters at Lützen, detaching Pappenheim to Halle in order to relieve the strain upon the commissariat. Seizing the chance of attacking a divided opponent, Gustavus at once marched to attack. The resemblance to Zizka before Kutna Hora will not be overlooked.

The last battle of Gustavus began with an army that was only 18,000 strong (wastage due to losses in battle and by sickness had been fearful) against the 20,000 of Wallenstein, who was suffering from gout and whose primary intention was to inflict sufficient delay to allow time for Pappenheim to join him. Adopting the customary formation of infantry squares flanked by cavalry, and placing his artillery to the fore, Wallenstein entrenched a line of musketeers in a ditch crossing the front. The contest opened with the routine artillery duel (there were about sixty guns on either side), the guns mixing their smoke with a thick early morning mist. Gustavus could make no apparent attempt to manœuvre because his left flank was impeded by Lützen (which Wallenstein burnt to add more smoke to the confusion) and his right by a canal. In the fighting which flared up across the entire front, the ditch was cleared, Wallenstein's cavalry shaken and his central gun battery taken and then retaken amid a general mêlée. Personally leading his men into action, Gustavus was at once involved in physical combat and thus deprived of the ability to function coolly in over-all command. Indeed it was while riding to re-establish control that he was caught and killed. Command reverted to Saxe-Weimar who so inspired his men that they fought even harder than when Gustavus was alive. The arrival of Pappenheim with his 8,000 merely postponed the decision, and he, too, was killed. Then the Swedes rushed forward again, overrunning Wallenstein's guns for the last time, capturing the baggage and taking full possession of the field. Wallenstein's army virtually disintegrated but departed unpursued since the Swedish Army was itself in complete disarray and exhausted. Every element had become fully engaged and its numbers were reduced to a mere 8,000 effective soldiers.

The political results of the Thirty Years War, which dragged on with ever-increasing violence until 1648, was the sating of religious enmity and the crystallisation of rivalry between Habsburgs and Bourbons, Spain and France. In the process Europe was converted into an unprincipled charnel-house in which, as Fuller puts it, "The peasants revolted, soldiers alone could live, and soon hordes of starving women and children, like packs of jackals, followed the army"—quoting 127,000 camp-followers to 38,000 fighting men in one instance.

The most significant change in the military balance came about with the final discrediting of Spanish arms and the revelation that the France of Richelieu's shaping was set to become the future military leader of Europe. In 1643, five months after Richelieu's death, a Spanish army advanced upon Paris from the Netherlands and besieged Rocroi. With 23,000 men the French commander, twenty-one-year-old Duke Louis d'Enghien, attacked the 27,000 Spaniards under Francisco de Mello. The ensuing battle was in two quite distinct phases—a wild encounter of charge and counter-charge between the rival cavalry, in which the Spaniards were driven from the field, followed by slow reduction of the Spanish infantry squares under the combined fire of the French and captured Spanish artillery until the Spaniards (who had repelled earlier infantry assaults) asked for terms. Unfortunately some Spanish troops opened fire upon d'Enghien as he rode forward to negotiate a surrender with the result that the French attack was renewed until the Spaniards were annihilated.

An important trend of the day was the inclination towards limitation of combat which appeared after the Thirty Years War—the attempts by d'Enghien and de Mello to make surrender possible with a saving of life being but one of several such incidents. The exorbitant cost of war both in material and life was generally deplored along with knowledge that people were tired of war.

Ministers of finance perpetually sought to keep military expenditure in line with commercial growth—and as often as not failed. Nevertheless, the armies which fought at the latter end of the war were far more professional in their outlook than those at the beginning—and good professional soldiers tend to eschew killing for killing's sake.

The first attempt at codifying international rules of war came in 1625. A Dutch lawyer, Edward Grotius, published a book called *On the Law of War and Peace* which established principles that remain valid to this day—the concepts that fairness in war should produce rules with a sense of moderation. But even Grotius could not evade the pressures of his day: though he declined to accept Catholic appointments he did become the Swedish Ambassador to France in 1634 where his principal task was seeking French aid for the Swedes in the war. It is ironic that he was excluded from the peace delegation which tried to end the war in 1643. He lived on the threshold of a new arms race. The French Army which, in 1600, had been only 15,000 strong, began recruiting vigorously. By 1678 it was to be 280,000 strong and in 1690 over 400,000 drawn from a population of only 20,000,000.

Edward Grotius

Sebastian Vauban

The most prominent signs of acceptance of a code of conduct in battle were to be found in connection with siege warfare, under French leadership and, above all, the influence of the Marquis Sebastien Vauban. Richelieu raised the French Army to a strength of nearly 100,000 in 1635. The child King Louis XIV, under the guidance of Cardinal Mazarin, continued French expansion as well as improvements to the Army.

France's most famous commander, Henri de Turenne, began his career in 1638. But an analysis of Turenne's campaigns reveals mainly brilliant strategic manœuvres— from one siege to another—with open battle only occasionally intervening as often as not as the by-product of a siege and its attempted relief.

Vauban won no campaign laurels nor does he have major literary works to his credit, either upon fortification or the military art. Yet his influence as a military engineer in the French Army from 1653, and above all as director of the engineering branch after 1687, dominated war in his own lifetime and for generations to come. He is credited with the construction of over 100 fortresses and the conduct of more than 40 sieges. Through the length and breadth of France, and wherever the French Army moved, Vauban's star-shaped fortresses were to be found— and may be seen to this day. Not that Vauban, who was born in 1633, originated a revolutionary system. By sheer industry and application he rapidly improved upon current methods which had slowly grown with experience since the fall of Constantinople in 1453. He modified existing fortresses and evolved new systems to defeat the contemporary methods of bombardment, sapping and assault. In parallel he devised sophisticated ways of defeating his own brand of fortress. Indeed, he so reduced the art of siege warfare to a science that it became virtually calculable how long a fortress could survive a well-conducted attack. From this precision stemmed the practice of honourable surrender by the defenders when defence was recognisably no longer economically justifiable.

Fortifications had primarily to be made proof against artillery, secondarily against mining and finally against direct assault. Artillery loopholes had been cut in the original stone walls during the mid-fifteenth century, but were quite ineffective since vertical walls themselves were far too vulnerable. The old stone walls came tumbling down with each succeeding campaign and were replaced by widened ditches with cannon mounted in low silhouetted, sloped bastions sited so as to sweep the bare approaches (the glacis) with fire; above all to act in a counter-battery capacity. Men sought safety underground and began to devise wedge-shaped bastions (not unlike those of the English archers at Crécy) to apply mutually supporting fire across rather than straight towards the front. Vauban's particular genius was to be recognised not only in the perfection of this system but because he introduced depth to defence by increasing the number and size of bastions within each sector.

The besiegers had primarily to establish their artillery in protected positions from which:

● They could dominate the defenders artillery.
● Batter down the walls and ditches.
● Support workmen who dug trenches towards the enemy lines.

In practice the advance to an attack took place below ground level, with the throwing up of mounds of earth to protect men and guns within range of the enemy, and the posting of guards against sallies directed at capturing or spiking the siege artillery. The initial advantage usually lay with the defenders, who could fight from long-established fortifications against hastily improvised excavations. Until Vauban put his mind to solving the problem, an energetic defence could easily unsettle an attack. He established siege artillery in carefully constructed emplacements some 600 yd (550 km) from the fortress, linked by trenches dug parallel to the fortress defences. Under cover of artillery fire more trenches (saps) would be cut in a zigzag direction to within 300 yd (270 km) of the fortress, where yet another "parallel", containing fresh battery positions, would be constructed. Then the bombardment would be resumed at yet closer range, concentrated against a selected weak spot in the fortress walls. Sortie and counter-sortie would now ensue, with brisk hand-to-hand fighting in the trenches for possession of the guns. The next parallel pushed

forward would take the assailants to within easy musket-shot of the
defences, and from there aimed fire would be directed against the defenders to make their forward position untenable. From there, too, tunnelling might be attempted until, at last, either the assault was launched
or the defenders gave up.

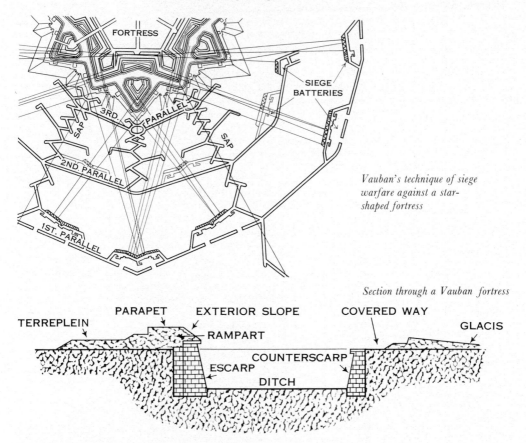

Vauban's technique of siege warfare against a star-shaped fortress

Section through a Vauban fortress

Vauban's masterpiece is the fortress at Neuf-Brisach where its defences were deeper and its artillery
more closely integrated by cunning emplacement than anywhere else.

The first trial of assault by parallels was at the Siege of Maestricht in 1673, which fell after very
short resistance. From this moment the balance of strength, which before
had been overwhelmingly in favour of the modern fortress, swung the
other way. Sieges continued to be expensive operations in all respects, but
they could be prosecuted with every chance of success and therefore were
relegated to devices of delay in the course of a campaign, a pivot round
which armies manœuvred up to the point of inevitable surrender. Between 1701 and 1714, for example, the combined English and Dutch
armies overcame at least sixteen Vauban-designed fortresses and only
once had to lift a siege in a period when the victories of Blenheim, Ramillies, Oudenarde and Malplaquet were won. Yet successful sieges such as
these were as much attributable to sound logistics as to the tactics of the
besiegers.

Among the last walled castles to fall to artillery were those of the British, brought down by Oliver Cromwell's men during the Civil Wars of the 1640s and 1650s. Cromwell's task, in this respect, was easy. His real claim to fame as a great captain was the creation of the first up-to-date British Army since the days of Agincourt. For the most part the armies of Royalists and Parliamentarians were ragtag and bobtail militias who suffered from lack of equipment—above all modern equipment. The best unit on either side was Cromwell's because he instilled hard discipline and staunch, religious morale into a well-equipped force of mounted men—the Ironsides—which could manœuvre in an orderly way under his control.

The first genuine regular British Army was created by Parliament at Cromwell's persuasion in 1645 and called the New Model. It was a balanced force of 22,000 men, of whom 14,000 were infantry and 7,600 mounted, supported, if it was lucky, by a small collection of antique heavy artillery. Though there was a tendency to organise musketeers and pikemen on the Swedish model, the artillery fell below the Swedish standard since its organisation and methods were a century out of date. The cavalry, too, eschewed firearms, preferring to charge with the sword and use its pistols mainly in by-play. Some English soldiers have a tendency to express a romantic preference for cold steel instead of hot powder.

The New Model Army was more than a match for the Royalists and was to prove its worth against continental armies, too, in the campaign of 1658 alongside the French against the Spaniards in the Netherlands. Yet, in the Battle of the Dunes near Dunkirk, the technological balance was tipped in the British troops' favour by the guns of the Royal Navy firing in support from close off shore.

Typical, if supreme among the campaigns of the day, was the one crowned by the Battle of Turckheim in 1675. It took place in the continuing contest between Bourbons and Habsburgs and against the backcloth of Louis's claim to the Spanish Throne. Pressure against France's eastern frontier began to increase in May, but was reduced when Turenne crossed the Rhine in June, defeated an army under General Enea Paprara at Sinsheim and as rapidly withdrew across the river. A fortnight later he repeated the manœuvre, won a victory near Heidelberg and laid waste the countryside. His opponents, now under Prince Alexandre of Bournonville, riposted by taking Strasbourg late in September, forcing Turenne to march to the area. On 4th October Turenne, with only 22,000 men, attacked Bournonville's well-entrenched army of 38,000 men, supported by 50 guns, at Engheim and not surprisingly suffered severe losses—some 3,500, of which the majority were incurred among his Irish and English battalions. Although Turenne camped on the field he could hardly claim a victory since his opponents were intact and had suffered only 3,000 casualties. Winter quarters were then adopted behind the shelter of the fortresses guarding the Vosges Mountains and Rhine River, but Turenne (like Gustavus before Lützen) made one more manœuvre. Suddenly he infiltrated his army in small parties southward of the mountains via Belfort to appear abruptly in his enemy's rear at Colmar. At Turckheim on 5th January 1675, Turenne again made a frontal assault but this time prevailed in full, crushing an army whose men had been dragged, all unexpectedly, into the cold and whose fighting spirit was low. This campaign is sometimes referred to as **one of the most brilliant in military annals.** It certainly rates very high as an example of successful mobile

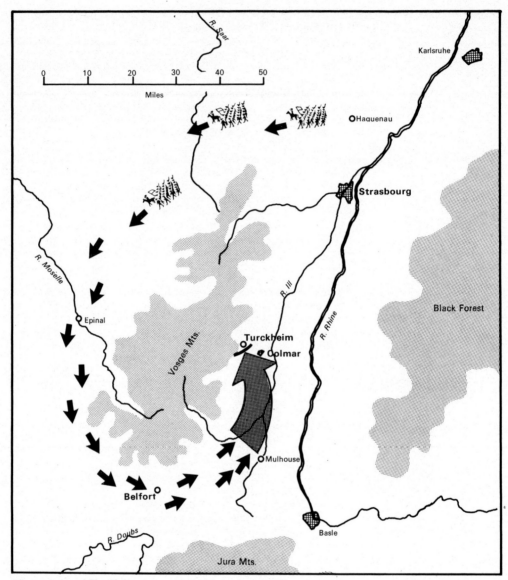

The campaign of Turckheim

offensive/defensive operations by a numerically inferior force. Its portent for the future was also immense since, among the English forces at Turenne's side was Colonel John Churchill, busily studying a great captain at close quarters.

IMPROVEMENTS TO WEAPONS

John Churchill, who was to become the first Duke of Marlborough, rose to high command at a moment of marginal but significant change in the affairs of land warfare, when improved weapons affected tactics.

The first bayonet seems to have been produced somewhere about 1640, perhaps, it is said, when the musketeers of Bayonne went at the enemy with knives stuffed in the muzzles of their empty firearms. Certainly this sort of "plug" bayonet came into fairly general use during the 1660s.

The first "ring" bayonet—a "sword" with a slip ring to one side that fitted round the muzzle and thus allowed it to remain in place during firing—appeared in 1678 and by 1687, at Vauban's suggestion, was adopted by the French.

The most celebrated flintlock musket of all time—the "Brown Bess"—came into British Army service in 1702 and gave Marlborough's infantry a useful fire superiority over the French who persisted, on grounds of economy as much as conservatism, with their older matchlocks.

The net result of combining ring bayonets with flintlock muskets allowed Marlborough virtually to dispense with pikemen while increasing the number of musketeers. Higher rates of flintlock fire also enabled him to improve the flexibility of fire control. Whereas the French fired by companies to achieve maximum shock effect, Marlborough could afford to decentralise fire control to platoons and thus raise the rate of volley discharge without material degradation. The true successor to the archer—the self-sufficient infantryman—had been rediscovered.

The Siege of Landau,
1703—bombardment from
the second parallel

Improvements to cavalry by Marlborough also diverged from French practice, which continued to employ a modified form of *caracole*. He insisted upon the Cromwellian system of deep penetration combining the action of pace and sword— and rationed each trooper's ammunition in order to restrict his use of the pistol for protection only when out of action.

John, Duke of Marlborough

Very little else in weaponry had changed in 1701 when the War of the Spanish Succession between France and Bavaria, on the one hand, and Britain, Austria, Prussia and the Netherlands, on the other, began in earnest. Artillery development was on a plateaux, communications still restricted, at short range, by the time sound took to travel and at longer distances by the pace of riders on horseback. To achieve massed fire effect men were compelled to move in dense formations which were subject to chaotic disruption on uneven ground or by well-concentrated enemy fire. The temptation to evade fire had to be shunned because survival seemed better assured by maintaining mass and thus the power to strike back. In any case, so rigidly was discipline imposed upon soldiers who were, in the majority of cases, sweepings from the streets, that once let them out of sight of their officers and they tended to deteriorate into a barbaric rabble.

The most important invention to facilitate co-ordinated manœuvres was that of the first spiral spring balance by Christian Huygens to regulate clocks and watches. Prior to the fourteenth century, when mechanical clocks first appeared, timing had been by sun dial, candle and water-clocks—none of which were portable and suitable for use on campaign. Domestic clocks appeared later that century and the first spring drive, invented by Peter Henlein of Nuremberg, in late fifteenth century. Clocks then became more portable though remaining distinctly inaccurate. The spiral spring balance, however, not only made possible exact regulation of spring-driven timepieces but also allowed miniaturisation—**the first "watches"** appearing in France and Germany about 1675. From this moment onward commanders could control their formations and units by reference to a common time base. No longer was it absolutely necessary to depend upon a visual or audible event or some forecast occurrence as the signal to actuate orders.

Marlborough is often rated among the greatest—if not the greatest—of all English captains, not simply because his victories at Blenheim, Ramillies, Oudenarde, Malplaquet and Ne Plus Ultra overcame opponents of the prowess of Tallard, Villars, Villeroi, Vendôme and Boufflers (most of whom were once his comrades in arms), but because he combined military talents with innate political skill, powers of persuasion and charm which enabled him to dominate an alliance of nations with divergent views and intentions.

The most celebrated of Marlborough's campaigns took place in 1704 when, leaving the quaking Dutch protected by only 60,000 men, he advanced up the Rhine with the British Army to join forces with the Allied armies under Prince Eugène, on the Danube, and knock Bavaria out of the war. The direction of the English advance, parallel with the French frontier, was enough to pin Louis's armies in defence of their homeland until it was too late to prevent Marlborough striking eastward—instead of westward as they feared. Yet so protracted an advance by waterway and foot would have been impossible had not meticulous logistic arrangements thoroughly supported the British Army throughout a march of 280 miles (450·6 km) in thirty-five days. Taken by stages of three to four days at 12 miles (20 km) a day

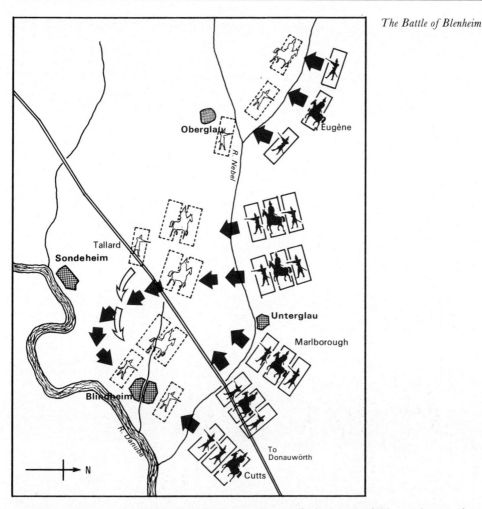

The Battle of Blenheim

and then a day's rest, the technical triumph of this march was to be recognised in the care lavished on man, beast and equipment, particularly with regard to food, footwear and hoofs.

The combined movements by the Allied armies began in Bavaria on 22nd June and continued for six weeks until they physically joined forces near Donauwörth. With 56,000 men they were thus opposed to the Franco-Bavarian Army of 60,000 under Tallard and Marshal Marsin and, despite this disparity in numbers, were resolved upon attack. This in itself was a surprise to Tallard who expected Marlborough and Eugène to manœuvre in order to avoid combat. The battle, as it evolved on 13th August, first took the character of head-on conflict since both armies rested their flanks upon the River Danube to the east, near the village of Blindheim, and the wooded hills to the west of Oberglau. Eugène attacked towards Oberglau, Marlborough towards Blindheim (which the English corrupted, as so often they do with foreign pronunciation, into Blenheim). Thus heavy fighting flared on the flanks and attracted the mass of Tallard's reserves until Blindheim, in particular, became packed with his infantry to the detriment of his centre which was almost denuded. It was in the centre where Marlborough concentrated his main strength, steadily massing infantry and cavalry on the south bank of the Nebel Stream. To this Tallard had no ready response since his artillery could hardly impose much fire upon this ground and his cavalry were easily repulsed by the British musketeers. By late afternoon Marlborough had deployed 80 fresh cavalry squadrons and 23 infantry battalions against 60 expended French squadrons and a mere 9 infantry battalions. Moreover he had moved up artillery to support his next advance. Instantly, by the combined action of all arms, the British broke through and fanned out, with the cavalry exploiting to cut off their opponents in Blindheim and Oberglau. The completeness of the victory can be gauged by the count of 38,000 Franco-Bavarian casualties to less than one-third that number on the Allied side. Tallard was made prisoner and the prestige of the French Army shattered with the same thoroughness by which its own victory over the Spaniards had ended an epoch at Rocroi.

Blenheim—the grapple

The largest siege campaign conducted by Marlborough was that at Lille in 1708, between August and December, after the Battle of Oudenarde. The actual reduction of Lille was by Eugène, but Marlborough commanded the covering force of 70,000 to prevent the main French Army of 110,000 under Vendôme from intervening. **For the first and only time** Marlborough, on 5th September, was compelled to contemplate a defensive battle. So it is interesting to find that, even in these circumstances, he deprecated suggestions that his infantry should dig in, though eventually permitting them to create bastions at key points in the centre and on the flanks of his position. He placed his cavalry and artillery to the fore and held his infantry mass in rear, clearly intending to fight an aggressive battle if the French attacked. But the French refrained due to divergencies of opinion among their commanders. At this time Eugène delivered the main assault on Lille, losing 5,000 men in breaching the outer defences and forcing back the garrison to the inner works. The campaign now evolved into a race with the besiegers trying to reduce Lille under Boufflers, before Vendôme could cut the Allied lines of communication with the sea and starve or deprive them of ammunition. It was a close-run thing with Boufflers grudgingly giving ground and Marlborough forcing convoys through from the coast against every intervention by Vendôme. It led to a brilliant Allied victory at Wynendael, at the end of September, when a large convoy from Dunkirk was escorted to Lille against strong French opposition—the French trying to debouch upon the convoy through a gap in the woods and being slaughtered in a matter of minutes by deadly English musketry from front and flank.

Wynendael sealed the fate of Lille which nevertheless held out until 9th December amid a whirl of activity by Marlborough in protection of Eugène. The cost in killed and wounded to the besiegers was about 12,000.

The genius of Marlborough's greatest victories at Ramillies (1706) and Oudenarde lay in his ability to establish preponderance of strength or fire power against weakness in the enemy position almost regardless of the inhibitions imposed by technical factors. At Malplaquet, in 1709, however, he was unable to find a weak spot or room to manœuvre round the flank of the French Army of 90,000 under Villars, and became embroiled in a head-on collision. Villars held breastworks with infantry in a 4,000 yd (3,600 km) gap between woods. His artillery was sited to bring cross-fire to bear, his cavalry posted in rear. Marlborough and Eugène planned to assail the breastworks while also bringing flank pressure to bear through the woods on the right. However, the frontal attack by Dutch infantry on the breastworks was stopped with appalling slaughter, despite the gallantry of the attackers. Then the advance through the woods, enmeshed in undergrowth and a fierce defence, lost its impulse and failed as a factor in manœuvre.

Malplaquet—the struggle among the breastworks

One of the most bizarre incidents in the Wood of Taisnières was an encounter between the French-employed Royal Irish Regiment (the "Wild Geese") and Marlborough's Royal Irish. The two sides, recognising each other at close range, exchanged volley for volley, but the "English" fire, being the heavier and better directed, prevailed. Thus the third "French" volley was only scattered as they took to their heels. The casualties gave testimony to the greater effectiveness of the English musketry system: they lost but ten men whereas their opponents lost at least forty.

Marlborough's main assault at Malplaquet finally developed into a direct attack by cavalry supported by men and guns close to the wood against the breastworks. At considerable loss it swept through to fall upon the French cavalry under Boufflers. Fierce charge and counter-charge ensued, sword against sword, with the French having the best of it because they timed their charge to coincide with the moment when the British and Dutch horsemen were still forming. Indeed, but for the disciplined fire of British infantry near at hand, the issue might have been decided in the French favour. As it was both cavalry forces expended themselves without result, leaving a few battalions of British infantry, along with their artillery, the sole fresh troops available. Totally exhausted, Boufflers (who had taken command when Villars was wounded), ordered a withdrawal and conceded victory. However, the Allied cavalry was so tired that it could not pursue and take advantage of the situation, while the French cavalry possessed just sufficient strength to cover the withdrawal. French losses were 12,500; those of the Allies 20,500—another clear indication of the perils inherent in a policy of attacking unshaken infantry in protected positions.

The emergence of a great military power in the East took place in parallel with the confusion in the West caused by the War of the Spanish Succession. Under Peter the Great, Russia began a series of wars against the Turks, Poles and Swedes which was to lead to the creation of a modern state as well as the curbing of Turkish, Polish and Swedish power along her western frontiers. Peter implemented major reforms of the economic, military and administrative services, besides bringing improvements to education. Increased industrialisation and encouragement of trade went hand in hand with a policy of rearmament and the reconstruction of a regular army by conscription. By 1724, it stood at over 170,000 from a population of 17,000,000 and at 4,000,000 roubles per annum was the greatest item of public expenditure. The Russian contribution to the art of war was therefore ordained as the application of inanimate mass—a philosophy which had its drawbacks against skilful warriors of the calibre put into the field by her various opponents. Victories against the Swedes were counterbalanced in the early eighteenth century by defeats at the hands of the Turks. The most remarkable achievement by both sides was their ability to conduct operations in deep midwinter—an indication not only of their physical toughness but also of the logistic efforts which made survival possible.

For no matter what transpired in weapon technology the main advances in the the art of land warfare were due to logistic improvements. Increasingly more attention had to be given to supply and to the maintenance of the morale of professional armies whose men were shown to fight better if properly cared for.

The last great conqueror in the East, prior to the twentieth century, was Nadir Shah of Persia. At the beginning of the eighteenth century, because of craven disunity

King Gustavus at Lützen. The Swedish infantry formation is well depicted in this contemporary painting

within the governing circles, Persian power had virtually dissolved and her frontiers had shrunk under constant outside pressure. Though Turkish power was also on the decline and that of Russia only just on the ascendant, both nations chiselled among the Persian defences where they were weak at the same time as the rising aggression of the Afghan tribes from the east (themselves breaking away from Mongol rule) posed the greatest threat of all. By 1725 Persia was virtually brought to her knees by successive invasions from three directions. Then it was that the Shah's son, Tahmasp, helped later by Nadir Kuli Beg, began to re-establish Persian prestige, repulsing the Afghans in successive battles until, by 1730, the Afghans were under control and the Turks rebuffed. With Tahmasp as Shah and Nadir the *de facto* ruler of the country, a process of reconquest began in a series of ding-dong campaigns. Persian arms were almost as often unsuccessful as successful but, throughout, Nadir's ascendancy both in the political and military field steadily improved. By 1735 he was strong enough to arrive at terms with Russia, to neutralise her aggression and then invade Turkey in support of Russian attacks upon the Turks. In 1736 he negotiated peace with the Turks, after defeating them in battle, on the understanding that he would not join again with the Russians. Therefore, in 1737, he felt free to invade Afghanistan, took Kandahar and followed up by invading Mogul territory in India as reprisal against the Moguls for supporting the Afghans. Here Nadir's true military genius was at work, for he won his greatest battles—at the Khyber Pass and at Karnal—by manœuvre though in difficulty from an inferiority of numbers. His armies penetrated to Delhi where a rising of the population was suppressed by massacre. Drunk with power, Nadir entirely abandoned all pretence to humanity and sought to impose his every idea by main force, attempting to dictate though lacking the administrative apparatus to enforce his will other than by constant land warfare. Inevitably he made still more enemies as he expanded his territorial possessions and overstretched his power. Inevitably, too, the Turks tried once more, in 1743, to reconquer what they had lost. It took all Nadir's military prowess to defeat this foe, who was superior in numbers, at the Battle of Kars in 1745. In 1747 Nadir was assassinated. Within three years the empire he had built by the sword had been torn to bits by civil war and all his conquests had reverted to their original owners. From the ruins emerged what, today, is Afghanistan, while to the south the hotchpotch of states filling the Indian subcontinent began gradually to fall under the influence of the European nations as they expanded their trade and martial power.

The essential feature of the Persian conquests and their aftermath gained nothing from startling innovations in the art of war; they were won with weapons that were largely outmoded in Western Europe. The introduction of European politics and martial experience to the Eastern peoples at last reversed the trends of the past. For the first time in history those in the Far East were to suffer major incursions from the West.

The first working machine-gun was produced in 1718 by James Puckle. It was intended as an anti-boarding weapon for naval warfare—to produce a large volume of flying metal by precise mechanical means instead of by random scatter as applied by the naval blunderbuss. Ammunition was fed to the chamber by a hand-rotated magazine; ignition was flintlock. It was inefficient but worked; yet it was not adopted. Indeed the Puckle gun was but one of numerous technical inventions which were appearing without finding immediate application by industry or armies. For example, the first practical steam-engine was made in 1698 by J. Savery (who coined the term "horsepower" as a measure of performance), but it was years before it was fully exploited.

The Puckle machine-gun

The leading military philosopher of the middle eighteenth century was Maurice de Saxe, who fought in the French Army at the age of thirteen at Malplaquet, in Eugène's army against the Turks at Belgrade in 1717 and in numerous campaigns with the French Army, rising to command of an army as Marshal of France during the War of the Austrian Succession in 1745. Saxe, one of 354 illegitimate children by Augustus II, the Elector of Saxony and King of Poland, was himself no mean exponent of seduction besides being a brilliant soldier and author of the definitive *Reveries upon the Art of War*. Saxe was technologically aware, eager to adopt the latest and best weapons, such as breech-loading weapons of all calibres, along with the improved kinds of musket which gave greater accuracy. Like Gustavus he embraced schemes to integrate artillery with infantry, but he improved on it organisationally by devising a permanent, all-arms formation—the division. The infantry he fostered by advocating improvements in their training, to enable them to pick their targets by aimed fire rather than hoping to score by a massed inanimate volley. From this evolved his concept of trained marksmen to skirmish to flank and front of the infantry mass. As for the mass itself, he demanded marching to musical cadence (such as had fallen into disuse after Roman times) in order to conserve their stamina while increasing their pace. Above all Saxe drew attention to the need for intelligent leadership, to produce high morale and a reasoned response from the rank and file—without conceding the essential need for strict discipline in order to prevent looting and desertion. Flogging remained in full force. Laughed at by the conventional soldiers of his day he was, nevertheless, taken seriously by one of the greatest of commanders—**Frederick the Great of Prussia**.

Maurice de Saxe

Frederick, the son of an autocrat, trained the Prussian Army to standards of precise discipline which remain symbolic of the method to this day. Yet, while the French Army retained the death sentence for desertion, Frederick abolished it in favour of flogging. Discipline in the

Prussian Army was geared to technical efficiency. With their musket of 1718 (that was slightly superior to the Brown Bess because it was loaded with the help of an iron ramrod) the infantry could achieve twice the rate of fire of the French because their loading drill was so much more efficient. Frederick accelerated the trends of a century by making his artillery more mobile, but at the same time he put greater emphasis on high-angle fire by howitzers to hit an enemy located behind cover or high ground. He was **the first to introduce the technique of calculated indirect fire.** Thereby he implemented accurate, remote intervention in the battle, by separating the executioner from sight of his victim and setting a new standard of callousness to warfare.

Yet Frederick at first down-rated firepower in favour of the effect conferred by manœuvre against enemy weakness, failing to see that a proficient enemy might, by firepower, restrict the power of manœuvre and thus make unavoidable the sort of fire fight he wished to circumvent. Saxe, who discounted infantry fire in attack, had misled Frederick: yet Saxe must surely have been aware that, in defence, accurate fire-power was deadly—as was his own use of it at Fontenoy in 1745 when he shattered the Dutch, British and Austrians.

The moment of victory at Rossbach. Captured French standards are brought to Frederick as his cavalry, supported by artillery, make the final charge

The first "modern" maps began to appear during the reign of Frederick and not only facilitated the aiming of artillery but also revolutionised tactics since good maps made campaign planning and manœuvre much more precise. **The first printed maps** appeared in Italy in 1540 along with a topographic survey of Europe. In 1730 came the **first recorded use by Samuel Cruquius of contours**, as a means of illustrating heights, and in 1750, in France, **the first Government-sponsored maps**—the Cassini edition. **The first official British maps** were published by the Ordnance Survey in 1791.

The artillery and infantry of Prussia

The first campaigns of Frederick were against Allied forces under Russian control. They began with a battle in Silesia in 1741 when, at Mollwitz, Frederick was compelled to quit the field on the advice of Marshal Kurt von Schwerin when the latter thought all was lost. Thus Frederick forfeited the chance of seeing how the firepower of Prussian infantry utterly destroyed a large force of Austrian cavalry. Later, however, Frederick gained such advantage, by manœuvre, despite numerical inferiority, that in June 1742, Maria Theresa of Austria sought peace and ceded Silesia to Prussia.

The reputation of Frederick as a tactician is founded upon a manœuvre called the "oblique order" —intended as a drill deployment of his army against an enemy flank straight from the line of march at the risk of being itself caught in flank before completing the movement. Only twice did Frederick fully employ this method—at Leuthen in 1757 and Zorndorf in 1758—and only then because his approach against the Austrian left flank was concealed by a line of hills. Napoleon was to deride those who were taken in by Frederick's parades at Potsdam which demonstrated the oblique order, for Napoleon realised that so good a general as Frederick would never be slave to pre-conceived notions in battle. It is Frederick's strategic insight and flexibility, for fighting nearly all his campaigns at a disadvantage in numbers, for which he is revered. An analysis of comparative strengths and casualties at selected battles makes significant reading:

Date	Battle	Against	For	Comments
1741	Mollwitz	20,000	20,000	Won by the skin of his teeth
1745	Hohenfriedberg	80,000	60,000	Won. Casualty ratio 16:1
1756	Lobositz	50,000	70,000	Won. Casualty ratio equal
1757	Kolin	60,000	33,000	Lost. Casualty ratio 8:12
1757	Rossbach	64,000	22,000	Won. Casualty ratio 8:½
1757	Leuthen	80,000	36,000	Won. Casualty ratio 27:6
1758	Zorndorf	45,000	36,000	Won. Casualty ratio 22:14
1758	Hochkirch	90,000	37,000	Won. Casualty ratio 8:9
1760	Liegnitz	90,000	30,000	Won. Casualty ratio 10:1. Night attack
1760	Torgau	64,000	45,000	Drawn. Casualty ratio 11:13

For sheer brilliance of execution the Battle of Rossbach is Frederick's masterpiece. The Seven Years War which began in 1756 was, in the simplest terms, an attempt by Russia, France, Sweden, Austria and Saxony to curb Prussian expansion.

The only major power to stand at the Prussian side (also for expansionist reasons) was Britain, though her contribution was mostly indirect—on the sea and in minor land operations in India, America and Canada. Frederick, though surrounded by his enemies, enjoyed the advantage of a central position and the ability to operate outwards to its periphery on what are known as "interior lines". Thus he might switch his strength rapidly from one threatened place to another and, if he got his timing right, deal with separate enemy armies in turn which, because they were separated by space, had the greatest difficulty co-ordinating their own activities on "external lines" due to the paucity of long-range communications.

In 1756 Frederick had absorbed Saxony and in 1757 invaded Bohemia and laid siege to Prague. But this siege had to be raised when Allied armies began to invade from all directions, moving on Berlin. Yet such was the respect of the invaders, who overwhelmingly outnumbered Prussia, they almost invariably avoided battle due to logistic failure or withdrew whenever Frederick approached them. On 16th October, however, 3,500 Austrians slipped through to Berlin and had to be "bought off" after looting the city. At last, on 5th November, a combined Austro-French army of 60,000 under Prince Joseph and the Duke of Soubise found themselves in a position at Rossbach in Saxony from which they believed they could envelop the Prussians by a flank march against a rise overlooking the Prussian rear. The Allies, however, based their moves on an assumption without knowledge of Prussian intentions or movements. Frederick, on the other hand, was well supplied with information from his cavalry scouts and from possession of good observation posts. He was thus enabled to preempt every Allied move and benefit from his ability to shift much more swiftly. Unobserved he redeployed on to a reverse slope behind the crest for which the French were making—and lay there in ambush. With perfect timing, moments after the Prussian cavalry under General Wilhelm Seydlitz had suddenly charged the Austrian cavalry and broken it into

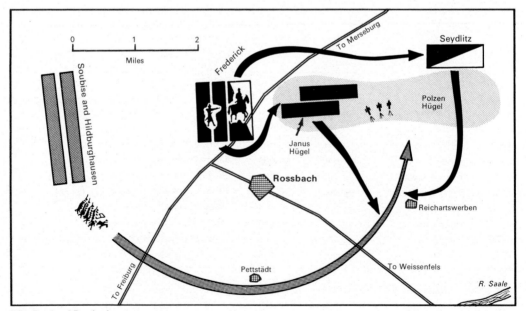

The Battle of Rossbach

rout, the Prussian artillery moved forward and came into action from the top of the rise to pour fire into the French infantry columns moving ponderously below in packed column, quite undeployed. To this was added musket fire as the infantry next came into range. Frederick's entire army rolled pitilessly towards the shambles, firing as they came. The Allies collapsed and bolted. In less than an hour and a half all was over. The day belonged to the artillery, while the cavalry, who had re-formed after their first charge, joined in to spread the rot among those of the enemy who had been too late to suffer the impact of the initial disaster. The French lost sixty-seven guns, and in defeat were to display a frightful degeneration in discipline, plundering and murdering with a bestial abandon such as had the Russian Army in East Prussia but a few weeks before. At Rossbach, as J. F. C. Fuller writes, ". . . emerged the spirit of German Nationalism, which found its focal point in the person of Frederick. . . ."

Least well known and yet highly significant within Frederick's armies was the "Freikorps" which he raised for deep raiding behind the enemy lines. Composed of cavalry and infantry they were recruited from irregulars whose loyalties were occasionally in doubt (some battalions deserted *en masse* to the enemy). Nevertheless they could achieve success out of all proportion to their numbers. Freikorp von Mayr, for example, with 1,500 men and 5 guns struck deeply at Pilsen in 1758, destroying enemy stores, causing immense alarm and confusion and evading a force of 6,000 men who tried to intercept it.

Some of the most important acquisitions to the British Empire were made during the Seven Years War, though the vital battle for the Indian subcontinent was decided not so much by generalship in the Prussian manner as by a technicality caused by a shower of rain. When 3,200 troops and 10 guns of the British East India Company under Robert Clive became surrounded by an army of 50,000 with 53 French guns under the Nabob of Bengal at Plassey on 23rd June, the only hope for the British lay in a battle fought defensively from behind entrenchments. As the French guns opened fire in preparation for an assault by native Indian infantry, a heavy rainstorm soaked their powder with the result that they all ceased shooting. But the British covered their powder with tarpaulins and maintained a steady bombardment and caused the Indians to lose heart and retire. Even then there might have been stalemate had not a local advance by a detachment (contrary to Clive's orders) begun a reciprocal enemy withdrawal which spread fast, far and wide among the Indians as increased pressure turned retirement into rout and disintegration of the Indian command. The importance of the Battle of Plassey lies in the interpretation that, from this moment onward, the British in India were on the ascendant for the next 150 years—and all because somebody could not keep his powder dry.

The future of North America was also decided by a small battle—at Quebec in which the losers, the French under General Montcalm, though superior in numbers, were deprived of technical superiority by the French garrison commander who would not allow Montcalm to use the fortress guns in the line of battle. Thus Montcalm disposed only three cannon and, as a result, the French infantry assaulted head-on against an unshaken line of British infantry (supported by only one gun) and, quite inevitably, were ruined by intense musket fire. But if Quebec fell to an outburst of conventional European-style warfare, the rest of Canada and America was to be infested by fighting of another more basic and yet also more sophisticated kind of sufficient intensity to change the course of history in one of its greatest upheavals.

SECTION V
The Rise of Industry
1760–1860

In 1776 a Scotsman called Adam Smith founded a political economic philosophy with the publication of his book *The Wealth of Nations*. The book crystallised the economic theories of the day—defining division of labour; the rules governing wages and the accumulation of stock in the form of capital; the commercial or mercantile system of trade; the functions of colonies in trade and the part to be played by Central Government in directing the economy. Fundamentally he urged *laissez-faire*, the system which exploited liberty and self-interest in a world which progressed by a combination of industrial expansion through its utilisation by the European nations. From this period can be dated a noticeable increase in the pace of progress and with it a compression of events in time. Cyclic affairs which once took a century might from then on be completed in a decade.

The Seven Years War which had overspilt into North America and led to the erosion of French power in Canada also infected what is, today, the United States of America. A war of manœuvre and siege, the image in miniature of major European campaigns, took place in Virginia in 1754 and steadily spread.

George Washington's first campaign began when he built a timber fortress on the location of present-day Pittsburgh (Fort Necessity). There he **lost his first battle** when the French compelled his surrender. In scattered campaigns with armies that rarely exceeded 10,000 men and as often as not were less than half that number, military proficiency was retarded. Most armies comprised a small cadre of well-trained regulars bolstered by an amateur, though intelligent, militia raised from the local populace.

A deadly part in the war in North America was played by the local natives, the Red Indians, who executed a highly efficient brand of self-interested guerilla combat besides providing both sides with excellent scouting services, plus skirmishers of high quality. Armament in the so-called French and Indian Wars embraced the full range of existing weapons from bow and arrow to musket and cannon.

The first effective "rifle" began to make its appearance during the 1750s. The so-called Pennsylvania rifle, made in that state by German craftsmen, was a long-barrelled flintlock originally designed for sporting purposes but proven as ideal for picking off stalking Indians. Yet it was merely one of a number of different, advanced types. By 1775 there were about 1,500 of this kind of accurate weapon in the hands of North Americans who developed skirmishing into a profession.

Among the first European "armies" to be overcome by combined French and Indian forces was that of General Edward Braddock which, 1,850 strong, was ambushed and routed by 900 fleet-footed opponents at Monongahela in 1755. Braddock was killed though part of his defeated force was saved by the skill of Washington. Studying this defeat in conjunction with evidence from other engagements, the British concluded that regular skirmishers must be selected from the best shots and armed with the most accurate weapons. They formed special "light companies" at a time when another sort of infantry specialist was also becoming known—the grenade-thrower or grenadier. Thus, once more, specialists had to be created to the detriment of the concept of the universal infantryman who had to be sacrificed to advanced technical and tactical expediency. Also money shortage, enforcing a deficiency of the good "rifles", made it inevitable that the musketeer in massed formation dominated because a thin line of skirmishers did not possess sufficient firepower to hold a position against heavy attack. Furthermore skirmishers were liable to be neutralised in the early stages of an engagement by hostile skirmishers before the main forces became engaged. Just as in 1758 the Battle of Fort Ticonderoga was decided in Montcalm's favour by conventional musketry and artillery fire, so did Wolfe beat Montcalm at Quebec with the same weapons. It is mere legend that sharpshooters won Canada and decided the campaigns in North America. Each of these campaigns were eventually concluded by forces of combined, conventional arms led by orthodox soldiers.

The first steam-driven road vehicle appeared in 1769—a tricycle invented by a Frenchman, Cugnot, that ran for twenty minutes at a speed of 2·25 mile/h (3·6 km/h) with a load of four passengers.

The sudden increase in Western industrial productivity which marked the 1760s was largely caused by substantial improvements to the steam-engine introduced by James Watt in 1763 and 1769, improvements which themselves had to await the invention by the ironmaster, John Wilkinson, of a machine which could bore the type of cylinder required. Rising populations, greater output of coal fuel and rationalised organisations and methods that were financed by the immense wealth pouring in from the colonies of India and the Americas, produced vast quantities of new materials, among them armaments. Rising populations also filled the ranks of larger armies whose manpower expenditure might no longer have to be conserved so closely as in the past.

First among the military thinkers with ideas geared to the new age had been Saxe, but schemes which were generally acceptable to educated opinion began to appear only in the latter half of the century from soldiers who had been involved in the Seven Years War—above all from Frenchmen who resented their defeats at the hands of Britain and Prussia. In France every arm of the service was scrutinised and brought up to date. Jean de Gribeauval began to do for French artillery in 1765 what Frederick had already largely accomplished for the Prussians—lightening gun-carriages, improving mobility by increasing wheel diameter, harnessing horses in pairs and "regularising" the gun crews. However, he also introduced vital technical improvements—providing standard parts which were interchangeable between pieces in battle, instruments which not only would improve accuracy of delivery and enable guns to fire in co-operation against selected targets, but also rationalised production in the factories. Organisation was reformed by Marshal de Broglie (who had conceived the fatal French manœuvre at Rossbach): under his direction, and that of the Duke of Choiseul, the army was grouped into "divisions"—permanent organizations of infantry and artillery which could move in co-operation with other divisions with distinct advantages in flexibility for the over-all commander.

Most precise and authoritative among military manuscripts were Frederick's *Military Instructions for the Generals*—standing orders in a limited edition of fifty copies which stated his philosophy of war, regularised methods and routine and formulated a strategic and tactical doctrine. Written in 1747 they remained secret until a copy was captured by the Austrians in 1760 and published in German in 1760, by the French in 1761 and the English in 1762. Though a strictly practical document, without pretension to literary merit, it by no means insisted upon utterly rigid procedures, as the sequence of Frederick's execution of command had demonstrated. Nevertheless its publication lent ample scope to imitators.

The best-known military philosopher of his day was the Count of Guibert who served in the Seven Years War with de Broglie.

    Guibert did for French military philosophy what Vegetius had tried to do for the Roman Army in its fall from grace. In his *Essai général de tactique* of 1772 (written when he was twenty-nine) he formulated the concept of a popular, citizens' force that was imbued with an aggressive spirit such as characterised the pagan armies of old. Not that Guibert believed that so Spartan an organisation could exist as part of civilisation as he knew it. He simply dreamed of a nation, which went part way towards his concept, overcoming one which retained the old order. In reality Guibert, who toyed with revolutionary concepts, was a codifier of Frederician practice who put into lucid, literate form what the Master had evolved. In effect he exploited a vogue which he happened to enjoy in Parisian society. He would command greater respect today if he could be shown to have maintained his opinions, but in 1779 his *Défense du système de guerre moderne* rejected the idea of the citizen army, reverting whole-heartedly to the orthodox concept of manœuvre by disciplined, professional armies in the Prussian way. Guibert is not to be criticised for changing his mind if the change reflected profound study and not merely a reflection of opinions held by more experienced contemporaries. One feels, however, that he was the victim of ill-considered opinions which, unfortunately, were widely read and believed by influential men of his day. This failing on his part is by no means unique among inexperienced military philosophers and he did inspire those who required the existence of citizen armies as instruments of a civil revolution they sought.

The Guibertian theory of 1779, that wars would stay true to type—and limited—may well have been conditioned by knowledge of contemporary events divorced from a true examination of trends into the future. In 1778 France had intervened against Britain in the American War of Independence when citizen armies were doing rather badly. And between 1777 and 1779, in the War of the Bavarian Succession, Frederick's Prussian armies had manœuvred against his Austrian opponents for two years, without fighting a battle—perhaps **the longest war without major combat**—in what was derisively called "The Potato War" because of a certain monotony in the rations.

Among the longest series of wars were those prosecuted by the Turks. Between 1400 and 1800, apart from frequent and bloody internal conflicts, they were almost continuously engaged at one time or another against Albania, Austria, Bosnia, the Byzantine Empire, Egypt, Hercegovina, Hungary, Persia, Poland, Russia, Serbia and Venice. Mostly these wars were on land, though naval influence was frequent in a theatre of operations centred upon the Mediterranean Sea: indeed Turkish decline can be dated from their defeat by an Austrian fleet at the Battle of Lepanto in 1571. But Lepanto by no means put an end to Turkish dreams of expansion in the cause of the Moslem faith. Located as they were at the crossroads between Europe and Asia, they felt free to thrust outwards in the same way as their opponents were tempted by the prospect of seizing the relatively small but vital strategic and political centres located along the Bosporus. But as time went by the gains from constant war were cancelled out by the expense of prosecuting campaigns which demanded an ever-increasing industrial backing. Turkey, like Assyria of old, depended upon captures and imports to maintain her army. When it became almost impossible to defeat technologically superior enemies—as it did with the failure to take Vienna in 1683 after a siege of two months—she found herself lacking in either indigenous wealth or prosperous colonies. Buy arms from Europe though she might, those imports would never be sufficient to satisfy her traditional predatory let alone her defensive needs. Such atrophy as Turkey began to suffer in the eighteenth century was an indication that bravery—of which her soldiers had a super-abundance—was no longer enough against sheer numbers armed with modern weapons.

THE NEWEST ARMY

The first encounter in a war between citizens and regular forces which was to change the course of history by the creation of the U.S.A., took the form, not unrealistically, of minor uprisings and disturbances aimed against British authority. The first was in New York in 1770 when British troops put down demonstrations. **Combat was first joined** at Concord on 19th April 1775 when British troops, making a raid to seize arms from the colonists, were fired upon by a local militia. This militia was at once dispersed by aimed volleys. For the rest of the operation, however, the British column rarely had the opportunity to fight mass with mass since the insurgents dispersed and harried their enemy from cover along the line of march, causing 273 British casualties against 93 of their own in several days' skirmishing. None of this was decisive. Indeed, under leaders of Washington's calibre, the first aim of the dissidents, once launched upon open warfare, was the creation of disciplined forces—which the farmers and huntsmen of America certainly were not. It was one thing to shoot

game with a steady hand (reloading a musket at leisure) but quite another
to fire against regular soldiers and reload proficiently when under a deadly
fire. Often the rebels were known to forget the ramrod and fire it in haste
against the enemy; frequently fully charged muskets were abandoned in
panic.

Regulars versus irregulars—the Battle of Bunker Hill

The first formal battle of the American War of Independence was fought at Bunker Hill on 17th
June, 1775, when British regulars under General Thomas Gage tried to
raise the blockade of Boston then being attempted under Washington.
The Americans, however, seized Breed's Hill (adjacent to Bunker Hill)
and entrenched a force of 1,500. Landing from the sea, supported by
naval bombardment, 2,200 British regulars, despising both the trenches
and their "irregular" defenders, stormed uphill to the assault—and twice
were thrown back by a hail of fire. They might have been beaten again had
not the defenders run out of ammunition. So it was that a badly arranged
attack finally succeeded against a poorly administered defence. Boston
was not relieved and British casualties were 1,054 while those of the Americans were 441. The British learnt respect for their new enemy while the
Americans acquired an unrealistic valuation of irregular troops. A long
war with too much over-confidence on both sides was in prospect. But a
new army—the Continental Army under Washington—was in the making,
its principal training almost invariably taking place in battle.

The escalation of the American War of Independence must be viewed against a series of disastrous
defeats inflicted by regular troops upon irregulars; the injection of numer-
ous foreign professional soldiers and mercenaries to both sides and the
merging of the central conflict with Anglo-French rivalries throughout
the world, until the guerilla war became a struggle dictated by regular
forces on both sides. Nearly always when it seemed the British were about

to win the decisive battle at the end of a successful campaign, something went wrong—and usually because the Americans showed more imagination and improvisation culled from a higher, general intelligence that waxed strongly within the ranks as well as among the commanders.

● **In 1775** the invasion of Canada by 900 Americans under Benedict Arnold was utterly routed, though the Siege of Boston was maintained.
● **In 1776** the arrival of strong reinforcements from Europe permitted the British to take the offensive at three points.

In Canada at Trois Rivières a force of 2,000 Americans, under General John Thomas, disintegrated against 8,000 British under General John Burgoyne.

At New York, in the summer, 32,000 British under General William Howe drove back Washington's army of 13,000 and inflicted heavy defeats at Long Island, Harlem Heights, White Plains, Fort Lee and Morristown. Washington was lucky to escape across the Delaware River with 3,000 men in December, the victim of a struggle in which superior numbers, brought to bear by sea power, had overcome his inadequately trained and armed men. Yet his riposte towards Trenton, when he recrossed the Delaware in a snowstorm on 25th December, resulted in victory over a garrison of 1,400 and the capture of large quantities of guns and munitions. This re-established confidence when hope was at its lowest ebb, just as another small victory, at Princeton on 3rd January—a hit-and-run affair in the guerilla mode with 1,600 regulars backing up 3,500 irregulars, proved psychologically decisive in consolidating the American cause. It should not be overlooked, however, that from this moment onward Washington enjoyed almost dictatorial powers.

At Charleston in June a British invasion was defeated at the outset because shore batteries repelled its ships.

George Washington with the ragged Continental Army at Valley Forge

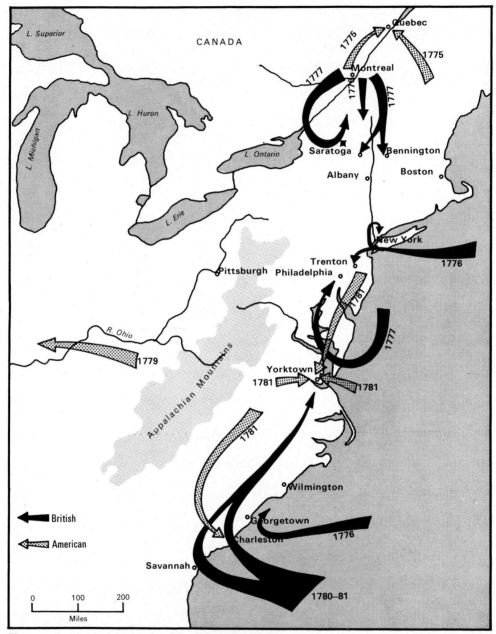

The successive phases of the American War of Independence

● **In 1777** the French and Spanish material assistance to the Americans became increasingly effective, even though the generals and soldiers remained largely indigenous despite attempts by the French to acquire command of the Continental Army. The British, however, were a hotch-potch. For example, Burgoyne's army of 7,200, which took Fort Ticonderoga in July, included 3,200 German troops. British strategy was shaped into a two-pronged attack upon the American forces in the Hudson Valley—Burgoyne moving south from Ticonderoga and Howe supposedly coming north from New York towards Albany. But Howe's orders were vague and so he left Burgoyne alone to advance harassed by ambushes until, with only 4,500 men, he encountered 20,000 Americans entrenched on the Bemis Heights. The fortifications were the work of a Polish engineer called Tadeusz Kosciuszko, but the battle was conducted on the American side by the English-born General Gates. A conventional turning movement by Burgoyne was, in essence, a forlorn hope against heavy odds. The American riposte, led with dash and courage by Benedict Arnold, was the common-sense flank approach though appallingly costly because, instead of enveloping the British right flank, it ran straight into a cauldron of artillery fire. Losses were higher on the British side than the American, but the latter were too shaken to pursue. Finally, however, Burgoyne was forced to surrender because he delayed his final retreat too long in face of an opponent three times his own strength.

A prime cause of British failure, all along, was the slow remoteness of their centralised command in London compared with the swifter closeness of American control on the spot. At a time when speed in communication over long distances was little faster than in primitive times, the Americans were assured of advantage—and doubly assured since they usually conducted their land operations on interior lines.

The immediate consequences of the surrender at Saratoga, in addition to stimulating the Americans, was encouragement to France to conclude a treaty of alliance with the Americans and declare war against Britain in March 1778. From this moment the conduct of the land war by Washington came increasingly under the influence of soldiers who had been educated by European combat. Line of battle with volley-firing, the scientific use of artillery and the construction of forts swiftly superseded the irregular methods which had done service in the opening campaigns.

The first Frenchman of distinction to make an impact on the War of Independence was the Marquis of La Fayette who arrived in America in 1777, acquired Washington's liking and trust and fought most courageously. Wounded at the Battle of Brandywine he fervently sought glory and so won the admiration of Americans and his own countrymen that it was he who was sent to Paris in 1778, when France declared war on Britain, to co-ordinate plans for sending a French expeditionary force. Next to Washington, this twenty-year old idealist (who nurtured a healthy hatred for the British because one of their cannon balls had cut his father in half at the Battle of Minden in 1759) is the most celebrated foreign hero of the war, a confirmed advocate of the American concept of freedom. Nevertheless the actual command of the French Expeditionary Force and the practical training of the Continental Army were put in the hands of fully seasoned soldiers—which La Fayette was not.

The most experienced in irregular warfare was a hard-swearing Prussian, Baron Friedrich von Steuben, who arrived in America on 1st December 1777 and in May 1778 was appointed Inspector-General. By then he already had started an intensive course to create a "model company" to act as a demonstration squad of standard manœuvres on the European pattern. Steuben had joined the Prussian Army in 1746 and gained extensive experience both in orthodox as well as *Freikorps* raiding during the Seven Years War. He acquired diplomatic practice in the negotiations between Frederick

and the Russians which brought the war to an end. A first-class staff officer and leader, he it was who turned the heterogeneous Continental Army into a cohesive fighting formation and, under Washington, became the progenitor of the first disciplined United States Army. **The first victory won by the army Steuben had shaped** at Valley Forge was at Monmouth in June 1778. **The first drill manual of the U.S. Army**— the *Blue Book*—was the bible of his instruction. The tendency to rigidity of doctrine and execution occasionally detected in operations by the U.S. Army ever since could well stem from Steuben's Prussian methods.

Baron Friedrich von Steuben

The first commander of a French expeditionary force to North America during the War of Independence was the Count of Rochambeau, who had fought against Steuben in the Seven Years War and who had also served under Saxe. With four regiments of infantry, some artillery and a handful of cavalry he arrived in July 1780—though it should perhaps be added that the 14,000,000 francs previously sent to Washington were rated of greater importance since unpaid American troops were beginning to mutiny. Nevertheless it was Rochambeau, with Washington, who designed the impeccable manœuvres which deluded the British of American intentions. A British army of 8,000 under the Marquis of Cornwallis was kept cooped up in Yorktown. There, in the only major campaign fought by the French contingent (under American command), the British surrendered—a surrender which led to the conclusion of peace in 1783 and the recognition of the United States of America as a separate nation. Revolution by a unified people had been shown to pay.

The first act of violence in the first "people's war" was the storming of the practically unde-fended Bastille on 14th July 1789. The storming of the Tuileries on 10th August by a Republican mob, however, was the urgent signal for an alliance composed of Prussia, Austria, Russia and Sweden to invade France in an attempt to restore the monarchy. The French Army was but a shadow of the one which had been worsted in the Seven Years War— except in two crucial respects. The artillery branch, equipped to the scale introduced by Gribeauval, was excellent and the roughly trained infantry imbued with revolutionary fervour possessed an *élan* far surpassing that of the established armies with their all-consuming respect for the devasta-ting effect of modern firepower.

The first test of the new Republican Army came swiftly on 20th September, 1792. In August some 42,000 Prussians and 30,000 Austrians, commanded by the Duke of Brunswick, began to advance on Paris through the Argonne until 34,000 of the Prussians came into collision with 36,000 fractious and unreliable French under General Charles Dumouriez and General François Keller-man at Valmy. At that moment the French were engaged in pushing forward a light screen to cover their withdrawal from what was reckoned a weak position, but Kellerman, caught on the wrong foot, decided to fight where he stood and posted his artillery in the front line to engage the Prussian infantry as it advanced through early morning fog. Piecemeal the armies came face to face across a valley and the guns, at their extreme effective range of 1,300 yd (1,183 m), opened an intensive fire. But the shot did little damage and, indeed, not until the Prussian infantry began to advance were many casualties inflicted. The Prussians advanced slowly against Valmy Ridge into a wall of fire discharged by expert French professional gunners. Confusion began to appear and with it a loss of confidence among the commanders of the Allied side. Prematurely the Prussian assault was recalled and the two sides drew apart with less than 500 casualties to share between them. By admitting defeat, the Allies flattered an untried opponent whose steadiness was in doubt but whose artillery dominated the battlefield.

The personification of the new model citizen army as developed in France was Lazare Carnot,

Lazare Carnot

an engineer (as Vauban had been) who became a captain in the engineers in 1783 and won notice by disputing the theories of Vauban. In 1793 he became Minister of War to the revolutionary Committee of Public Safety and proceeded to implement, by iron-handed organisation, the concepts of war which had evolved since the Seven Years War. Accepting the flood of manpower endowed to the Army by the August decree of nationwide conscription—the Lévée en Masse—he drafted it into **the first all arms divisions** composed of both infantry, artillery and cavalry. His was to be the citizen army Guibert had envisaged and rejected as impractical, a force to defend France against invasion from all quarters. He nevertheless built an army rich with offensive capabilities inherent in the shock effect of tight-packed columns, that bore down upon the enemy like armed crowds, and was assisted in its advance to close quarters by the same kind of crack-shot skirmishers who had appeared in America. Armies of this type could be quickly raised and needed no more than two months' training. The spirit of ruthlessness ruling these surging columns has been admirably appraised by General Hackett: "Their aim was the total destruction of the enemy and humanitarian scruples were few. The age of limited war was over." In parallel with conscription, Carnot created a logistics system which, although it depended upon central depots for its munitions, gathered the bulk of its supplies by requisition from the countryside—a policy that could never long be tolerated at home even if it was acceptable by *force majeure* on campaign abroad. It was a sign of the internal strength of the French Army that, despite losing the major aristocratic part of its officer corps in the turmoil of revolution, it could rapidly identify and promote a number of excellent professional junior officers and senior non-commissioned officers to high command and win battles under their leadership. From these sources would come Soult, Jourdan, Ney and a host of hard young men who resurrected the spirit of the French Army. Significantly, too, at a time when technology and the artillery arm were in the ascendant, it was a professional gunner who outshone them all.

Napoleon Bonaparte was a young, industrious and intensely professional gunner who studied every aspect of war with burning enthusiasm. Like all great captains he analysed the campaigns of his greatest predecessors—Hannibal, Caesar, Turenne, Eugène and Frederick—and being a man of his day adapted their principles to the modern techniques suggested by Saxe and Guibert. As a true professional he insisted upon making systems work: under him the projected divisions of Carnot were kept intact and not dispersed. Above all he practised high mobility and persisted in strengthening the artillery arm.

The first demonstration by Napoleon of his artillery methods, personal bravery and leadership was at the Siege of Toulon in 1793. A combined British and Spanish fleet had seized this important port, its arsenal and a third of the French Navy in August. A French army then laid siege to the port on 7th September

The French assault on Fort Mulgrave at Toulon

and began the slow reduction of those outer forts in Allied possession. On the 16th Colonel Napoleon, passing through on his way to the Italian front, was intercepted and put in charge of the artillery. Both the British commander, Lord Mulgrave, and Napoleon appreciated that the two forts sited on high ground overlooking the harbour were the keys to the whole garrison. Mulgrave strengthened the forts and Napoleon, entering upon his new task with furious vigour, gathered guns and munitions to batter the western fort—Mulgrave—into submission—laying the guns himself to achieve the desired accuracy and effect. By mid-November an assault was judged possible and would have succeeded had not the local French commander beaten a retreat at the critical moment. Napoleon accused this officer of cowardice and began the train of intrigue which led to the appointment of a replacement. On the night of 17th December a renewed assault went in with Napoleon in the lead. He was bayoneted in the fight, but the attack was successful. Since the harbour could now be brought under direct fire its evacuation was inevitable. At once Napoleon was promoted brigadier-general. Within six years, as the French dream of revolution turned to deeds of conquest, he was made the virtual Dictator of France.

The most effective revolutionary in Eastern Europe was Kosciuszko, who had taken part on the American side in the War of Independence. In 1794 he began in Poland what he hoped would be the equivalent of the American and French Revolutions—for successful ideas are catching and lead to many imitations. Poland had suffered a series of repressions and partitions under the weight of Prussia, Russia and Austria. In 1768 a civil war had provoked a Russian invasion, the fighting taking the form of a local guerilla struggle

Tadeusz Kosciuszko

with French connivance. In 1794 Kosciuszko led a revolt against both Russians and Prussians, basing his political and military concepts upon American practice and calculating that, throughout Eastern and central Europe, the oppressed would range themselves alongside the Polish standard in the French model, and that the French would feel emotionally compelled to assist. The Polish people responded to Kosciuszko in his desperate bid because they felt they had nothing to lose by fighting. Yet material support from external sources was lacking (the French themselves were hard pressed just then) and the Polish National Army itself suffered from the disease which aggravates all guerilla movements when under pressure. It would disperse and, at a crucial moment, when it had need to stand shoulder to shoulder for a conventional battle, would disintegrate.

The first Polish success was achieved in April at Raclawice by 6,000 of their men over 5,000 rather astonished Russians. The arms captured and the subsequent taking of Warsaw by the rebels cemented the revolution. Within three months their numbers had risen to 36,000 men with about 22 guns. Although they were penned into a small zone centred upon Warsaw by over 100,000 Russian and Prussian men with nearly 300 guns, they fought with a determination that was peculiarly Polish when enthused by the nationalist ideal. They held Warsaw for twelve days and managed to break the siege on 6th September. But in open battle at Maciejowice, Kosciuszko was caught, in October, by an army of 16,000 Russians and, with but 7,000 badly co-ordinated men, suffered the inevitable defeat.

The first major campaign by Napoleon took place in 1796 as part of the general outward movement of the new French armies throughout Europe. In 1793 the political situation within France was stabilised through terror and a series of victories against foreign invaders won. At Fleurus, in 1794, a large Allied army was repulsed and Belgium brought into French hands along with the Rhineland. But though, in the winter of 1795, the Netherlands were annexed by a cavalry raid, an invasion of Germany was frustrated and, in Italy, operations made only slight progress. This pattern was repeated in 1796. Fresh French penetrations were made into Germany, with Vienna as the objective, but of the several battles which ended in the French favour none achieved decisive results. In Italy, however, where Napoleon took command of 45,000 ragged soldiers in March 1796, he was opposed by some 60,000 enemy spread in four pockets, of unequal size, along the western French frontier with a mobile reserve 60 miles (96·5 km) in rear. Napoleon recognised the weakness of this dispersed defence but first drove his commanders to stiffen discipline in the Army, to bring in reinforcements and re-establish a working administration. He exhibited no histrionics, such as sometimes is suggested, but just gave firm orders and received strict compliance by generals and men who recognised the ability and authority of a leader who obtained the supplies they needed and moved constantly among them. The invasion had long been planned by Napoleon when he was in Paris, so the bewildering series of manœuvres and battles which successively divided and broke the scattered enemy armies were no fluky improvisation. If by manœuvre he could not get astride the enemy communications or take them in flank, Napoleon concentrated more men and intensified artillery fire against opponents who stood in weak detachments to bar his way—and led the crucial assaults in person. The numerical advantages which he engineered by subtle leverage in battle speak for themselves—the French victories against odds being devised by the factors of surprise and morale over an enemy who failed to concentrate.

French cavalry against a Scottish square at Waterloo

	French	Opponents
Montenotte	12,000	6,500
Dego	17,000	4,500
Lodi	5,000	10,000
Mincio Crossing	28,000	19,000
Lonato	30,000	18,000
Castiglione	32,000	25,000
Bassano	20,000	10,000
Caldiero	13,000	17,000 (a lost battle)
Arcola	18,000	20,000
Rivoli	23,000	28,000

Napoleon

In less than a year Napoleon won control of northern Italy and defeated all comers even though his army was starved of reinforcements and supplies by Carnot—despite his vehement, dogmatic plea ". . . that victory lies with the big battalions and that the supply line gets longer and longer". In March 1797, reinforced at last to 53,000 men, he was leading the invasion of Austria, driving through the Julian and Carnatic Alps, winning minor victories in a rapid march until the Austrians, faced also by another French force, under Joubert, approaching Vienna from the west, sued for peace in April. Napoleon's reputation was irrefutably made. As a reward (or more likely a sop) he was given command of an army which was intended to invade England but which never sailed in face of the British fleet.

The initial strength of French ambitions for conquest under the new regime were epitomised by Napoleon's invasion of Egypt in 1798. For the 40,000 men who accompanied him could travel only on a sea voyage fraught with danger from the British fleet—an appalling gamble by a soldier with scant maritime appreciation. Yet even when he got through and prevailed in combat against the Egyptian Army at the Battle of the Pyramids in July 1798, and against the Turks at Mount Tabor and Aboukir in April and July 1799 respectively, he merely established a tenuous base which began to crumble once the French fleet had been destroyed by Nelson in Aboukir Bay in August 1798. Unlike the indigenous American partisan armies which had survived in the midst of a friendly population, supplied with French arms through the British blockade, the French Army in Egypt was cut off (its siege-guns captured at sea) amidst a hostile population. Escape by land via Constantinople was unthinkable because lack of siege-guns made it impossible to reduce Turkish forts. Therefore the Army was ripe for the defeats at Heliopolis in 1800 and Aboukir in 1801 at the hands of Anglo-Turkish forces. Of those who had sailed with Napoleon (nearly all of them veterans of Italy) but 26,000 were shipped home to France after their capitulation in August. A year before, however, Napoleon had returned to Paris and, in November, had been appointed First Consul. From that moment the military destiny of France was to be merged with the civil and diplomatic wings under the dictatorship of one man. And that man, consumed by megalomania, would pursue cultural targets in addition to military objectives like so many of his kind.

Alexander Suvorov

Reverses for France in Egypt in 1798 and 1799 ran in parallel with a total reversal in Italy when a combined Austro-Russian-Neapolitan army. backed by Britain, projected an invasion. Though the Neapolitans mutinied and the French enjoyed an initial success, the big battalions at once made their decisive impression. **One of the most ingenious Russian commanders** was Marshal Alexander Suvorov. Under him the 90,000-strong Austro-Russian Army, swept away less than 40,000 French and, at Cassano in April, won a battle which put Milan and Turin into Allied hands. At a stroke Suvorov, skilfully employing the Napoleonic method of divide and conquer, had retrieved all that Napoleon had taken in 1796. Again, by June, when the combined French forces defending the approaches to southern France had risen to 50,000 and Suvorov's army had been reduced to 40,000, he was able with 25,000 from that 40,000, to tackle and defeat a French force of 35,000 at Trebbia. In August, too, he concentrated 50,000 to rout 35,000 French at Novi—driving them through the Apennines in a fiery pursuit. And when later Suvorov (under protest) was diverted to Switzerland his work was completed by Marshal Mélas who, with 60,000 Austrians, defeated 30,000 French at Genoa.

The last campaign of Suvorov in Switzerland was his most skilful since, in compliance with bad orders, he was compelled to enter a trap between French forces which blocked the mountain passes. Yet, with a mere 22,000 men in declining autumn weather, he was able to struggle clear. In reward the Tsar relieved him of command. Within a few weeks, on 18th May 1800, this great commander who knew how to win victories with inferior forces, had died of grief and exhaustion.

Napoleon's swiftest riposte took place in Italy in 1800 to recover the territory lost to Suvorov. On 8th March his new army of 37,000 began to assemble at Dijon and, to check further Austrian successes during April, was launched through the snows of the St. Bernard Pass on 14th May to debouch into the North Italian Plain, aimed between Turin and Milan. Soon Napoleon was to be joined by another 15,000 coming through the Simplon and St. Gotthard Passes plus 5,000 through the Mont Cenis Pass. Not only was his approach march dangerously dispersed but it took place through deep snow and under appalling road conditions. Guns and carriages had to be loaded on to mules and sledges, the latter hauled by manpower with twenty men to a sledge. Ammunition supplies were cut to half the normal scale. On 25th May the fort at Ivrea, guarding the entrance to the Plain of Lombardy, was taken by surprise when artillery, with wheels bound with straw, was hauled in silence (fifty men per gun) to within close range of the defences. On 2nd June Napoleon was in Milan, straddling the Austrian lines of communication between Genoa and the frontier. But it was too late to save the French garrison, besieged in Genoa, which was forced to surrender on the 4th.

Napoleon's luckiest victory (if as such it can be described) came from the St. Bernard manœuvre. He spread his small army—some guarding the roads, others foraging for supplies, but with few in reserve—to maintain a barrier behind the Austrians. On 9th June 14,000 Frenchmen, under General Jean Lannes, attacked 18,000 Austrians at Montebello and threw them back on Alexandria. Napoleon drew the conclusion that the Austrians were in full retreat on Genoa and set out in chase with 18,000 men. But Mélas was also fixed upon attack and was advancing against Napoleon. On 13th

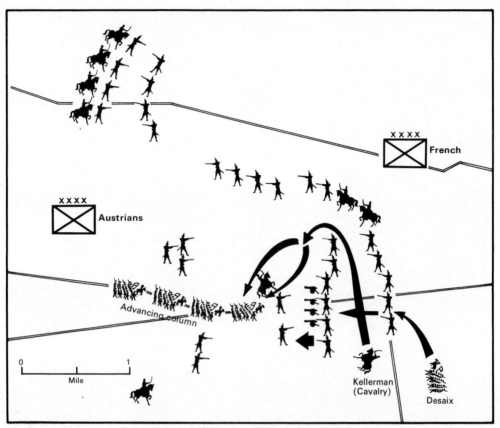

The Battle of Marengo—the late arrival of Kellerman and Desaix saves the day

June contact was made between advance guards (Napoleon interpreting
Mélas's advance guard as a rearguard). On the 14th, at Marengo, 31,000
Austrians hit the French and drove them back in heavy fighting. By mid-
afternoon Napoleon, short of artillery and beaten, was calling desperately
for his distant detachments: "In God's name come back if you can still
do so." They did—in the nick of time and by flank attack and charge
threw the Austrians into confusion. Yet the Austrians were still unbeaten
even though they had suffered 13,000 casualties. The French themselves
had lost 7,000 and Napoleon was still in direst peril, so he can hardly have
been more delighted when, next day, it was the Austrians' turn to miscal-
culate—to ask for a premature armistice and negotiate their withdrawal
from Lombardy. Lombardy was regained but the Austrian Army remained intact. Napoleon had been frustrated by bigger battalions.

The predominant feature throughout Napoleon's conduct of war remained his fixation
with the application of superior force at the point of impact at a time when
the influence of machines over muscle and courage became oppressive.
Each nation strove to turn economic and technological sources to its
advantage as a mechanical defence against the frenzied enthusiasm of

revolutionary armies. Britain financed the masses of Europe and her industry poured out guns and munitions which were transported to the theatres of war under the protection of a fleet which dominated the oceans.

'The Battle of Maida'—a victory by a British army, in support of Calabrian guerillas, in 1806, over the French

Vital increases in industrial power allied to inventions marked the period of revolutionary struggle as man's ingenuity was stimulated in all walks of life.

The first flow-line engineering works was laid down in 1796 by the English firm of Boulton and Watt and called the Soho Factory. It enormously raised production by creating workshops that were functionally specialised—for drilling, turning, pattern-making and so on—and for devising the easiest possible flow of materials throughout the complex.

The first precision screw-cutting lathe was invented by Henry Maudsley (an ex-employee of Woolwich Arsenal) at the turn of the century. It set a measure of accuracy that was self-perpetuating, and also allowed semi-skilled workers to apply standards of precision previously only within reach of a craftsman.

The first manned ascent of a lighter-than-air craft was made on 15th October 1783 when François Rozier went aloft in a Montgolfier-designed balloon. **A balloon was first used for observation in a military capacity** at the Battle of Fleurus in 1794 by Capitaine Coutelle. No longer was a military position on the other side of the hill secure from enemy view.

The first shell which could be exploded in mid-air and spray bullets among the enemy below was invented by Henry Shrapnel in 1784. This would revolutionise artillery tactics because of its effect at long range on troops in the open.

The first mass-production of muskets was begun in 1798 by Eli Whitney of New England, U.S.A. Sufficient weapons might now be made to arm the immense conscripted masses.

The first percussion cap was made possible by the discovery of fulminate of mercury. It was invented in 1805 by the Rev. Alexander Forsyth though its first practical application was delayed until 1816 when it was exploited by an American sea captain named J. E. Shaw. This invention, allied to copper cartridge-cases, would originate the next more devastating generation of firearms and artillery.

The first breech-loading carbine to go into service was the Hall flintlock type, adopted by the U.S. Army in 1817.

The first visual signalling by semaphore was begun in France by Claude Chappe in 1792 and rapidly developed to carry messages at a speed of 150 miles (241·3 km) in fifteen minutes throughout Europe via chains of relay stations. Central government was thus provided with a new dimension of information and control through speed of contact with its peripheries. Even battlefield control could be improved when visibility was suitable.

The first practical rocket missiles were used by Haidar Ali of Mysore against the British in 1780. As a result an Englishman, William Congreve, produced rockets in 1805 which were used in a naval bombardment of Boulogne in 1806. Thereafter, despite their inaccuracy and relatively short range of 1,500 yd (1,365 m), they were to be found on many battlefields in use by both the British, a few European and the United States forces. Rockets had been a long time coming to service for they are **first observed in military use** by Arabs in 1241: their development was slow because missiles fired from guns were so much more accurate.

A vision from 1806 of future war

The cult of the military college also received a boost in Napoleonic times. Ironically it was Britain, the big power with least interest in its army, which produced the first of a new generation of military institutes in 1802 at Sandhurst. In the same year West Point was founded in the U.S.A., in 1808 the French college at St. Cyr, and in 1810 the Prussian War Academy.

Highly fanciful impressions of future wars also began to appear at the turn of the century, triggered off, it seems, by the demonstration of man's ability to fly. Whereas a projection of future war penned in 1763, *The Reign of King George VI, 1900–1925*, merely envisaged battle in eighteenth-century shape, there appeared, in France in 1795, a play called *La Descente en Angleterre* which dwelt on invasion by air. Soon innumerable drawings of massive balloons, each carrying 3,000 men in their gondolas, were being printed and also of armies under bombardment from balloons.

    The intensity of war in the early nineteenth century matched an increase in the size of armies, their artillery content and the frequency of their engagement in combat. For example:

	Av. size of armies	Guns per thousand men	Av. battles per month
Thirty Years War	19,000	1·5	0·24
Seven Years War	47,000	3·33	1·40
Napoleon's	84,000	3·5	7·00

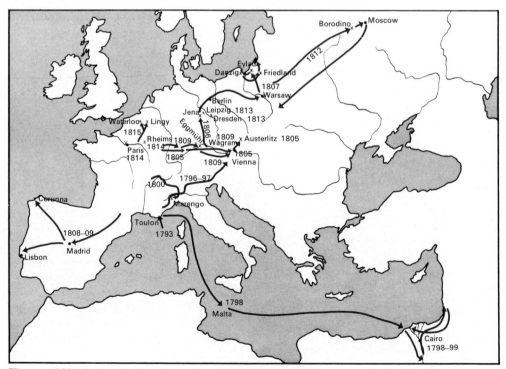

The axes of Napoleon's major campaigns and some of the important battles

The first major turning-point in the Napoleonic Wars had as its derivation the undefeated presence of the British fleet, which convinced Napoleon that he could not invade England in 1805. Once more he plunged eastwards into Europe to engage the coalition of Austria, Russia and Sweden which British diplomacy and money had ranged against the French. It was axiomatic that, although Napoleon had a balanced land force of 200,000, he was incapable of asserting his superiority over an inferior British Army because, lacking a viable fleet, his forces actually were unbalanced in the truly international sense.

The French proceeded to fight some of the most brilliant land campaigns in history—without achieving a lasting result. Yet it is rewarding to analyse Napoleon's plans and relate them to the military decisions achieved in the key engagements.

Place and date	Forces engaged French ('000)	Opponents ('000)	Method employed	Result
Ulm 1805	130	50	Flank attack to place barrier behind enemy.	Total victory
Austerlitz 1805	73	85	Deception by Napoleon to draw opponent out of position. Then attack on flank and centre.	Total victory
Jena 1806	96	55	Mass attack.	Total victory
Auerstadt 1806	27	63	Defensive in conjunction with Battle of Jena.	Successful
Eylau 1807	53	72	Head-on after failure to turn flank.	Costly draw
Friedland 1807	80	58	Head-on riposte after enemy attack.	Total victory
Aspern-Essling 1809	70	111	Head-on attack	Defeat— Napoleon's first
Wagram 1809	154	158	Massed assault supported by greatest artillery bombardment ever (554 v. 480 guns) in conjunction with flank movement	Costly half-victory
Borodino	130	120	Largely a head-on assault supported by artillery.	Costly half victory

A significant military trend to develop during the Napoleonic Wars was the upsurge in guerilla warfare. Although it first took strong root in Spain, in objection to occupation by the French in 1807 on their way to attack Portugal (and gained its name from the Spanish word meaning "small war") mutterings of insurrection were already prevalent throughout Europe. People of independent mind objected to foreign occupation under the guise of benevolent government when they recognised that Napoleon's aim was suppression and not the granting of liberty. Bitterness increased along with resistance to foraging by the voracious French armies. Carnot's logistic system might have been productive for armies in the short term, but it was self-destructive for France in the long. Support, without which the guerillas could not survive, was always forthcoming from Britain—with arms, money and armies in Spain and Portugal, although mostly only with money to those parts of Europe where resistance to France was endemic. But where regular forces collapsed before the might of the regular, disciplined French Army, guerilla forces also tended to fade. Take as examples:

● *Prussia*. When she was compelled to make terms with France in 1807 after the Battle of Friedland and cede her slice of Poland, there was no local resistance movement. But in 1811, when she was forced by Napoleon to collaborate with France, a secret organisation of local militia (the Black Reichswehr) sprang up under General Gerard von Scharnhorst and prepared for an opportune moment to fight in the open. Yet a safe moment was not recognised until after the French Army had been rebuffed at Moscow and was retreating in disorder to central Europe.

● *Russia*, which also fought a desultory guerilla warfare against the French invasion in 1812, where the perseverance of the guerillas was assured only because the main Russian armies remained intact after the Battle of Borodino. It was combined action by predominantly regular forces in support of the irregulars which caused the disintegration of the retreating French regulars whose logistic system already had fallen into disorder before they reached Moscow.

● *Spain*, where an army of local conscripts dependent upon a small regular cadre and supported by guerillas, not only absorbed great numbers of French, by compelling them to waste troops in guarding vital points on the lines of communication, but won victories in open battle. At Baylen, in 1808, 20,000 French were surrounded and surrendered to the Spanish: in keeping with the unbridled violence which typified the guerilla war as practised by both sides, the prisoners were either massacred on the spot or sent to die in prison.

The most highly disciplined forces to make their appearance in the Iberian Peninsula were the British army of General Sir John Moore, which was repelled by Napoleon in person in 1809, and that of Sir Arthur Wellesley, which landed at Lisbon in 1808. Wellesley, whose army only later exceeded 35,000 and often was much less (but aided by an ill-disciplined Spanish guerilla swarm that was often more than 100,000) launched invasions of Spain in 1808, 1809 and 1810 which, in succession, were driven back into Portugal. In defeat or victory, however, the principal lesson of the Peninsular War was the superiority of British musketry practised by men deployed in "line" or "square", against the solid French columns and cavalry charges. Time and again Wellesley's soldiers, who frequently saved themselves from decimation by artillery by occupying sheltered positions on a rearward slope, devastated numerically superior French armies. At Talavera 36,000 Allied soldiers held 46,000 French and inflicted losses of 7,400 against 6,000 of their own. At Salamanca, in 1812, Wellington's 46,000 (he had been appointed Viscount in 1809 after Talavera) defeated 42,000 French, causing 13,000 French casualties against his own 6,000 and bringing about the taking of Madrid where 180 French guns were captured.

Duke of Wellington

The Battle of Borodino

The final collapse of Napoleon's first regime stemmed partly from national war exhaustion, but was largely due to the impact of innumerable European battalions that were far larger than his own, recruited from the nations he had antagonised. Skilfully manœuvre as he did in a withdrawal to the Rhine in 1813, with an army that had not fully recovered from the Russian débâcle, he found his force of 185,000 and 600 guns threatened with envelopment at Leipzig by 300,000 Russians, Prussians, Austrians and Swedes with 1,400 guns and a rocket battery. French losses were 70,000 and 150 guns. Napoleon would win more tactical victories in the ensuing months, but nothing could halt the incoming tide of immense hosts rolling in from Spain, Germany, Italy and the Netherlands. At the end of March, 1814, Paris lay under threat of bombardment by Allied guns. A week later Napoleon abdicated and the war was over—or so it seemed.

Napoleon's last battle, at Waterloo in June 1815, is the epitome of the contests which industrialisation had enforced upon war. When Napoleon returned from exile at Elba and resumed power in March, he was almost at once made master of 500,000 soldiers of whom about 250,000 were veterans. Against him came Allied armies of nearly 700,000—but arriving piecemeal whereas Napoleon's troops, for the most part, were concentrated. In Italy a French army was defeated by the Austrians, but in Belgium Napoleon turned swiftly to the strategic offensive, before the Allies could concentrate, and attacked the assembling armies of Britain, Holland and Prussia. Napoleon advanced with 124,588 men and 344 guns aiming to penetrate, by surprise, between the Prussian concentration of 120,000 men, with its 312 guns at Ligny, and the 92,477 Anglo-Dutch, with 196 guns, assembling south of Waterloo. He intended to deal with them separately before they could fully co-ordinate their strength and activities. But at the dual battles of Ligny and Quatre-Bras, on 16th June, the French suffered from communication difficulties which led to the breakdown of Napoleon's original plan. Once his corps were committed to specified lines of approach, Napoleon, from a central position, found it almost impossible to impose direct command over a battle-front that was 10 miles (16 km) wide. Committing his main force against the Prussians, under Marshal Blücher, and giving Marshal

Ney the task of holding the British in check, Napoleon suffered the chagrin of having d'Erlon's corps shuttle to and fro between the two battlefields without coming into action. There was no decision at either location and the Prussians escaped from a serious situation intact. In consequence, when Napoleon attacked Wellington's Anglo-Dutch army on the 18th at Waterloo, with 72,000 against 68,000, he had not the strength simultaneously to interpose forces that were large enough to hold off the Prussians from the east and indulge in an overwhelming head-on assault against an unshaken and skilfully positioned opponent. It speaks volumes for French gallantry that, with scant numerical advantage, they pushed the British back, charging up the slopes with their old *élan*—and falling in swarms. Again it was lack of adequate co-ordination among the French corps which prevented their cavalry and infantry working jointly to exploit local successes. Eventually it was the one accurately directed, strategic flank attack, of a campaign of tentative command and control, which decided the issue in a matter of minutes. When Blücher advanced from the east and struck the French right flank late in the afternoon, pressure upon Wellington was at once relieved and he was presented with the opportunity to counter-attack and roll back a demoralised opponent. Allied losses at Ligny/Quatre-Bras and Waterloo were 41,500; those of the French 51,000. But the French were irrevocably defeated, their spirit destroyed and Napoleon forced to abdicate for ever on the 21st.

The sating of French expansionist aims and the emergence of the combination of British naval power and industrial strength led to what is

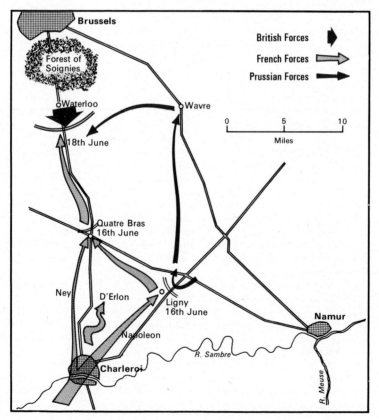

Ligny, Quatre Bras and Waterloo

sometimes known as the Pax Britannica. The term is as misleading as Pax Romana. From 1812 to 1900 there occurred several major wars involving all the principal European nations, as well as numerous countries in North and South America and in the Middle East. In addition there was persistent international friction caused by the colonial expansion of the major European powers and the U.S.A. which led to a plethora of minor frontier confrontations in which well-equipped and trained professional forces usually overcame the amorphous armies of the non-industrialised world. Such limitations as were imposed upon these encounters stemmed not so much from humanitarian considerations as from a temporary standstill in military evolution retarded by economic policies which rejected the production of the new, more powerful weapons and facilities offered by a constantly burgeoning technology.

The most important technical developments of the period prior to 1861 were in respect of:

● *Small arms* which were vastly improved by the introduction of the percussion cap fitted to expanding metal cartridge-cases. This ensured complete sealing of the breech and also kept powder dry. In terms of weapons these improvements introduced:

The first effective repeating pistol with revolving chamber, made by Samuel Colt in the U.S.A. in 1835.

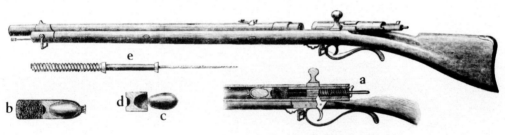

The Prussian "needle gun" of 1848:   (a) Section of breech   (b) Cartridge   (c) Bullet
(d) Pasteboard sabot containing fulminate
(e) Needle and spring

The first serviceable breech-loading rifle, in which a paper cartridge was inserted into the bore by a "bolt" action, percussion being obtained by a needle. Designed in 1827 by Von Dreyse (a Frenchman) it was adopted by the Prussian Army in 1848 and was technically ahead of the celebrated Minié, muzzle-loading rifle with its expanding cartridge-case which went into service in 1851 in several armies including the British. Incidentally it was the Minié cartridge which, inadvertently, started the violent Indian Mutiny in 1857, beginning an internal war which lasted for over a year at great cost in life. Hindu soldiers of the East India Company objected to biting the greased cartridge-case (as part of the loading process) because the fat in use came from cows and was taboo to their religious customs. Refusals led to punishments which incited revolts, massacres and then a full-scale war of battles and sieges.

● *Artillery*, for which the introduction of **the first successful breech-loading cannon**—a 6-pdr made by the German firm of Krupp in 1851—was a milestone. It was swiftly followed by rifled cannon made by Armstrong and Whitworth in Britain whose guns doubly exceeded the range of smooth-bore pieces. At about the same time, too, the Russians produced "bursting" shells—thin-walled missiles packed with explosive and detonated on the target by fairly reliable time and impact fuses.

● *Mass-produced steel*, the processing discovery of Henry Bessemer which, in 1856, made available almost unlimited quantities of this superior material to satisfy all manner of engineering demands in addition to armaments.

● *Steamships, the first of which appeared* in France in 1775, accelerated the long-range development of overseas possessions and made possible rapid maritime deployment of land forces regardless of the elements' vagaries.

● *Steam-driven railway trains* whose first public employment in 1825 in England, carrying both freight and passengers, led to vast construction programmes throughout the developed countries and made possible immensely expanded trade as well as the solution of enormous military logistic programmes. In 1846 the Prussians executed **the first full-scale rail movement of a corps** of 12,000 men, including their horses and guns, to Cracow. During the revolutions of 1848 railways were extensively used, too, for troop transport, in Austria, France and Russia.

● *Telegraphic communication*, which was first demonstrated in 1838 by K. A. von Steinkeil and rapidly developed into land networks of communication systems, linked political and military systems in close contact. The land telegraph system, despite the inflexibility inherent in fixed cable routes, made possible intimate command and control of lower formations in land battle long before anything so sophisticated was attainable by navies. Generals began to complain of excessive interference by their political masters.

Cowan's armoured fighting vehicle

● *Steam cross-country tractors*, **of which the first at war** was Boydell's, with its "footed" wheels, in the Crimea in 1855. Based on this agricultural prime mover James Cowan proposed **the first armoured fighting vehicle to be propelled by something stronger than muscle power**. Lord Palmerston rejected it as "uncivilised".

● *Gas, for which a proposal was made to suffocate the defenders of Sevastopol* with sulphur fumes. It was turned down by the British because "no honourable combatant would use such means".

● *Mines and booby traps which*, with new, simplified fuses, could be laid inconspicuously in a war zone to inhibit enemy movement and, by harassment, undermine morale.

● *Machine-guns*, the development of which since 1718 had been slow but came to fruition in 1860 when a Puckle-type, manually operated weapon, designed by Williams in the U.S.A., was first used at the Battle of Fair Oaks in 1862 during the American Civil War. It was rated, at first, as an offensive weapon in the artillery role as a substitute for grape-shot. Eventually no less than eleven different types of manually operated machine-gun, were employed during the Civil War—the famous Gatling coming into service shortly before its end.

The first aerial photograph was taken from a balloon by Gaspard Tournachon over the outskirts of Paris in 1858. This ushered in the possibility of conclusively establishing enemy dispositions from the air as a more reliable method of reconnaissance than reports from observers.

One of the most prolific of nineteenth-century military historians was Antoine Jomini—a

banker of Swiss nationality who became Chief of Staff to Ney until he deserted to the Russian Army in 1813. Not only has he more than thirty books on the history of war to his credit but also many pamphlets and two major works on military theory—the latter his *Traité des grandes opérations militaires* and *Précis de l'art de la Guerre*, published in 1828. His ideas were based on the campaigns of Frederick and Napoleon, though he was more a pragmatist than Clausewitz whose name is more closely associated with the heart of military theory. Yet he had immense vision. Contemplating the advent of railways he forecast in 1836 that they would lead to "a most bloody and unreasonable struggle between great masses equipped with the weapons of unimaginable power".

Karl von Clausewitz for all the esteem in which he was held for the profundity of his famous and voluminous *On War* (published posthumously in 1832) was among the most misunderstood of military philosophers. He crystallised the doctrine of war as an expression of total national effort aimed at the shaping of universal combat—the harnessing of entire populations to struggle both in peace and war and he captured the imagination of statesmen and soldiers in an age when the expansion of frontiers and the building of empires were at a peak. Under these conditions *On War* was wide open to misinterpretation by diverse, self-interested people.

Karl von Clausewitz

The most celebrated and influential political philosophers of the nineteenth century were Karl Marx and Friedrich Engels whose fame is based upon the teaching in *Capital*, but those thoughts were frequently consumed by military strategy. Still more than Clausewitz they were convinced of modern war's totality, visualising in political, economic and psychological warfare elements of struggle which were stronger than actual physical combat. They envisaged people's wars as an extension of the eighteenth-century revolutionary movements. Insurrection they foresaw as the final arbiter of class struggle, a method which would overcome the kind of formal positional warfare as waged by regular armies. They sought to strike at a nation's brain instead of hacking off limbs.

A peak in revolutionary warfare was reached in 1848, a year which witnessed revolution in Paris in February, an insurrection in June and the election of Napoleon's nephew as President in December—himself, to become, in due course, a sort of war-lord. In Schleswig-Holstein, in March, a revolt, stirred up by the Prussians, involved Austria, Sweden and Russia in efforts to preserve Danish sovereignty. In Vienna, Milan, Berlin and parts of the weakening Ottoman Empire, too, sympathetic insurrections flared up almost simultaneously in response to news which darted like wildfire along the new postal and telegraphic routes into the newspaper's columns. A series of local events which, before the telegraph, might have been isolated or spread over half a century were suddenly telescoped into a few months. Their pace caught everyone by surprise. But disorganised mobs led by amateur intellectuals were no match for trained soldiers controlled by professional officers. Revolts were put down by main force, a few volleys in the streets proving sufficient to end resistance. At the culmination of a revolt against Austria by some of her Italian possessions in 1848, there occurred:

The first aerial bombardment of a city under siege. When the rebels were defeated by the Austrians at the Battle of Novara, in March 1849, Venice came under siege by the Austrian Army and fleet. The city would not, however, surrender and the Austrian artillery was unable to destroy the defences. During a stalemate, in which both sides became ravaged by cholera, an Austrian artillerist, Oberleutnant Franz Uchatius from Wiener Neustadt, arrived with several score of paper balloons designed to carry a 30 lb (13·5 kg) bomb which could be released over its target by a time fuse. After a long wait for a favourable wind the first attempt was made in mid-July; an event which aroused much interest, caused neither casualties nor panic among the Venetians (as claimed) and merely reduced the aerial delivery of explosives to obloquy as a waste of military effort. The experiment was not repeated and Venice eventually surrendered to the combined effects of artillery fire, ammunition and food shortage and cholera.

A war of interim classification—between the Napoleonic type and that of the forthcoming intensive industrial kind—took place in the Crimea between 1854 and 1856. Although the great powers of Britain, France and Turkey were pitted against Russia, and in the end some 100,000 men a side were involved, the conflict stayed within territorial bounds—mostly within the Crimean Peninsula, the Caucasus, the Black Sea and along the Baltic coast. Two strict limiting factors were at work. The Allies did not feel strong enough to invade Russia, bearing in mind Napoleon's experience: the Russian Army was too poorly equipped to embark upon ambitious operations, fearing a crushing defeat at the hands of a technologically superior opponent.

The first astonishing feature of this ineptly conducted war was the lethargy of the Russians, who made no effort to resist an Allied landing on the Crimea, and their acquiescence to being penned behind fortifications within the port of Sevastopol. It was true that their relieving forces from the north, which were preponderant in artillery and virtually besieging the besiegers, made desultory attempts to fight a way through, but they were repulsed in a series of bloody battles. The Allies, meantime, conducted a formal siege in dreadful winter conditions and, particularly on the British part, amidst logistic chaos. Supplies, which could so easily have been brought in by sea, failed to arrive. The suffering of the wounded and sick raised a scandal and led to a complete overhaul of the British Army's administration.

The first time chloroform anaesthetics were used to save the wounded from pain, nevertheless, paradoxically, occurred during the Crimean War.

The dominating features of almost every battle were the devastating effect of rifles loaded with the new Minié bullet (in their first major operational outing) and the impact of the latest shells. The biggest battalions in attack seemed no longer big enough to overcome defences even when supported by artillery fire in the Napoleonic manner. It took nearly a year to overcome Sevastopol, the final assault by the Allies on 8th September 1855 giving a frightening glimpse of the depths to which men had sunk in relation to material. Three days fire by massed artillery was aimed to pulverise the Redan (where the British would assault) and the Malakoff position (where the French would attack). The front-line trenches were but 30 yd (27·3 m) apart when the time for assault came, the moment judged by synchronised watches so that the Russians would not be forewarned. Even so the British were repelled and the French prevailed only after a desperate fight among the fortifications where the Russians fought to the death. The city fell that night at a cost of 10,000 Allied and 13,000 Russian casualties.

Perhaps the most important result of the Crimean War was an awakening of public conscience towards the welfare of the common fighting man. Large-circulation newspapers printed their correspondent's report (notably those of William Russell of the London *Times*) shortly after the event and brought home to a more profoundly educated public the actualities and bestialities of war. Whereas in previous wars mainly the officers' view had been heard, while the men suffered in silence in barbaric conditions, from the Crimean War came descriptions which stirred humanitarian feelings among people with educated sensitivity. If the first reaction was merely to rectify administrative ailments this was a step towards imposing legal limitations upon the conduct of war.

The carnage at Solferino

Among the most influential books affecting the conduct of war was *Un Souvenir de Solferino* by a Swiss observer, Henri Dunant, published shortly after the battle in 1859. In this culminating encounter of Austria's war against France and Piedmont (over the ejection of the Austrians from Italy) armies of roughly 80,000 apiece clashed headlong in a soldier's battle which was barren of attempts by the generals to effectively manœuvre. The French half-victory (they remained in possession of the field) was simply the product of dogged bravery by their soldiers, driven into battle by bull-headed commanders, over an opponent only slightly less determined. An all-day struggle cost the French and Piedmontese about 17,000 casualties; the Austrians about 22,000. Public revulsion at news of the enormous losses and the agony of the wounded and prisoners persuaded politicians slowly to take action. In 1864 sixteen nations met at Geneva and founded the Red Cross as an international society dedicated to the relief of suffering.

For the first time formal recognition was given to the inviolability of official medical and care agencies on and off the battlefield. The flag of the Red Cross became a symbol of sanctuary at a time when the outright destructiveness of war was demonstrating the increased power of the latest generation of weapons.

Sinisterly the Solferino War, **the first in which extensive troop movements to the front were made by railway**, amply justified Jomini's worst fears of an oncoming "bloody and unreasonable struggle".

SECTION VI

The Epoch of Totality
1861–1915

The most extensive war fought on the North American continent began on 12th April 1861 when South Carolinian forces opened fire upon Fort Sumter and its garrison of eighty-three U.S. Army men. This first engagement, in an enlarging struggle which, eventually, was to cost an estimated 618,000 soldiers' lives, was remarkable in that nobody had been killed when, thirty-four hours later, the garrison surrendered for lack of supplies.

The root cause of the American Civil War was an attempt to resolve the right of individual states within the Union. Slavery and the underlying rivalry between the Southern, slave-holding, agricultural states (who were to form the rebellious Confederacy) and the Northern more heavily industrialised, non-slave-holding states were but the central issues round which emotion and propaganda were ranged. In an industrial age, the Southerners, with only 7,000,000 whites, were at once and increasingly at a disadvantage in matters of supply. Northern sea power gradually, yet effectively, blockaded Southern ports and prevented the import of arms and munitions. Indeed the Southerners, led by President Jefferson Davis (who was a soldier by training) felt compelled to adopt a defensive strategy, hoping to erode the 20,000,000 Northerners' resolve; implying, therefore, the probability of a long war of attrition. The Northerners, under the lawyer, President Abraham Lincoln, budgeted for a short war, staking their greater potential industrial and manpower as guarantee of early success. But U.S.

The French assault on the Russians at the Malakoff in 1855

A small battle of the Indian Mutiny at Paudoo Nudee in 1857.
Notice the more open order conducive with increased fire-power

regular forces in 1861 amounted only to 16,000, spread across the country
and mostly as cavalry engaged in guerilla-type anti-Indian operations. In
1857 alone there were thirty-seven such campaigns and they went on
throughout the Civil War. The Army did contain, however, a leavening of
experienced officers, the best of whom gave allegiance to the Confederacy.
Hence rapid expansion by both sides was feasible while quality in leadership and training was at first slightly in the Confederates' favour. The rate
of build-up of forces in the first two months came to:

	April	**June**
Confederates	314 regulars (officers only)	112,000 volunteers on a one-year engagement
Federals	15,000 regulars (only 3,000 available)	152,000 volunteers on a three-month engagement

Many volunteers could already shoot straight though, naturally,
countrymen from the South had advantages over townsmen from the
North, while leaders from both sides, with an inherent bent for mobility
learnt in the wide frontier spaces, instinctively sought a decision by manœuvre in closer combat. Yet in the end all were compelled to employ
conscripted masses to sustain a war of attrition.

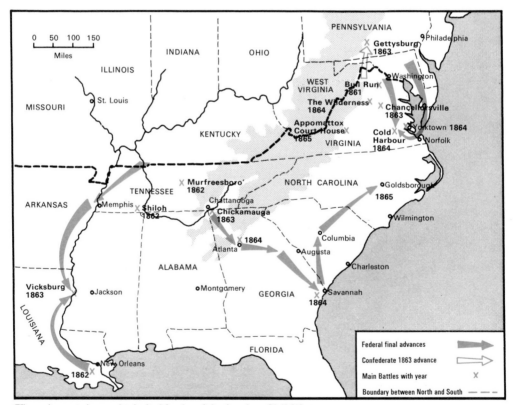

The main campaigns and principal battles of the American Civil War

The first major battle of the war occurred as a result of the first Federal invasion of the Confederacy aimed at their capital, Richmond. At Bull Run, on 21st July 1861, the mutual unpreparedness of both sides was exposed. Generalship on the Federal side was revealed in its ineptitude by comparison with that of the Confederates, but there were innumerable cases on both sides of communication failure as well as indiscipline by raw troops. Technology won a victory by making possible the **first ever tactical delivery of troops to the fringe of a battlefield by railway**. After the initial attack upon the Confederates, under Brigadier-General Thomas Jackson, had been repelled (winning Jackson the nickname "Stonewall") the arrival of 1,900 Confederates by rail at Manassas Junction from the Shenandoah Valley turned the tide and initiated a rout, which ran like wildfire to the outskirts of Washington and created such panic that the Federal capital itself and, perhaps, the will to fight were in peril.

General Lee

The vital theatre of land war became the area of 150 mile^2 (240 km^2) which contained the two capitals. In this well-populated terrain, intersected by wooded valleys and rivers, and comparatively well served by railways, the principal battles of the war were fought by armies of ever-increasing size, ever-mounting fire power and ever-improving prowess under generals with immense latent talents, a few of whom rate places in the list of great captains. Battles of wide manœuvre were to be fought in faraway Mississippi and beyond—battles which were to win vast territories for the Federals, as they implacably drew a net round the Confederates, but which would have been valueless had one side or the other come absolutely to control that vital 150 mile^2 near the eastern seaboard. Within this box were fought, in 1862, no less than twenty-two battles, under the direction of the Confederate General Robert Lee and General George McClellan for the Federals. They included Winchester in May, when the Federals lost heavily and, of vital importance to the Confederates, disgorged quantities of arms; the Seven Days Battles, between 26th June and 1st July, when at a price of over 20,000 casualties in almost continuous fighting (**the longest battle then on record**) the Federals were repulsed from Richmond at a cost to themselves of 16,000 men: the Battle of Antietam in September when Lee's 50,000 stopped McClellan's 70,000 with combined losses of 26,000 in what

The massed dead after the Battle of Antietam, 17th September 1862

may have been **the bloodiest day's fighting of the war**: Fredericksburg in December where about 13,000 Federals fell casualty after making no less than fourteen abortive charges into a remorseless storm of fire.

The causes of the holocausts of the American Civil War are many and yet not difficult to understand. Poor maps led to blundering approaches; inadequate communications prevented commanders from closely controlling the unwieldy forces at their disposal; the hatreds of fratricide inculcated terrible attitudes of vengeance; the sheer volume of fire which could be generated by an increasing assembly of the latest weapons of mass destruction made it impossible for men long to survive outside cover. Perhaps, above all, there was a pathological faith in Napoleonic tactics by inexperienced generals. It was a habit of these generals to adopt Napoleonic poses when being photographed. Large armies tied by administrative necessity to existing road and railway communications found it almost impossible to strike out in wide flanking movements of indirect approach. During the Seven Days Battle, for example, the contenders were funnelled by a confluence of roads to the point of impact and compelled to employ direct assaults aided, but rarely adequately, by concentrated artillery fire. It was commonplace for infantry to emerge from cover in mass formation against unshaken enemy guns, to be torn to shreds by "case" and "shell" ripping through their ranks. Frequently the attackers were denied close combat because it was impossible to advance more than a few yards without being hit. The bayonet lost its importance; even the sound of musketry fire became less in evidence, particularly when the new machine-guns came into action and overawed the infantry.

One of the most successful cavalry raids of the war was undertaken by the Confederate General J. E. B. Stuart's division between 12th and 15th June 1862 when it passed across the rear of McClellan's army, discovering its dispositions and strength, capturing or destroying stores and causing terrible alarm and confusion.

The largest cavalry duel of the war took place on 9th June 1863 at Brandy Station in the preliminary moves of Lee's Gettysburg campaign. Stuart, with 10,000 horses, was screening the redeployment of the main army after Lee's victory in May at Chancellorsville (where Jackson had been killed). However, he was caught by surprise in a sudden raid by 12,000 Federal cavalry under Brigadier Alfred Pleasanton. Charge and counter-charge rode over a key hill which had been occupied by Federal artillery; the cavalry milling round the guns, cutting down the crews and spiking the pieces. For some time the result was in doubt, but it was the discipline of Stuart's men which finally told: when the Federals were worn out he could still gather enough survivors into an effective body and drive his opponent from the field. Stuart's subsequent total recovery was also quick. On the 26th he was circling the flank of Federal forces moving towards Gettysburg—at one instant screening Lee's flank and engaging prying cavalry, the next cutting Federal lines of communication in an independent operation which lasted seven days. Yet, for all its audacity, the raid had small influence upon the battle which opened at Gettysburg on the 30th. No worthwhile intervention in the main encounter was attempted: cavalry, the most vulnerable of all targets, could exist only where the enemy was absent, extremely frail or against its own kind.

The genesis of Lee's Gettysburg campaign was the failing strength of the Confederacy and its realisation that dire shortages caused by the blockade, the loss of Vicksburg on the Mississippi in May and general war-weariness mitigated against the original defensive strategy. It was hoped that a dramatic victory, far into Federal territory, might shatter support for Lincoln, divert world sympathy from the Federal cause and promote a compromise peace. With 76,000 men, Lee struck deep into the rich Pennsylvanian countryside where the living for his men was superior to anything they had known for two years. Surprised, the Federal Army of 115,000 men could but follow and impose itself between the enemy and Washington. On 27th June, when Lee was at Carlisle and swinging east towards Harrisburg, and Stuart (right out of touch with Lee) was causing fear and trembling in central Maryland, telegraphic messages from Hooker, the Federal commander, revealed a desperate lack of confidence. He was replaced at once by Major-General George Meade. Both armies were wisely seeking battle from a posture of tactical defence, endeavouring to entice the other to attack. But the fight's commencement to the north of Gettysburg was accidental since neither side was properly aware of its opponent's location. A brush between cavalry on 30th June, just when the armies were spread thin in line of march on the approaches north and

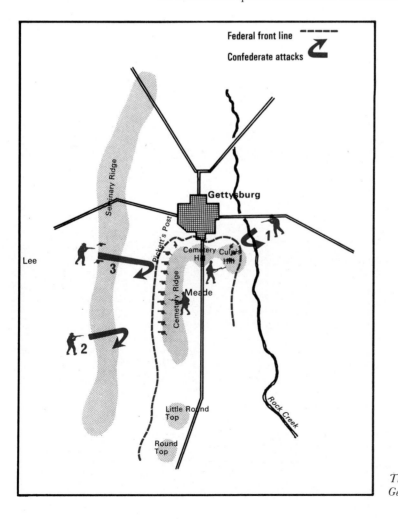

The three-day struggle at Gettysburg

south of the town, brought infantry columns and their artillery marching piecemeal into battle. The Federals retired under pressure to the high ground overlooking Gettysburg from the south.

The key feature of Lee's handling of the war's greatest battle was the abandonment of strategic manœuvre in his search for combat from a defensive posture, and his projection of ill-co-ordinated flanking attacks (which inevitably became head-on), without the benefit of overwhelming artillery preparation, against strong, elevated positions. First, through close country, he attacked the Federal right and was repulsed; then the left, with the same result; and finally the centre with a residue of unsupported reserves. The longer the struggle lasted the stronger the Federal positions grew as they built up accumulated strength behind stone-wall barricades. Because Lee's corps commanders held divergent opinions it was impossible to launch an immediate, co-ordinated massed assault off the line of march. The road-bound Confederates spread their attacks over three days, crossing open ground in the final assault against Pickett's Post where the assailant's gallantry alone made it possible for them to come to grips. The outcome was bound to be a repulse followed by retreat. This was the Civil War's turning-point, characterised by uninspired command decisions of which Meade's failure to pursue the departing Confederates was last but not least.

The most effective commander the Federals produced was Ulysses Grant who won the bloody Battle of Shiloh in 1862, took Vicksburg in 1863 and, in 1864, assumed over-all command. Grant conceived the pattern of the campaign to end the war. While continuing to seek a solution by close combat in the vicinity of Richmond, he sent an equally brilliant colleague, General William Sherman, in a 700-mile (1,126·9 km) march from Dalton to Savannah in Georgia, carving a swathe 50 miles (80·5 km) wide through the heart of the Confederacy in seven months. Sherman fought for possession of railways—cutting his opponent's tracks to prevent concentrations against his moving army; rebuilding stretches which were useful to him but largely feeding his army off the country; employing foraging parties which paid no regard to the welfare of the Southern people.

General Grant

The most costly campaign of the war was waged by Grant against Lee in the summer of 1864, grimly seeking intensive combat as a way to wear down the Confederate Army pitting 105,000 men against 61,000. In six weeks' fighting and four major battles (Wilderness, Spotsylvania, North Anna and Cold Harbour) he lost 55,000 to Lee's 30,000, and almost broke his own army's spirit by the magnitude of the slaughter. Indeed when, early in June, he at last cleverly outmanœuvred Lee in the strategic sense, the sheer war-weariness of his men frustrated victory in the tactical battles which consummation of the manœuvres demanded. Attacks broke down from faulty execution and the reluctance of men to expose themselves to apparent suicide. The Army of the Potomac had become veterans to the extent that their experience was a disadvantage.

The chief cause of higher casualties, however, lay in the fact that, whereas in 1861 the infantry mostly were armed only with smooth-bore muskets, by 1864 they nearly all carried far more accurate and reliable repeating rifles (such as the Spencer carbine) in addition to several types of the new manually operated machine-guns.

The largest single tactical explosion of the war took place before Petersburg on 30th July 1864 when the Federals detonated 4 tons of powder under a Confederate fort. They had tunnelled 511 ft (152·4 m) to lay the mine but, as so often was the case with an unusually powerful weapon, placed over-much trust in its effect. The follow-up troops casually entered the big crater through a 500 yd (457·2 m) gap in the defences, but went no further due to lack of initiative by their leaders. When, a few hours later, the Confederate counter-attack took place the Federals were caught entirely by surprise, penned in the crater and massacred. Confederate losses, the majority coming from the explosion, were little more than 1,000: those of the Federals were about 4,000.

The crucial lesson of the American Civil War—a war in which the future of land combat stood starkly revealed—may well have been the inability of military observers, critics and statesmen to recognise its obvious lessons. The entire range of modern weapons had been used—some in abundance—with results that were plain enough to see if only by reading the casualty figures. Experts from every important army in the world were present—some to advise and some simply to assess. However, European pundits chose to despise the military efforts of the New World. Arrogantly they discounted the effect of industrialism on battle, preferring to believe in man's infallibility over material, assuming that American soldiers were tyros in the art of war and that the apparent martial and administrative failures were the results of incompetence. Myopically they failed to understand that the immensity and complexity of modern war had outstripped the existing means of control, that head-on-clashes were all but inevitable because the sheer size of armies forbade extensive manœuvres too far distant from lines of communication, and that fire power in defence was bound to be more superior to an equal weight of metal in the attack unless some extraordinary factors of surprise or technology were introduced to redress the balance.

One of the most far-reaching of military reorganisations in the nineteenth century was the appointment, in 1821, of the Prussian Chief of the General Staff as supreme adviser to the Monarch who was himself Commander-in-Chief, by-passing the Ministry of War with its political functions. Thus political power was given to a military deity on the eve of a renewed bid for expansion by Prussia. The first example of this ambitious system in action appeared when Prussia intervened in Schleswig-Holstein in 1848 (see Section V above). But when, in 1864, with minor Austrian involvement, the Prussian Army invaded Denmark to settle some small outstanding territorial differences and, at little loss to itself, defeated the Danish Army, the Prussian generals, Helmuth von Moltke and Albrecht von Roon, and the Chancellor, Otto von Bismarck, felt satisfied that the instrument of their creation, with its modern weapons, was capable of dominating central Europe and creating the amalgamation of all the Germanic states into one nation under one Monarch—Wilhelm I.

The first outright challenge by the new Prussian Army came in 1866 when Bismarck engineered war against Austria.

The essence of land warfare, as Moltke, the Chief of Staff, saw it, lay in pre-battle movement. Realising that instant total concentration at the point of impact was no longer possible he promoted a system of movement by rail and road so scheduled as to make corps and divisions arrive simultaneously to envelop the enemy in a pre-selected battle zone. The Army was geared to rapid mobilisation in its peacetime locations. Each corps and division was recruited locally. In 1860 it was doubled from 200,000 to 400,000. Strategic movement was governed by railways whose alignment within Prussia came to assume a military configuration. Although Moltke claimed that he did not view strategy as a science, he nevertheless planned to wage war with unheard-of precision and calculation, based upon railway timetables and telegraphic communication and, to implement this practice, strengthened the Great General Staff as a highly erudite military élite. He realised, however, that in battle it was the local commander whose decisions alone would be viable, because communication systems were still far too inadequate for detailed, centralised control. Encouraging initiative in subordinates, Moltke merely sought to instruct them from above with outline schemes moulded by sufficient sound information.

The first campaign employing Moltke's methods began the cycle of victories by encirclement which are the symbols of Prussian military prowess. Their armies seized the initiative, when war was declared against Austria on 15th June 1866, by a lightning concentration of troops against Austria's ally, Hanover, aided by Italian intervention against Austrian Trent in the south. At once, the Hanoverian Army, readily located because it moved slowly in mass, became the target for converging Prussian forces which achieved a well-timed concentration at Langensalza on 27th June. Complete surrender was assured when the Hanoverians became entirely surrounded by Prussian forces in a modern Cannae.

The decisive pre-combat manoeuvres of the Austro-Prussian War were remotely controlled by Moltke from Berlin. Three Prussian armies, totalling 221,000, invaded Bohemia, intent upon crushing the 205,000 Austrians under General Ludwig von Benedek. Feeling their way towards the supposed location of Benedek's army, the Prussian prongs ran successively into detached Austrian corps, pushing them back indecisively. At once, at the baptism of the latest Prussian "needle guns", the Austrians found themselves at a fatal disadvantage. When on the defensive they had to stand up to recharge their muzzle-loaders, and when walking forward on the attack, in mass, were swept away by a storm of fire. In either case they were far more vulnerable than Prussian infantry who could load and fire while prone. At last, on 3rd July, Moltke received definite information of his opponent's location at Sadowa and launched his three armies in concentric columns, aiming at a complete encirclement. But while the Army of the Elbe and the First Army moved in concert, the Second Army stood still for lack of orders because the telegraph had broken down and could not transmit the vital message in time. Thus Moltke, who had arrived with the King in the battle zone, had the chagrin of watching but two-thirds of his force fighting at a disadvantage in numbers. And at a technical disadvantage, too, because the Austrian rifled artillery well outranged Prussia's smooth-bore guns (the penalty for parsimony in not procuring the latest Krupp guns) and dominated their formations.

Had Benedek then struck back the Prussians must have been defeated. As it was the Austrians stood, rooted to the spot, until hit in the flank by the Second Army when it tardily arrived in response to horse-borne orders. At last the superiority of Prussian rifle fire could be brought to bear and this, added to Benedek's failure to provide reserves to check the Second Army, led to a fatal Austrian reverse, at a cost of 65,000 men

General Helmuth von Moltke

against the Prussians' 10,000. Yet the bulk of the Austrian Army escaped—indeed completely broke contact since the Prussian cavalry, reluctant to pursue in the face of brilliantly handled Austrian artillery, allowed Benedek to retire on Vienna, avoiding Moltke's pincers as they groped concentrically to enmesh him. On 21st July, with French diplomatic encouragement, an armistice was signed, leaving the Prussians and the world with an impression that they had won by superior skill. In fact they had prevailed by luck rather than judgement, helped more than a little by the incompetence of Benedek.

Moltke's valedictory campaign was fought in 1870 when France, goaded by Bismarck's provocation, declared war on Prussia. That summer, because the Prussians extensively used the railway, nearly 500,000 men could be put into the field at extremely short notice to confront a mere 224,000 Frenchmen whose commander, Napoleon III, and staff deluded themselves with dreams of past glory. They hardly deigned use railways, relegating them to the evacuation of refugees from the battle zones.

The latest French weapon was the Reffye mitrailleuse with its 25 rotating barrels capable of pouring out 75 to 125 bullets per minute at ranges of between 500 and 1,250 yd (455 and 1,137 m). Used as artillery, of which it constituted a quarter the number engaged, the mitrailleuse was contemplated as a vital factor on the battlefield. Superior, too, was the French rifle. But it was the Prussians, learning the lesson of Sadowa and putting their artillery arm to rights, who enjoyed a marked technical superiority over the French.

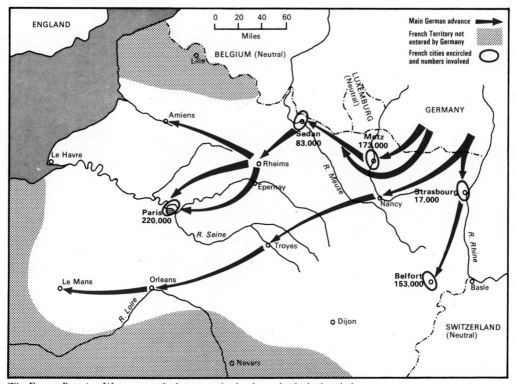

The Franco-Prussian War—axes of advance, major battles and principal encirclements

The first major battle of the campaign, was fought at Weissenburg on 4th August and set the tone for those to come. A French corps under Marshal Marie MacMahon was surprised by a Prussian army and forced back—both sides suffering heavy casualties. Successive battles produced a pattern of dominant superiority by Prussian fire in conjunction with their overlapping flank moves against the less mobile and poorly directed French. At the Battle of Spicheren, on the 6th, Marshal Achille Bazaine's army was worsted by two Prussian armies—even though Prussian casualties were the higher. Shaken by this engagement and those at Borny on the 15th, Mars-la-Tour on the 16th and Gravelotte St. Privat on the 18th, Bazaine abandoned hope and took his army of 100,000 into Metz where it was thankfully encircled by the Prussians. At Gravelotte the inability of the French High Command system to penetrate the fog of war, compounded by poor communications, threw away the chance of victory. Frontal attacks by 100,000 Prussians against 23,000 French condemned the Prussians to massive losses. Yet Bazaine declined to exploit an advantage by using his reserves to attack the demoralized enemy. In effect the manifestation of firepower was the suffocation of bold offensive spirit. Commanders of sensitive calibre became reluctant to commit their men to annihilation. Only ruthless leaders like Moltke (who, at Gravelotte, led the Prussian reserves in person) could succeed—or so it was thought.

The most celebrated encirclement battle of all—Moltke's Cannae—was completed on 31st August. MacMahon with 120,000 men had advanced on the 21st to the aid of Bazaine, who was instructed to break out from Metz. The latter, however, lay virtually comatose while MacMahon, his movements disclosed to the Prussians by uncensored press reports, found himself, on 26th August, the target for 190,000 Prussians with 426 guns. On the 30th he was forced northward towards the Belgium frontier to be cornered in a loop of the River Meuse at Sedan. The French position was hopeless from the start for they permitted the Prussians to occupy the dominant hills surrounding the town, thus allowing artillery fire to play at will upon packed men, horses and guns milling in the plain below. Every French attempt to break out on 1st September was at once observed and checked by rapid fire from guns and rifles. Charges by cavalry were cut down, infantry assaults beaten into the ground. On 2nd September the Emperor Napoleon, who had accompanied his army in the field, surrendered. He was followed into captivity by 83,000 men with 449 guns. The loss to the Prussians was but 9,000. This could justifiably be termed a classic victory.

The aftermath of Sedan was a tale of sieges, forays, skirmishes and small-scale guerilla warfare— the despairing attempts of an utterly defeated nation to rescue pride and acquire faint bargaining power at the peace conference. Paris was encircled but held out under bombardment behind a ring of forts from 19th September until 28th January 1871. Metz surrendered on 27th October 1870. Attempts by the French Army of the Loire consistently failed to relieve Paris, while the activities of guerillas against the Prussian lines of communication led only to an escalation of hatred and bestiality without in any way shaking the Prussian grip. In the meantime, under the shadow of defeat, revolutionary elements within France took the opportunity to raise insurrections aimed at upsetting the established Government. Within Paris the activities of the 300,000 locally recruited *gardes nationales* were as dangerous to defenders as besiegers. For example, in a sortie on 19th January, they fired upon their own side. After an armistice had been concluded **the first commune** was set up and Paris became ridden by civil war at the barricades until regular forces moved in to restore order.

One of the most perplexing problems besetting military commanders after the Franco-Prussian War was that of the future of fortifications. Experience had demonstrated the negative influence of such costly structures even though Metz, Paris, Belfort, Strasbourg and many lesser fortifications had long resisted the Prussians—in cases to the end. It was true that the Prussians were ill equipped for this type of combat, deafened as they were by the call of mobile warfare. It was also undeniable that an army surrounded in a fort could but apply indeterminant influence on the final outcome of a war. Nevertheless, fortress systems could not be ignored and the tendency for cities to lie safely out of artillery range behind a ring of well-sited strongpoints rather suggested that, in the future, vast areas that harboured threatening armies, might be put into a state of defence and pose a menace to field armies which lacked an adequate siege-train. It was symbolic that the French in the 1880s were the leaders in experiments to assess the relative merits of fortifications and the Germans who put most effort into studying the effects of heavy artillery upon the strongest forts.

An early experiment with howitzers to test their ability to breach fortress defences had been made by the British in 1824, but was inconclusive because the shells fell too widely dispersed—the normal state of the gunnery art in those days with the pieces available.

The increasingly effective range of artillery impelled the construction of forts at far greater distances from the vital places they were intended to protect. For example, Washington D.C. had been protected during the Civil War by a perimeter of sixty-eight forts out to a radius of 12,500 yd (11,000 m), while the forts guarding Paris in 1870 were 10,000 yd (9,000 m) from the city centre with minor field works, containing artillery, interspersed between them. And from Crimean War days far thicker walls,

French infantry fighting from the roof-tops in 1870

reinforced by iron and steel plate, were being introduced. Nevertheless, heavy artillery could still cause a breach. At Belfort 1,000 Prussian shells, fired from a range of 800 yd (728 m), created a 30 yd (28 m) wide gap, though the French managed to defend it for 105 days even without hope of relief.

Extensive experiments were carried out in the 1880s to assess the future usefulness of forts. Greater depth which demanded more forts to cover a longer perimeter and the need to increase protection to defeat heavier shells raised the costs of construction enormously. For example, guns and searchlights had to be mounted in expensive rotating steel cupolas. And when all was done the fort was quite immobile and therefore of only limited use in the sort of decisive war of movement envisaged by the pundits. In 1885 and 1886 the Germans and French conducted two important trials:

● *The Germans* fired 164 rounds from a 21 cm gun at a 430 ft (130 m) square target—and failed to score a hit.
● *The French* subjected the old fortress at Malmaison to fire from 20 cm guns as a basis for establishing the standards of optimum protection in steel, concrete and earth—thickness of 6–10 ft (1·8 to 3 m) being deemed necessary.

These trials helped decide the construction of the next generation of forts, obliterating the pleas of those who claimed that simple field entrenchments were almost as good and certainly far cheaper.

Major changes in the application of firepower, mobility and communication were imminent:

● **Heavy guns** with ranges up to 15,000 yd (13,650 m) and field guns with ranges up to 9,000 yd (8,190 m) all with higher rates of fire, were on the way from the armouries of Germany, Austria, France, Britain and America, along with much-improved shells and fuses. To the invention of the Krupp breech-loading gun was added the hydraulic system which absorbed the shock of recoil, permitting the gun-carriage to remain stationary instead of heaving backwards from each discharge and thus saving crews the labour of returning it to the original point of aim. First devised by the Siemens brothers in 1862 this system attained the point of definition in the French 75 mm quick-firing gun of 1897—a weapon for which rapid loading was also made easier by combining shell and case in one "round".
● **The first smokeless powder which appeared in 1885** was not only a far more efficient propellant but of vital importance in making possible **the first fully automatic machine-gun** as demonstrated by Hiram Maxim that same year. **This gun was first used seriously in action during** the Boer War in South Africa.

A Maxim machine-gun in South Africa

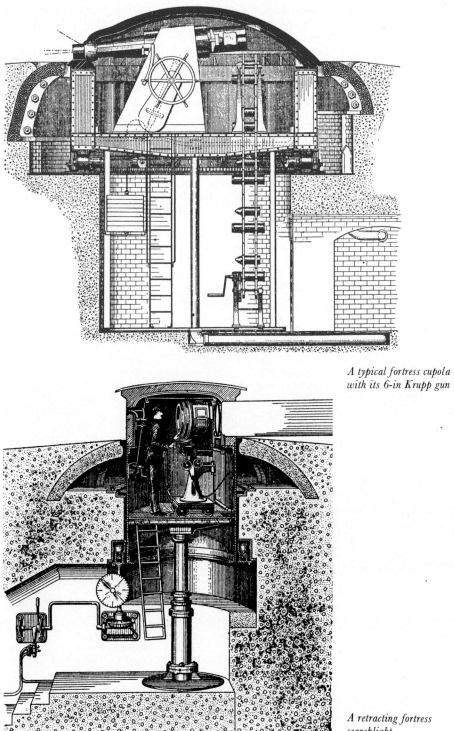

*A typical fortress cupola
with its 6-in Krupp gun*

*A retracting fortress
searchlight*

● **The first successful oil-well** was drilled in Pennsylvania in 1859 introducing ample supplies of liquid fuel.

● **The first petrol-driven vehicle**—a 3·5 hp model designed by Karl Benz powered by a Gottlieb Daimler engine ran in 1885 and opened **the greatest transport revolution in history**. In 1902 **the first fully armoured fighting vehicle** was made by an Englishman, F. R. Simms, armed with a Maxim machine-gun and a 1-pdr pom-pom gun.

● **The first demonstration of a sound-transmitting instrument** activated by electricity goes to the credit of a German, Philip Reis, in 1860. But not until 1875 were **the first practical telephones** patented (within hours of each other) by Alexander Graham Bell and Elisha Gray— the former taking the credit as first in the field after a fierce legal battle in the United States courts. Development was rapid and immediately recognised as an important aid to military communication both for command and control—particularly of long-range gunfire. For example, German artillery experiments in 1885 were controlled by forward observers using telephones which were connected with the gun positions.

● **The first wireless transmission** was performed by Sir William Preece in 1892 over a range of 0·25 mile (400 m). In 1895 Guglielmo Marconi sent a message 1 mile (1·6 km) and in 1901 a transmission of 3,000 miles (4,800 km) were achieved.

The realisation that the power of the latest weapons might overwhelm past practices in war was revealed by a Polish banker, Ivan Bloch, in his book *The Future of War in its Economic and Political Relations: Is War now Impossible?*, published in 1898. Scant attention was paid to Bloch when he suggested that the qualities of modern weapons would neutralise battlefield movement. He was out of harmony with the euphoric outpourings of writers like Sir George Chesney who, in 1871, published *The Battle of Dorking*—the first of a proliferation of such books by many authors projecting wars of the future. Chesney envisaged an invasion by Germany of Britain at a moment when the Royal Navy was weakened. His was an appeal, therefore, to strengthen the Navy. His successors strongly visualised air warfare after 1906 when **the first man-carrying, powered, sustained flight** was accomplished by the Wright brothers at Kitty Hawk, North Carolina.

The first military specification for an aeroplane was drawn up in 1908 by the U.S. Navy Department—an act which, along with U.S. purchase of a Wright machine in 1909 and the firing of a rifle and the dropping of missiles (lead darts) from the air in 1910, began the intrusion of air power into the land battle. **The first military operation by aircraft** was an observation flight by the Italians in Libya in the war of 1911 against the Turks.

The first indication to the colonial powers of the end to their easy dominance over backward peoples, appeared in 1899 at the commencement of the Second Boer War in South Africa. The British Army, vividly dressed in colourful uniforms, rashly advanced to the attack against a determined, irregular army of Dutch farmers, clad indistinctly in drab clothing, who fired with deadly accuracy from behind cover. The Boer Army was a militia of about 35,000 operating in horsed, mobile columns (called commandos) and only rarely forming a genuine line of battle. They had but little artillery and were quite incapable of breaching the defences of the besieged towns of Ladysmith, Kimberley and Mafeking. They were, in fact, little more than guerillas, but equipped with good modern firearms. Moreover, in the first months of the war, they outnumbered the British by about two to one.

*Capture of British wounded
by the Boers*

The first repeater hand-gun was a breach-loader flintlock ingeniously fed from a complex revolving breech-block and three separate magazines (one for missiles, one for propellant powder and the third for priming powder) designed by Michele Lorenzoni of Florence in the seventeenth century. Due to cost and unreliability the idea fell into disfavour.

The first practical repeater rifles were those of Horace Smith and Daniel Wesson, produced in the U.S.A. in 1855. They led to a proliferation of their kind, notably the Henry and Winchester repeaters of great fame. But in the 1890s most armies adopted bolt-action rifles with magazines containing five or six conical bullets with the centre percussion-cap cartridge.

The first time magazine rifles were used in action by both sides on a large scale was during the Boer War—the Boers equipped with Mannlichers and Mausers, the British with Lee-Enfields. On a rifle range in peacetime accurate small-arms fire could be applied out to about 800 yd (728 m), but only after intensive training. In battle trembling hands drastically spoiled accuracy and led to the tactical application of fire in volume at closer ranges.

A disastrous period of British arms—called "Black Week" by the hysterical Press—occurred between the 10th and 15th December, 1899. In three battles—Stormberg, Magersfontein and Colenso—the British lost more than 2,000 men (including a general and nearly a score of guns) at a cost to the Boers of a little above 100. Uphill frontal assaults by infantry, who were already exhausted after long marches, once again were proved suicidal against even an amateur opponent. A professional approach, that made use of rail and horsed mobility, to equal that of the Boers, was adopted by the new British C.-in-C. Field-Marshal Lord Roberts and his chief staff officer, General H. H. Kitchener. Throughout 1900 the British Army, after suffering more reverses at Spion Kop and Vaal Kranz in January and February, began to outmanoeuvre its opponent and round up the Boer "commandos". Yet at Paardeberg on 18th February Kitchener, when he launched a frontal assault against a Boer waggon laager, (shades of Zizka and Hunyadi), was expensively repulsed. Gradually, however, the besieged towns were relieved and the main Boer forces destroyed whenever they were compelled, by undeniable political circumstances, to indulge in formal battle. By the end of the year the Boers were forced to resort to pure guerilla warfare, vanishing into the wide spaces to strike, thereafter, only through intermittent and ineffectual raids. Peace was concluded on British terms in May 1902, because no political solution favourable to the Boers was in sight. British casualties, out of an army some 500,000 strong, had been about 28,500; those of the Boers, out of some 83,000, about 60,000 of which 40,000 were prisoners.

The Japanese assault on the Turban Redoubt at Port Arthur

The most impressive "new" army to appear among the world's military powers at this time was that of Japan in the aftermath of the Westernisation initiated by American influence following Commodore Perry's visit in 1853. A national army was formed in 1873: conscription followed and with it the emergence of expansionist ambitions. In 1875 Japan invaded Formosa and in 1876 provoked an incident with Korea. By 1888 there was trouble with Russia and in 1904 war—large-scale naval operations against the Russian fleet and a massive land campaign in Manchuria in connection with the celebrated Siege of Port Arthur. The Japanese sought prestige as much as territorial gain—the satisfaction of her ambition to shake off Western influence in Asia and her determination to win back Port Arthur from which she had been expelled in 1894. Heavily outnumbered in population, the Japanese nevertheless could restrict the relative size of Russian armies engaged by attacking the inefficient, low-capacity railway which connected Port Arthur and Manchuria to European Russia.

The most sinister trends of the Russo-Japanese War, compared with wars of old, were the lengthening periods of battle, the immensity of casualty lists, the inescapable conclusion that a thoroughly decisive military result was missing even when peace was declared in September 1905—the spectre, in fact, for those with imagination, of Bloch's worst prognostications. In a war of exhaustion, a table of battles in Mânchuria which led to Russian rebuffs (though never their total disintegration) tells its own story:

	Battle	Length in days	Casualties Russian	Japanese
June 1904	Telissu	2	3,600	1,000
August	Liaoyang	14	19,000	23,000
October	Sha-Ho	12	40,000	20,000
February 1905	Mukden	17	100,000	94,000

The most bizarre operation of the entire Russo-Japanese War was the Siege of Port Arthur which was heralded by an undeclared attack on the Russian fleet by Japanese torpedo-boats in February 1904 and foreshadowed by the gradual encroachment into the surrounding country by Japanese amphibious forces until, just before the end of May, investment was complete. The garrison contained over 40,000 men with more than 500 guns—but was somewhat low in supplies. On 25th May began the Japanese assaults —rolling waves of men flung against defenders who ruthlessly shot them down—though not always in sufficient quantity to prevent a few determined survivors seizing their local objectives. The Japanese sometimes achieved a manpower superiority of ten to one at the point of assault and were prepared to sustain 15 per cent casualties to win. The Russians impeded attack by adding barbed-wire defences to the conventional fortifications and having machine-guns sweep the wire while artillery played across the approaches to the trenches. The Japanese artillery, gradually recruiting its strength as heavy guns were brought in, increased the intensity of its efforts though rarely wholly subduing the defence. Finding it almost impossible for his men to survive in daylight, the Japanese commander, General Maresuke Nogi, poured them in at night and the fighting went on under illumination by flares and searchlights, the dead piling up, local objectives falling piecemeal and the garrison slowly weakening in numbers and physical strength. Yet the besiegers were weakening, too. Beriberi was at work and would claim over 20,000 Japanese. The customs of ancient war were practised. Before another major assault on 16th August, Nogi, under flag of truce, demanded surrender. He was refused. Minor territorial features began to assume an exaggerated tactical significance and were contested as if national survival depended upon them. Mines were dug beneath the defences, detonated and the craters fought over by assailants and defenders who raced each other for possession. When at last the Russians surrendered on 2nd January 1905, 31,000 men were casualties and the remaining vessels of their fleet lost, along with all the artillery and quantities of ammunition. Only 24,000 men survived and of these more than half were crippled. The Japanese had lost nearly 60,000 plus 34,000 sick.

The logical result of the Russo-Japanese War might well have been a common-sense re-examination of the art of modern war by all the military nations. Yet the armies which struggled throughout a series of Balkan wars between 1911 and 1913 (involving Italians, Turks, Bulgarians, Greeks and Serbs) and the hosts of Germany, Austria-Hungary, France, Russia, Britain and Belgium which entered the so-called First World War in 1914, all fought under the guidance of lessons from their own latest major campaigns.

General Maresuke Nogi

The most threatening, and yet the least well-formulated, type of war was the subversive kind which had been developing steadily under Marxist influence since 1848 and had found fresh impetus during the days of the Paris Commune in 1871. Assassination of heads of state was endemic. In 1861 serfdom had been abolished in Russia; in 1905, a serious uprising in Moscow led to heavy intervention by the troops along with small concessions to democratic pressures by the Monarchy. There was nothing new about civil insurrection; its difference with the past, in 1914, lay in a more universal and co-ordinated nature of response to skilful handling by professional instigators through the superior communications of the day. The Moscow riots, for example, spread through Russia in the succeeding years. The battlefields of the future, while subject to enlargement at the front, were also tending to spread rearward, involving entire populations in intensive struggles.

Massive peacetime armies depended, of course, upon universal conscription—the system by which a man was called up for a year or more of regular service and then released into the reserve from which he could be recalled in time of war as part of an established reserve corps or division. Thus the populace became merged with the armed forces, one becoming the close reflection of the other. In consequence, though martial routine began to inhibit a significant number of people against militarism, it also enthused those who, but for conscription, might never have become interested in military life. Whereas the educated "gentleman ranker" had been a scarcity among the old volunteer armies which had been drawn from the unemployed and the streetside sweepings, they now introduced a liberalising and humanising influence. At the same time the inventive among them felt compelled to improve weapons and organisations that would increase military destructiveness.

The most prevalent type of war was the colonial kind, waged against tribesmen and dissidents the world over. Until 1898 the U.S. Army was almost perpetually putting down risings by the Red Indians—Custer's death with 211 men at the Little Big Horn in 1876 is but one of a myriad small battles and notable because, for a change, the Indians won. In Russian, French, British, German, Italian, Spanish, Portuguese and Belgian colonies small professional armies were constantly engaged in petty invasions and punitive expeditions against numerically superior but technically inferior opponents. Only rarely did they suffer serious defeats—as had the Italians at Adowa in 1896 with a loss of 8,000 men out of 15,000 against 100,000 Abyssinians.

The most celebrated exponent of colonial warfare was General Louis Lyautey who, in 1900, published a paper called *Colonial Rule of the Army*. He advocated a policy of total occupation and sound administrative government of colonial territory as opposed to single-minded punitive raiding. Lyautey recognised that total oppression by military force could never be a long-term solution to civil disobedience in a so-called peacetime setting, because it was too costly and therefore self-defeating. He was prepared to relegate military means to political government and thus, in his way, was a truer disciple of Clausewitz's dictum that war merely acted as an extension of diplomatic policy. Yet by advocating a diminution of oppression against insurrection at a time when insurrectionists and terrorists were redoubling their energies, he merely restated an age-old conflict between the haves and have-nots.

General Lyautey in Morocco

The most far-reaching progress in formulating new rules of war was made at the Hague Conventions in 1899 and 1907. In 1868 the Declaration of St. Petersburg had forbidden the use of explosive projectiles of under 14 oz (0·4 kg). In 1874 a conference in Brussels outlawed the bombardment of open cities. The twenty-six nations which met at the Hague in 1899 at the call of the Russian Tsar (who is reputed to have been frightened by Bloch's prophecies), tackled international law on a wider front. It tried to codify the principles of Grotius, outlawed the use of poisons or poisoned weapons and defined the rights of combatants, non-combatants, irregulars and prisoners. However, the underlying motive of every nation remained basically unchanged: they subscribed to those rules which were advantageous to themselves and reserved their position over anything which tended to threaten their settled, military policies and the type of armament they had already bought.

The most prolific arms race the world had ever experienced began in the 1890s as a combination of national rivalries allied to economic strains and rising arms manufacture which led to an escalation of fear throughout Europe. The aggressive intentions of Kaiser Wilhelm II of Germany increased friction with France whose people were constantly educated to the need to avenge the disgrace of 1870. Recurrent wars in the Balkans, a general fear of Russian intentions and the imbalance caused by atrophy of both the Austro-Hungarian and Ottoman Empires brought power politics to the boil. The creation of **the largest peacetime armies the world had ever seen** went hand in hand with aggressive military policies. Vastly improved communications hastened decisions and events and still further hastened the cyclic processes of tension.

The German war-lords of 1914—Kaiser Wilhelm II and his Chief of Staff, Helmuth von Moltke

The overriding philosophy of the military commanders of 1914 was the pre-eminence of an attack syndrome. The Austro-Hungarian Empire, which began the conflict by declaring war upon Serbia on 28th July, had but one ambition under General Conrad von Hötzendorf—to attack the Serbs and the Russians. The Germans under General Helmuth von Moltke were intent upon attacking France and then dealing with Russia. The French under General Joseph Joffre and the Russians under Grand Duke Nicholas

Gettysburg—the fight for Pickett's Post

British Grenadier Guards defending Mons in August 1914—compare this painting with the one on opposite page

were determined to attack Germany while the British, strong at sea, were happy to place their little army under the French wing. All lay under the spell of Clausewitz and the theories of total war; the Germans guided by plans of the late Count von Schlieffen, with his fixation upon the quick knock-out of France; the French, who strongly influenced the Russians and the British in the concept of a simultaneous march upon Berlin, consumed by the aggressive philosophy of Colonel de Grandmaison and General Ferdinand Foch.

The activation of the aggressive plans of the combatants depended upon swiftly mobilised armies, composed of massed regular and reserve formations, being delivered, along with their weapons (above all their artillery), to the frontiers by railways the peacetime layout of which had been bent by military considerations. Within about fourteen days of the pronouncement of general mobilisation **the largest collision of armies the world had ever witnessed** was in progress. The line-up of effective forces (less militias) was as follows:

West Front			East Front			The Balkans	
France	1,150,000 ⎫		Russia		1,300,000	Serbia	190,000
Britain	100,000 ⎬ 1,367,000						
Belgium	117,000 ⎭						
			Germany	400,000 ⎫		Austria-	
Germany		1,485,000	Austria-	⎬ 1,500,000		Hungary	200,000
			Hungary	1,100,000 ⎭			

German infantry advance under British fire at Ypres on 30th October 1914

The key weapon—artillery—was not so evenly balanced as man-power. For every army corps placed in the field by the principal nations the number of guns amounted approximately to:

Germany	160	Austria-Hungary	130		
France	126	Britain	154	Russia	90

But that was not the whole story. Whereas the French Army's artillery consisted of a mere 300 heavy-calibre guns, that of the Germans comprised 3,500. Some were pieces of Austrian design, as well as those made by Krupp, and were up to a calibre of 42 cm, capable of accurately firing a 1-ton shell a distance of 16,000 yd (14,560 m). **The heaviest**, "Big Bertha", weighing 75 tons, was transportable by road, had a crew of 280 men and a rate of fire at ten rounds per hour.

"Big Bertha"—the 42 cm Krupp monster which cracked the forts of Liège, Maubeuge, and Antwerp

The first shots of the First World War were fired on 28th July, 1914 though the first major clash of armies had to wait until midway through August when mobilisation was nearing completion and the opposing forces met head-on in the north Balkans, in Poland and East Prussia, in Belgium and in eastern France.

The effect of heavy artillery on a Liège fort's cupola

The first major artillery duel began on 5th August at Liège. German cavalry, with intent to encircle this strong Belgian fortress town on the 4th, had been easily frustrated by a smattering of small-arms fire—the precursor of most cavalry rides to come. German infantry, advancing through the night, were illuminated by fortress searchlights and swept by guns. The 15 miles (24 km) gap through which the Germans hoped to pour their armies in the gigantic wheel of the Schlieffen Plan, deep into France, was closed to them. A system of twelve forts, designed in 1888 by the engineer H. A. Brialmont, had justified its existence. But Brialmont's forts had fallen into decay and, in any case, were built of 7 ft (2·1 m) thick concrete to withstand bombardment by artillery up to 21 cm calibre. Once the German heavy guns opened fire on the 12th it was only forty-eight hours before concrete roofs and steel cupolas had been cracked and dismantled with devastating efficiency. Each fort was tackled in turn and either surrendered at call or was ripped apart by internal explosions. On 16th August all was over at Liège.

The fallacy of fortresses in modern war was exposed not only there but at Maubeuge and Antwerp. Infantry could infiltrate between the forts and modern transport systems readily thread their way to supply the armies beyond. At their leisure the Germans cracked Maubeuge and Antwerp long after their mobile armies had progressed into the distance.

The most ambitious encirclement ever conceived by the Germans was projected against France through the celebrated Schlieffen Plan which aimed to throw a preponderantly strong right wing of their armies round the left flank of the French armies which, it was rightly assumed, would launch their own attack on the opposite wing against the German western frontier. Thus, while the French pinned themselves to one end of their country, the Germans hoped to envelop the entire nation by circling to the west of Paris, isolating the capital and taking the main French armies in rear. Their failure to do so may be accredited to a combination of frictional breakdowns such as had been common to every campaign since 1860, because:

● *These enormous armies* (General von Klück's enlarged First Army on the right wing alone numbered 320,000) were compelled to subsist off well-developed lines of communication. Thus their direction of approach was inevitably direct and predictable and this led to head-on clashes in which modern weapons in defence once again slaughtered the attackers. Had the French armies themselves not chosen to charge headlong during the opening battles on the frontiers, in Belgium and northern France, they might have won crushing successes similar to those of the British when, at Mons on 23rd August, their rapid rifle-fire from concealed positions stopped massed Germans in their tracks.

General Joseph Joffre (left), victor at the Marne, with General Haig and General Foch

● *As the German armies advanced* they could no longer be fed by rail. Marching men supplied by horsed transport became exhausted at the extremities of extended and crowded road communications. Their rate of advance slowed down and gave the French and British additional time in which to redeploy and tackle the threat to their left wing, engineering what is known as the Battle of the Marne which was in actuality a manœuvre aimed at an open enemy's flank.

● *Vacillation within the high commands* of both sides, which caused false conclusions to be drawn from insufficient information, and induced indecision which, finally, among the Germans, brought a complete loss of confidence and led to an abandonment of the Schlieffen Plan. It was significant that several crucial and correct decisions by the army commanders were based upon aerial reconnaissance reports rather than from the cavalry, and symptomatic that the precipitous German withdrawal, which began on 9th September, was to the order of a junior German staff officer who was acting as Moltke's emissary at the front. But the responsibility was Moltke's.

Some of the most complex manœuvres of the war were caused by the multiple head-on collisions on the Russian Front in August under the impulse of the Austrian von Hötzendorf, in his anxiety to gain glory for his country by humbling the Russians, and in the anxiety of the French to hurry the Russians into a premature offensive (before their mobilisation was complete) in order to distract German forces from the West. The Russians were bent upon a ponderous, broad-fronted approach into East Prussia and Austria-

Cavalry fighting on the Eastern Front—a Russian patrol pursued by Austro-Hungarians

Hungary, rather vaguely aimed upon Berlin, Budapest and Vienna. The Germans wanted to stand on the defensive. But the Austro-Hungarians, forfeiting German co-operation, tried on their own to envelop the Russian armies in Poland. Therefore the war on the Russian Front developed piecemeal. The Russian First and Second Armies, pushing into East Prussia against the German Eighth Army, suffered heavy defeat at **the first decisive encirclement of the war** at Tannenberg on 29th August. Simultaneously the Austrian First and Fourth Armies, rushing into southern Poland, were repelled by three Russian armies and hit in the flank by two more rolling in from the east towards the Carpathian Mountains.

Capture of a crater by British infantry at Aubers Ridge, 1915. German prisoners in foreground

The European scope of the war was most clearly demonstrated by events on the East Front. Because of the invasion of East Prussia, Moltke felt obliged to rail two army corps from the West at a time when they would have been vital in winning the campaign there. But though the German victory at Tannenberg encouraged Hötzendorf it also blinded him to the Russian trap which brought heavy defeat in a struggle of attack and counter-attack at Rava Ruska. Inevitably the victorious German forces in the north (which had totally liberated German territory) had to be diverted to the aid of their allies in the south as the Russian host began to enter the Carpathians on 12th September. By 29th September the Germans had redeployed and were ready to advance on the Austro-Hungarians' flank, making for Warsaw in an effort to distract the Russians from their weakening Austro-Hungarian prey—initiating another round of sweeping manœuvres in the Polish plain when the Russians riposted with a counter-attempt at encirclement which threw the Germans back. Here was a campaign of expansive manœuvre such as would have delighted the great captains of old. Never, however, did it produce such a decisive victory as would persuade either side to abandon the war. There was stalemate prolonged by national policies of determined resistance.

The most intractable stalemate of all was to be found on the Western Front where, after the Battle of the Marne, some thoroughly predictable attempts were made by both sides to outflank each other between Paris and the North Sea. The armies came face to face, each behind a continuous barrier of entrenchments, guarded by barbed-wire fences and an impenetrable barrage put down by rifles, machine-guns (of which the Germans had 12,500 Maxim types in 1914) and artillery. This was the beginning of **the most extensive bout of siege-type warfare in history** along a 475-mile front (764·3 km). The ancient practices of breaching operations supervened. Sapping, mining, intensive bombardment, the rush to seize a breach—all were in evidence during nearly four years of almost continuous action. The casualties reached enormous dimensions. Armies that were shifted by remote control by commanders who were compelled to operate from a telephone, telegraph or wireless terminal became locked in a blind struggle. The old-fashioned *coup d'œil* was impossible when men spent 99 per cent of their time out of sight below ground level. In this conflict the above-ground appearance of massed formations simply invited massacre.

Looking for advantage via an open flank, the Kaiser rewarded Generals Paul von Hindenburg and Erich Ludendorff for their successes in the East by switching Germany's main effort against Russia in the winter of 1914–15. Ample geographical space, of course, made easier the freer movements on a frontage of 500 miles (805 km), because there it was impossible to arm sufficient men to hold a continuous, invulnerable line of trenches.

The overriding influences at work upon the formulation of land campaigns, in addition to those imposed by care of the combatants' morale (which was ever at a premium in conditions of trench squalor) were technological.

● **A new dimension to the gathering of information** had been added by aircraft reconnaissance which was far more thorough and deeply ranging than had been previously possible with captive balloons. Though bombing of armies from the air was to increase as the war progressed it was never to assume decisive proportions: always the emphasis was on observation, reporting and artillery control. The air battles which developed between fighter aircraft over the battle zones were tightly related to a struggle for air supremacy to enable reconnaissance aircraft to function unhindered. Air forces were strictly under army control until the last months of the war.

● **The introduction of wireless telegraphy**, as an important medium for passing operational instructions and orders, made it possible for eavesdroppers to listen in on high-level conversations and planning. **The first example of a battle being read by the other side** occurred before Tannenberg when Russian orders, sent in "clear", were monitored by the Germans, enabling them to redeploy in confidence upon full knowledge of Russian intentions. The Austrians broke the Russian code system making it possible to study every impending Russian move in the future. In trench warfare, too, it became possible by induction, to overhear telephone messages passed from closely adjacent enemy trenches. In effect these abilities to overlook the enemy lines or to join in his thoughts made the acquisition of surprise on the battlefield increasingly difficult to obtain, with a consequent reduction in the power of the offensive. At the same time increased opportunities to deceive an opponent with false messages were presented by introducing a plethora of false messages and dummy military installations. Deception plans thus assumed greater importance than ever.

● **A new way to dominate the battle-front, almost regardless of infantry presence**, by positioning artillery, whose crews were protected by steel shields, permanently in the front line to hold the enemy at bay by direct fire supplemented by machine-gun and rifle fire. During the winter of 1915 the French used their 75s in this way. But, in general, both sides indulged more and more in indirect fire methods, directing the guns by telephone from observation posts or balloons and by wireless from aeroplanes. It followed that the possession of strong artillery and plentiful ammunition (of which every army was short in 1915) became recognised as the key to victory. By 1918 there would be 10 guns per 1,000 men (compare this with the figures on page 110). Conversely the Russian Army, which was desperately short of both guns and ammunition, was recognised by the Germans and, to a somewhat lesser extent, by the Austro-Hungarians, as easier prey than the French. This was another reason for the Germans choosing to concentrate against the East Front where, with technical superiority, a knock-out blow seemed within their capability.

● **The first use of irritant tear-gas** was made on a small scale by the Germans against the French during a battle near Neuve Chapelle in October 1914. Its employment passed unnoticed by the French who, themselves, had been experimenting with tear-gas grenades against the interior of fortresses. On 3rd February 1915 the Germans tried again with an improved 15 cm shell in the hope that a high concentration of the gas could be achieved—but this time against the Russians at Bolimov in very cold weather. Again there was no noticeable effect. The Germans had no need to use their primitive face masks, and were swept by rifle and machine-gun fire from an opponent who was not the least inconvenienced. At this time, however, the Germans were manufacturing poisonous chlorine gas that was to be released on to the battlefield from cylinders positioned in the trenches.

The forest of barbed-wire entanglements screening the Hindenburg line

● **The resurrection of flame warfare** seems to have been made by the French in the Argonne in October 1914, with a petrol spray ignited by incendiary bombs. It was the Germans, however, who pioneered a modern device which squirted flaming oil from a container under inert gas pressure. Ranges were only 20 to 40 yd (18 m to 37 m) and the equipment was so heavy that it was suitable only for use in trench warfare or against fortress embrasures. **It was first used** against the British at Hooge in the Ypres salient on 29th July, 1915, but with only limited success.

● **The biggest changes inflicted by technology on armies as the war progressed** were the results of widely increased mechanisation of the transport services as well as the fighting arms. During the initial German invasions both sides used petrol-engined cycles, cars and lorries to hasten the delivery of messages and supplies. The British Army took civilian lorries and passenger buses to France. **The French were the first to use a fleet of motor-cars to move a division to the front**, carrying them in 600 Parisian taxi-cabs on 7th September at a crucial moment during the Battle of the Marne. Had the Germans possessed more motor-lorries they might have maintained the momentum of their advance: undoubtedly they would have reacted more quickly to French counter-action.

● **First to put an armoured fighting vehicle in action** had been the Italians with a Bianci armoured car during fighting against Turkish troops in Libya in 1912. **First to use an armoured car in the First World War** were the Belgians, with a Minerva protected by armour plate and armed with a machine-gun, during their retreat into the fortress of Antwerp.

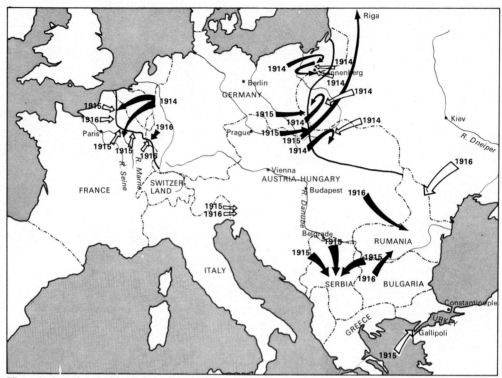

The main campaigns and battle lines of 1914–16

A crucially formative period for tactical development of trench warfare was the first six months of 1915. A succession of offensives launched by the Allies and Germans crystallised the methods which soldiers thought should penetrate the trench lines and reopen mobile warfare.

● *At Neuve Chapelle* on 10th March the British attacked with four divisions against two weak German divisions. The key to their attempt at obtaining complete surprise was the surreptitious registration, before the assault, of 340 guns to avoid arousing German suspicion, and then a bombardment of thirty-five minutes followed by an infantry advance as soon as the gunfire lifted to targets in rear. The assault involved the most thorough preparation yet attempted: meticulous efforts by the artillery to cut the German wire, terrorise the occupants of their forward trenches and knock out their guns; thorough aerial photography of the assault sector and the issue of prints down to junior leaders. Nevertheless, the attack broke down from shortage of infantry and ammunition reserves in face of quicker German reaction.

● *During the first poison-gas attack by the Germans at Ypres*, on 22nd April, the chlorine cloud, integrated with a conventional artillery barrage, drifted over trenches held by French colonial and Canadian infantry none of whom, of course, were provided with any sort of protective mask. This, incidentally, was **the first major operation by Canadians**. In panic, the French ran, opening up a gap more than 5 miles (8 km) wide, into which German infantry flooded. But, as was so typical of trench warfare, attackers who preferred to stay out of sight were slow to recognise a tactical opportunity and slower yet to exploit it. Quickly the Allies filled the gap and instructed their soldiers in anti-gas measures. When next the Germans attacked with gas on the 24th the defenders had improvised face masks of wet towels and blankets so that at least 75 per cent of their number were not incapacitated by the vapour and fought successfully to hold their position. In point of fact the Germans simply did not have the facilities to achieve a persistent cloud of gas at lethal density.

● *On Vimy Ridge*, where the Germans had dug a strong defensive position into the chalk, well protected by barbed wire, the French attacked on 9th May. The artillery preparation had begun on the 4th, working its way systematically across the German defensive positions—though chiefly against the gun lines because French gunners did not yet feel strongly obliged to closely support their infantry. The guns disrupted trenches but gave only low priority to destroying wire and located machine-gun nests. Hence, although the French assault made remarkable progress on the first day, it was fatally disorganised by uncut wire and hammered by surviving machine-guns: moreover, reserves which were too far to the rear could not intervene when the time came to exploit successes. There was no breakthrough. In this style passed a bloody summer and autumn laden with massive casualty lists which piled up for no gain worth the expense. At Vimy alone, in seven weeks, over 100,000 French and 60,000 Germans became casualties for an advance of 1·5 miles (1·9 km) on a 3·5 mile (5·4 km) front and only once, during the first two days, did the Germans feel seriously threatened.

The three best ways round the trench barrier seemed, to the Allies—above all to the British—a landing on the German Baltic coast, massive intervention on the Russian Front or (in aid also of the Russians) an invasion of Turkey (that nation having entered the war on Germany's side on 28th October 1914) by seizing the Dardanelles and Istanbul. Early in 1915 the Baltic approach was rejected, on naval objections, while aid to the Russians, who were to suffer catastrophic defeats at the hands of Hindenburg in the summer of 1915, was considered as best applied via Istanbul.

The largest amphibious operation of the war began at Gallipoli on 19th February with a naval bombardment of the ill-protected, under-armed and ancient forts guarding the Dardanelles. The dose was repeated on the 25th until, gradually, the forts were overcome by sheer weight of gunfire—the Turkish guns being outranged and thus incapable of fighting back. Under these conditions small demolition parties of Royal Marines were able to go ashore, almost unmolested, and complete the work of destruction. But after 4th March these landings were made impossible by the arrival of Turkish reinforcements. Quickly the Turks mined the waters and emplaced more guns to prevent sweeping. To eliminate these guns fresh and larger landings were deemed essential.

The first major landing on the Gallipoli Peninsula took place with more than a division of troops on 25th April. It produced several notable "first occasions".

● **It was the first major operation by Australian troops**—who put a brigade ashore at Ari Burnu.

● **It was the first occasion** in which a specially adapted ship—the S.S. *River Clyde*—was used to take assault infantry ashore. On "V" Beach her men suffered fearful casualties as they ran along the special gangways, though machine-guns, mounted behind sandbags in her bow, gave a measure of useful covering fire.

● **It saw the first impact of dynamic leadership by General Mustapha Kemal**, the commander of the 19th Turkish Division, whose intervention in the battle prevented a breakthrough and defeated the plans of the British commander, General Sir Ian Hamilton. Within a matter of hours trench warfare had set in along a narrow front which could be turned only by further amphibious operations. But whereas Hamilton told his men to dig, Kemal tried all he knew to drive the British off. Thus the would-be attacker was compelled to defend when to advance and expand the flanks was mandatory for success.

Failure by the British at Gallipoli occurred not only because they were incapable of breaching the Turkish trenches, but also because their subsequent flank landing at Suvla Bay in July was as ineptly conducted as the initial invasion. At the end of 1915 the force was withdrawn in **one of the most successful evacuations of an army ever attempted by sea**. Hardly a man was lost in the final stages; only burning stores were left to the Turks.

Austro-Hungarian field artillery dragged to the mountain peaks on the Italian Front

The first major mountain campaign of the war (and the greatest in history) began when Italy opened hostilities against Austria-Hungary on 23rd May. Along a 400-mile (643·5 km) front, running the length of Italy's common frontier with her opponent, only 20 miles (32 km) were unguarded by peaks. In the mountainous Balkans, where Serbia grappled with Austria-Hungary, there were quite extensive plains and valleys leading towards centres of strategic importance and so intensive mountain fighting was not entirely unavoidable. In Italy there was no alternative and so men had to learn to live above the snow-line, risking the avalanches caused by explosions, enduring the risk of frost-bite and exposure, compelled to haul practically every necessity, piecemeal, to the heights. Everything favoured the defensive since almost every attack had to be aimed against positions on elevated ground. Artillery could only be brought forward by the most laborious processes, often bit by bit to be assembled on some narrow, craggy site. There was a repetitive sterility to the offensives—no less than eleven in the River Izonzo sector within two and a half years not one of which threatened a decision. If ever an offensive did seem poised on the verge of success it failed at the crucial moment because the vital effort could no longer be sustained by weary men:

The most bizarre alternative to a conventional kind of offensive designed to capture ground

was the idea of Moltke's successor, General Erich von Falkenhayn. Appreciating, at the end of 1915, that victory in Russia was remote (the latest German-Austro-Hungarian offensives, after initially gaining vast territory, had run out of steam) and that it was more important to knock France out of the war, he devised a plan to "bleed the French Army white" in an artillery abattoir. By applying pressure against a location which, Falkenhayn correctly reasoned, the French could not afford to relinquish, he strove to attract their manpower into a killing zone of German heavy artillery fire.

General Erich von Falkenhayn

At Verdun the greatest ever assembly of artillery was pitted against its 20 forts and interrelated field-works—nearly 1,400 pieces of artillery and mortars along a frontage of 8 miles (12·8 km) among them 26 of the vast siege-guns such as cracked the Liège, Maubeuge and Antwerp forts. Close to the gun positions were piled ammunition stocks to last six days—the 2,500,000 shells allocated to the attack. Gas shells were to be fired at the French artillery to restrain its response. Even so, the German artillery commander, Major-General Schabel, considered the support insufficient by 408 barrels. To ensure full observation and deny it to the French, 166 aircraft, 14 balloons and 3 zeppelins were provided.

French 75s coming into direct action in open ground

To match the Germans, the French, at first, had only 270 guns in position with 20 infantry battalions initially to oppose 72 German. Moreover the forts had been denuded of infantry and machine-guns in the belief that they were impotent against the German heavy guns: only the turret artillery teams remained to fire a set programme against predicted German targets that were far from necessarily those which required the most urgent attention.

The French forts were the strongest in the world. The mighty Fort Douaumont, for example, was protected by 18 ft (5·4 m) of earth over 4 ft (1·2 m) of concrete, over 4 ft of sand which lay above yet another 4 ft of concrete. The pitiful main armament of a single 155 mm gun and two 75s, were retractable and encased in thick armour. This fort was able to withstand the German 42 cm shells. Yet when the German assault lapped against its walls on 25th February the nearest French infantry was a full 1,000 yd (910 m) away and the entire place was captured virtually by three men who found their way almost by accident into the subterranean part—**one of the most remarkable feats of individual achievement of the war.**

German trench mortar applying high-trajectory fire

The products of attrition in the Verdun battle were multifarious. It began on 21st February and dragged on almost ceaselessly under German volition until 11th July. In that period the German advance, thrown against mounting French resistance in a landscape churned to porridge, captured several forts and smothered numerous French counter-attacks. French casualties rose, but so, too, did those of the Germans at an almost equal rate. When the Germans called a halt it was the turn of the French to counter-attack. By the end of 1916, after the last French counter-offensive had died away, the casualties amounted to about 350,000 each. But not only the French and Germans were involved.

● In response to French cries for help the Russians launched a premature and thoroughly abortive offensive at Lake Narotch in March 1916 and lost 110,000 men against the Germans' 20,000. On 4th June they attacked again, but against the Austro-Hungarian Army to the south of the Pripet Marshes—and this time with startling initial success—enough to pin German troops in the East which might otherwise have moved west. On 24th June the British and French opened the Battle of the Somme with fire from 1,537 guns on a 30,000 yd (27,300 m) front in preparation for an infantry assault a week later that was to lead to:

● **The highest casualty figure ever recorded in a single day by the British Army**—no less than 57,470—on 1st July. Those for the French and Germans are unknown but were much lower, though by 10th July the Germans had to admit to 40,187, not including the lightly wounded as did the British statistics. The Somme battle, too, was to last into November and bring the tally of casualties on the Allied side to 630,000 by comparison with 660,000 for the Germans. Again there were no worthwhile territorial gains in a battle the sole strategic objective of which was to take life and relieve pressure from an ally.

A major turning-point of the war had been reached by the end of 1916 when, for the first time, it became apparent to the contestants that they might be near the end of their tether. The Russian Army was incapable of further offensive action; that of the French seemed capable of only one more offensive, the Italians were shaken as were the Austro-Hungarians; while the Germans appreciated that, having lost the cream of the Army, they must revert to the defensive in 1917 while rebuilding. Only the British possessed the capability to attack in strength in 1917 at a time when diplomats were searching for an end to the fighting. Yet, at a time when the bloodshed seemed endless amid **the most costly war in history**, a weapon, which had been used for the first time during the Battle of the Somme, had the potential to break the deadlock. Also at the same time combat methods were being revised.

● *Artillery fire* was being more systematically, accurately and flexibly directed using ammunition with fuses of greater reliability. Each gun was carefully matched against suitable targets. It was becoming possible to shoot accurately "off the map" without direct observation of the fall of shot against distant targets—a technique made feasible by the careful calibration and surveying into position of guns, improved intelligence and control methods and the introduction of accurate meteorological data to compensate for cross-winds and the like. This more accurate fire allowed infantry to advance closer behind a moving barrage of shells to arrive safely at the objective almost immediately after the last shell had burst; thus the enemy was given insufficient time to recover and shoot back. Counter-battery shooting improved to a high art—the precursor to every battle was a systematic attack upon opposing guns with high explosive and gas.

The revitalisation of artillery demanded centralised control. Every army evolved special artillery staffs to advise commanders and to implement complex fire plans which virtually dictated battle tactics. The British, for example, installed senior artillery commanders who superimposed their will not only upon the normal divisional artillery and over heavy artillery groups (which included the mass of medium, heavy and super-heavy batteries that could be moved from one location to another to suit the tactical situation) but also upon the army commanders' tactical plans.

Lewis machine-gun team wearing respirators

Almost as powerful in their own environment of direct fire were the machine-guns, among them the new light models. **The first one-man portable machine-gun** brought into service was the American gas-operated Lewis, which was designed in 1911 and weighed only 25 lb (11 kg) compared with 125 lb (56 kg) for the complete Maxim. Manufactured at first in Belgium and then in England, the British by 1916 had 40,000. The other armies mainly relied on heavier types—either Maxim or the French Hotchkiss or Chauchat (a much-disliked gun with a high propensity to jamming). The Germans developed a 22 lb (10 kg) Maxim but did not manufacture very many. In 1918, however, they made a twin-barrelled gun called the Gast with a 1,000-round-per-minute rate of fire as compared with the 500 normally fired by Maxim types. In effect rifles and bayonets became of lesser importance, particularly in enclosed trench fighting. Hand-grenades were much better area weapons which required no precise aiming.

German field artillery in action on the Rumanian Front during mobile operations

Infantry assault— 1916

⬤ *Infantry tactics* became more closely linked to fire support. The original concept of infantry waves ponderously advancing to occupy ground which had been "taken" by the artillery gave way to infiltration by picked men moving by rushes under the local support of fire from the new light machine-guns.

The return of armour protection against fire was, as described above, first manifested in gun-shields and armoured cars. Later the Germans were to make steel body-armour. **The first devices to increase the cross-country capability of vehicles**—footed wheels and chain tracks—had been mooted as long ago as 1770 by an Englishman, Richard Edgeworth, and the first commercial tracked vehicle sold by the Holt Manufacturing Co. of the U.S.A. in 1906. By merging the armoured gun with the armoured motor-car and placing them on "tracks", the British produced in 1915 **the first cross-country armoured fighting vehicle** to which, in the interests of secrecy, they gave the name "tank". **Used for the first time** on 15th September 1916 on the Somme they ushered in a new epoch of land warfare.

SECTION VII

The Epoch of Mechanisation
1916–1944

The first proposal for armed and armoured trench-crossing fighting machines was made by a British engineer, Lieutenant-Colonel Ernest Swinton, in September 1914 when he recognised that coming trench warfare would cause a stalemate. Swinton was thus ahead of a Frenchman, J. L. Breton who, in November, proposed a machine that would merely advance to cut wire, an armoured tractor without guns. In the months to follow the British and French developed their ideas in ignorance of each other. Moreover, the tanks they eventually produced, were quite different in shape and, to some extent, in purpose.

	Weight (tons)	Armament (mm)	Armour (mm)	Speed (mile/h)	(km/h)	Tactical purpose
British	28	2 × 57	10	3·7	6	Break wire, cross wide trenches, attack enemy artillery and machine-guns.
French	13	1 × 75	24	4·2	8	Break wire and act as an assault gun.

The first tank attack on 15th September 1916 involved only 36 British machines out of 49 available while the French were unable to get their first machines into action until 16th April, 1917, although they employed 128. Neither achieved much success since the first tanks were very unreliable, the crews quite inexperienced and numbers insufficient to achieve a concentration that would "saturate" the German defences. Nevertheless the basis of an operational mode was established. Tanks would advance ahead of the infantry but behind the artillery barrage, breaking lanes through the wire and dealing with enemy machine-guns. It was hoped that artillery fire would neutralise the enemy artillery (the tank's deadliest enemy) and that infantry would "mop up" pockets of resistance after the tanks had passed. In the event tanks found themselves involved in mopping up and also in their first-ever duels with enemy artillery.

The most significant pointer to the future occurred on 26th September 1916, when a single British tank, moving ahead of infantry and in the wake of artillery fire to attack a German trench, found itself in isolation and engaged by German infantry. At that moment a British aeroplane arrived and began low-level machine-gun attacks while the tank straddled the trench and moved its length, dominating the enemy below. When British infantry arrived they merely had to collect the prisoners.

An immense and extensive system of defence—called the Hindenburg Line—was developed by the Germans in the winter of 1916–17—not as a counter to the tank, which hardly impressed them, but as a modern version of "depth" such as had been forced by improved siege methods on fortresses of the Vauban period. Realising that by holding the front line in maximum strength they were merely offering packed men to certain destruction by artillery, the Germans spread their garrisons into groups within a prepared "battle zone" that was located some 1,500 to 2,000 yd (1,365 to 1,820 m) behind outposts. The inventor of this system was Colonel Fritz von Lossberg. Within the battle zone the groups were allowed freedom of action as well as interplay with prearranged artillery fire. Here and there isolated field-guns would be dug in, specifically as anti-tank weapons, while deep trenches and massive banks of barbed wire created what looked like an impenetrable, multi-layered barrier. Nevertheless tactical emphasis was placed on aggressive elasticity in the holding of terrain; ground might be surrendered if the tactical situation demanded but, if rated as vital, it must be retaken by counter-attack. The Hindenburg Line did not cover the entire West Front, only the vital sector from Arras to Vailly on the River Aisne—a distance of 60 miles (96 km)—and even this was not completed before the Allies attacked again in strength in April 1917. The rest of the West Front was only partially converted to the new system while, on the Russian Front, nothing so comprehensive was ever attempted. There the armies concentrated only on holding vital communication centres and essential ground, permitting a degree of manœuvrability such as was possible elsewhere only on the open desert flanks in the Turkish theatres of war in Mesopotamia and Palestine.

The justification for von Lossberg's defensive system was the failure of all but one of the major Allied offensives in 1917. At Arras and on the Chemin des Dames in April, and in the Ypres Salient from July until October, British and French infantry wallowed in mud that was the creation of their own pulverising artillery fire. At an immense cost in life—the Third Battle of Ypres alone claimed 300,000 British, 8,000 French and 260,000 German casualties—the battle lines remained all but static.

Yet vital changes in the methods of making war were about to bring a decision in sight.

Hindenburg

Italian soldiers hauling their artillery up new-made roads to positions on the mountains

The Dardanelles operations: The landing of the Australians at Gallipoli, April 1915

British 60-pdr guns amid the waterlogged devastation of the Third Battle of Ypres—autumn 1917

● *At Riga* on 1st September a German, General Oscar von Hutier, tried out a revolutionary attack system designed to overcome the Lossberg type of defensive layout and at the same time restore surprise and momentum to the battlefield. Instead of the prolonged preliminary bombardment such as featured in every offensive after Neuve Chapelle in March 1915, Hutier reverted to a short bombardment, under Colonel Bruchmüller, immediately prior to the infantry assault. This bombardment, however, was an enormous improvement on 1915 because of better and more guns and ammunition, indirect fire and silent registration techniques. **For the first time** "battle units", comprising infantry, machine-gunners, assault artillery and engineers, were grouped into *ad hoc* teams to ensure close co-operation by all arms. At the same time the leading groups—special Storm Troops—were instructed to by-pass strong opposition and leave its reduction to following echelons. Thus the advance would proceed like an incoming tide, surrounding and finally flooding centres of opposition instead of attempting to crush them simultaneously like a wave. Once a breach had been made it would be for the victorious troops to fan out and eliminate every vestige of enemy opposition. This was achieved at Riga. The Germans captured a mass of Russian artillery and 9,000 prisoners for losses of about 4,000 themselves. But the Russian soldiers, war-weary and distracted by the Revolution which had deposed the Tsar in March, made little resistance and so it was hardly fair wholly to attribute a German advance of 5 miles (8 km) in four days to the new tactics.

● *At Caporetto* on 24th October the new tactics were demonstrated far more conclusively by the Germans and Austro-Hungarians under General Otto von Below against the Italians under General Luigi Cadorna. Within less than three weeks the Italians had lost more than 300,000 men and 2,500 guns and been swept back over 70 miles (122·5 km). The catastrophe almost brought the country to its knees. Meantime Anglo-French divisions had to be taken from France to reinforce the Italians, thus removing the main strategic reserve from the West Front at a crucial moment. German and Austro-Hungarian losses were little more than 20,000.

A most remarkable example of infiltration tactics at the lower levels during Caporetto was performed by Captain Erwin Rommel who, in two days, captured a complete key section of the Italian Front along with over 9,000 men and 81 guns. By personal example he kept fatigued men constantly on the move, bypassing opposition and bluffing the enemy into surrender. Yet, even when deep among the enemy, he actually improved his safety by keeping on the move.

The most crippling effect of Caporetto, however, was the breakdown of Italian command and control when gas and high explosives brought confusion to communication sections. The Italians were never quite able to circumvent an enemy whose movements kept a step ahead of their defensive measures. It was exhaustion and attenuation of their reserves which finally brought the attackers to a halt when they failed to capture a vital Italian position in the rear and inevitably came up against increasing numbers of defenders whose pace of reaction at last matched that of the attackers.

● *At Cambrai* on 20th November where the new artillery surprise tactics, linked with a massed attack by 476 British tanks (the idea of Colonel J. F. C. Fuller who already had the reputation of a military thinker), swept a broad swathe 12 miles (19·2 km) wide and 4 miles (6·4 km) deep into the strongest sector of the Hindenburg Line in a matter of hours. Here again, in **the first tank offensive** in which these fighting machines were given a dominant role, initial losses to the attackers were much lower than those of the defenders; against 4,000 British (and 179 tanks) the Germans lost 10,000 plus 123 guns, 79 trench mortars and 281 machine-guns and a complete slice out of their highly expensive new fortified system. But the British did not practise infiltration tactics and tried to reduce each German strongpoint in turn instead of driving ahead in depth. The attack petered out in the customary stalemate as the Germans sealed the breach.

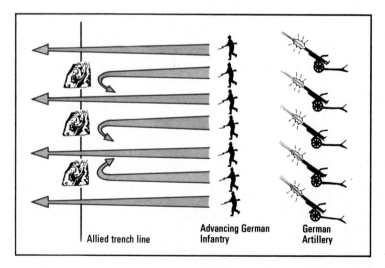

Allied trench line   Advancing German Infantry   German Artillery

The tactics of infiltration past entrenched opposition

As the war progressed, the most important factors limiting land warfare were those associated with mass both in connection with manpower and industry. When the U.S.A. declared war upon Germany on 6th April 1917 she added next to nothing immediately either in armies or munitions to the Allies: the U.S. Army was a mere 210,000. But support from a nation of vast potential redoubled Allied faith in the future and strongly influenced the Germans into one last desperate attempt to knock Britain out of the war in 1918 before an irresistible mass of 2,000,000 American soldiers could arrive in 1919.

The Germans, too, had to find reserves for the 1918 gamble and this became possible by harnessing subversive warfare—by injecting the virus of Communism under Vladimir Lenin into the Russian Revolution and thereby instigating Russia's withdrawal from the war in December 1917. This allowed the Germans to transfer vast reserves of men and material from east to west in the New Year. But at the same time it triggered off a civil war within Russia that was to turn into **one of the fiercest bouts of internecine guerilla warfare** in history.

The most important military product of the Bolshevik Revolution was the Red Army which was born of the struggle between the pro-Tsarist White Army in the fighting that raged from 1918 until 1922. It is impossible to compute the extent of the Russian Civil War because it embraced the entire expanse of the greatest land mass in the world—from Poland to Vladivostok and from the Arctic Circle to the frontier of Persia. Nor did the Red Army come into being as the result of one dramatic announcement, but was slowly and painfully welded together from a polyglot collection of conscripted masses whose major concern was desertion rather than fighting the sort of holy war which Communism postulated. Leon Trotsky, whose task it was to establish the Red Army, was clear about essentials; he knew that private guerilla armies were the antithesis of the orderly government which he and Lenin required. Against the wishes of confirmed Communists, such as Frunze and Stalin, he sought professional soldiers as officers even if that meant re-employing the old aristocracy. At the same time he was content to promote from the ranks truly professional non-commissioned officers. The similarity of the Red Army structure to that of the original French Revolutionary Army will not pass unnoticed. Nor was its task so very different, committed as it was to maintain a defence against German and Allied incursions from the west, Japanese and Allied intervention from the east, large Tsarist White armies operating with Allied support, and marauding Polish and Czech dissidents. It was also engaged in eradicating anarchist elements within its own ranks—those private armies which fought anybody who questioned their independence. In the midst of this ghastly turmoil, in which modern weapons were at a premium and a rare tank or armoured car dominated its locality, it would have been astonishing had important innovations in the art of war emerged. They did not. Simply there was a repetition of lessons from the distant past—that an army whose morale is upheld by a cause may well prevail over numerically superior but demoralised opponents; that in the absence of a superior technology, mass will prevail; and that amoral brutality is the inevitable dividend of irregular civil war. In Russia after 1917 such rules of warfare as were still respected almost disappeared. The country was, as the German General Max Hoffman said, "crawling with maggots".

The heaviest German offensive brought a swell of resurgent mobility which loosened the Western Front in March 1918 when Ludendorff unleashed the German armies, first, against the British. The highlight of every break-in battle was the use of the special siege batteries controlled by Bruchmüller. More extensive advances were made than at any time since 1914, hordes of prisoners were taken and for a few ephemeral days a final decision seemed in the offing—particularly when squabbles between the British and French generals threatened a fatal split. Yet Ludendorff's attacks merely heightened the tension without touching a single worthwhile objective in depth. The cold statistics of his offensive are revealing though without relating the story of appalling suffering caused by the outpouring of so much destruction.

Location of attack	Date	No. of guns	No. of attack divs	Casualties German '000	Allied '000	Comments
Somme	21 Mar	6,598	67	230	240	German failure to maintain mobility British failure to withstand outflanking attacks
Lys	9 Apr	5,000	35	95	100	As above plus deterioration of assault troops
Aisne	27 May	3,719	41	50	60	Stopped by exhaustion
Matz	9 June	4,500	23	30	35	Stopped by strong defence and counter-attacks
Marne	15 July	5,000	47	50	45	As above

The critical factors governing German successes and failures throughout five months of offensive warfare in 1918 were not only those of logistic number and mobility mentioned above, but of weaknesses and strengths

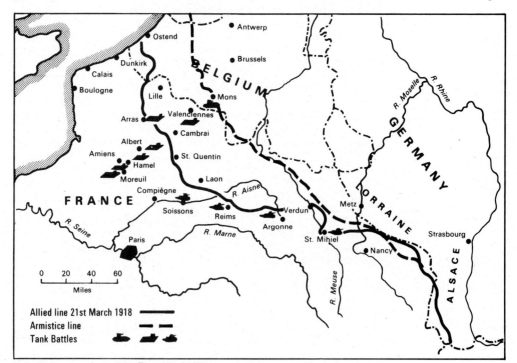

Allied line 21st March 1918 ———
Armistice line — — —
Tank Battles

Principal tank actions of the First World War.

Ludendorff

in personalities and organisation. At the strategic level the virtues of attacking weakness and by-passing failure (as was the norm with tactics), were too often ignored by Ludendorff who tended to butt against the strongest Allied bastions. For example, at the end of March when his troops were approaching Amiens and in need of reinforcement at points of profitable penetration, he diverted immense effort to attacking the strongest sector in the Allied line—the region of Arras and Vimy Ridge—and was repulsed. Hutier and Below, aided by Bruchmüller, repeatedly copied the relatively localised successes of Riga and Caporetto, yet the longest German advance never exceeded the 40 miles (64 km) achieved by the first offensive in March. After that the distances progressively declined as Allied soldiers, fighting back with growing confidence and efficiency, got the measure of German tactics which, in the final analysis, depended only on a rejigged formula of slow-moving men and guns.

For the worst deficiency in the German Army in 1918 was lack of armour and a sound mobile arm. They never produced more than thirteen tanks in any one battle and were totally devoid of cavalry divisions in the West.

A French Schneider tank advances along with infantry

The fastest expanding part of the Allied armies, on the other hand, was in their corps of armoured mobility. While retaining a reduced force of horsed cavalry, the British tank force had risen to a strength of 1,184 effective machines by July and that of the French to about 800, while the Americans had about 175 machines of French manufacture. Appearing in ever-larger numbers were tanks that were both lighter and faster than the original British 28-ton heavies. The French were to build 3,500 two-man Renault tanks weighing only 6·5 tons; the British a three-man medium of 14 tons called the "Whippet" which could travel at 8 mile/h (12·8 km/h) and had a range of 40 miles (64 km). The victory at Cambrai had convinced every army of importance that tanks in battle were essential, though mostly it was as an adjunct to infantry that soldiers regarded them.

However, the first tank philosopher, J. F. C. Fuller, visualised tanks as revolutionary weapons in their own right. He saw that they were essential to restoring strategic as well as tactical mobility to the battlefield, as the only possible means to obtain adequate protection against shell and machine-gun fire and as the most economical method for maintaining long-range momentum by injecting mechanical stamina in lieu of human muscle. It was Fuller who analysed the most efficient methods for using tanks both in attack and defence, wishing to employ them as weapons of aggression regardless of the tactical situation, and he who deprecated their use in small numbers for local counter-attacks during the Ludendorff offensive and who insisted they should be used in mass. Fuller wrote a paper in May 1918 entitled *The Tactics of the Attack as affected by the speed and circuit of the Medium D Tank*, a paper which called for long-range strategic attacks by tanks aimed at enemy communications and control centres, striking at artillery and other enemy troops *en passant*, but endeavouring, in essence, to swiftly paralyse the enemy's resistance instead of slowly destroying it piecemeal in the artillery fashion. "Plan 1919", as Fuller's concept came to be known, telescoped time in battle and was adopted by the Allies as the operational blueprint for the 10,000 tanks they were building for the campaign of 1919. Instead it was an embryonic version of Plan 1919 which started the rot in the German Army and a mere 2,000 British, French and American tanks, heavily and skilfully supported by artillery and infantry (with cavalry assistance), which ended the war in November 1918.

J. F. C. Fuller

The visions of the future of tank warfare most clearly projected in 1918 were:

⬤ **The first tank v. tank engagement** at Villers-Bretonneux on 24th April when three British Mark IV tanks fought a drawn engagement with three German heavy A7Vs.

⬤ *Innumerable occasions when* tanks, due to their ability to react quickly to a situation, were able, sometimes in co-operation with aircraft, to turn the tables upon a German infantry attack as it emerged more slowly into open country.

⬤ *The intensifying duel between guns and tanks* and the way the latter suffered fewer losses in proportion to the concentration of machines they achieved at the point of impact.

The largest tank battle of the war was fought at Amiens on 8th August when 604 Allied tanks advanced in unison to crush a surprised German Army which lay exhausted at the end of extended lines of communication. It was not only heavy tanks closely following the by now characteristically short bombardment which broke through the defence in a matter of minutes, but light tanks, armoured cars and cavalry infiltrating through the 20 mile (32 km) gap to drive 6 miles (10 km) deep into the German rear which brought chaos in their train. Artillery positions plus divisional and corps headquarters were overrun. The magnitude of the blow struck fear in the hearts of German front-line soldiers and their leaders. From this moment it was clear to the German Command that they were on the verge of abject collapse.

Perhaps the least effective of the "new" weapons turned out to be poison gas. Once every man was equipped with a mask and trained to deal with what turned out to be only an inconvenience, the emotive drama of its first surprise use was never repeated. Not even the introduction of liquid mustard gas, by the Germans in 1917, which attacked through contact with the skin, did much to alter this general conclusion. American casualties from gas were proof, indeed, of a certain "humanity" in their use: 25 per cent of their total casualties were from gas of whom only 2 per cent died, whereas 26 per cent of other wounded did die.

German assault troops (one with a pack flame-thrower) advancing behind a captured British Mark IV tank

Among the most dramatic of victories, both in nature and outcome, were those won over the Turks in Palestine by the British and Arabs. Throughout the war, apart from the rebuff of the Allies at Gallipoli and a victory over the British when they allowed a division to become besieged in Kut-el-Amara in Mesopotamia, the Turks had been losing. They had failed to cut the Suez Canal in 1915 and gradually been driven back by the Russians, in Armenia and Persia, and the British in the Middle East. German assistance helped stabilise them, but this was on too small a scale. Defeated at Gaza in October 1917, when a handful of British tanks were used, they had retreated beyond Jerusalem to the north and taken post in trenches defending the plain which lies before Nablus, Jenin, Megiddo and Haifa. At the entrenched front all the appurtenances of modern siege warfare, with the exception of tanks, were present. But on the wings were the elements of mobile warfare which drew their inspiration from warfare of the past. General Sir Edmund Allenby, the Allied commander, had at his disposal a force of 12,000 cavalry, backed up by armoured cars, and, in addition, some 6,000 or more Arab irregulars under the command of the Emir Faisal and the English Colonel T. E. Lawrence. Since 1916 the Arab rebellion against their Turkish overlords had manifested itself in persistent and increasingly damaging raids against rail communications and depots. The Turkish Army in Arabia was kept close to famine and almost totally isolated from the main Army in Palestine. The Arabs cut the railway with small explosive charges, wrecking trains and then riding in to the kill on their camels, supported by machine-gun fire from armoured cars. The British supplied a cadre of experts, the necessary munitions and considerable finance. What started as a small guerilla force developed into a highly mobile army which, in September 1918, acted as desert flank guard to Allenby's main force operating parallel and close to the coast. When Allenby broke through on the 18th and drove deep with cavalry among the Turks, cutting communications and roping in hordes of prisoners, the Arabs descended upon the Turkish flank and rear to sever the rail and road links with the main base at Damascus. Eventually three Turkish armies with 76,000 men and 360 guns were captured for an Allied loss of about 5,500 killed and wounded.

At the height of the Turkish débâcle occurred the **most highly concentrated and damaging single intervention by aircraft yet effected upon an army**. In the Wadi Fara, on 21st September, columns of the Seventh Turkish Army under Kemal were caught in the defile by British aircraft and heavily bombed and machine-gunned. The road became blocked. As time went by the soldiers began to abandon their equipment and seek escape in the open desert. Eventually, after a four-hour attack, 90 guns, 50 lorries and some 1,000 other kinds of vehicle were found destroyed or abandoned. Elsewhere cavalry charged with lance and sword— an ancient privilege which had been denied to horsemen almost everywhere else throughout the war, except with ghastly casualties. These charges, too, had portent for the future, encouraging the staunchest advocates of the unarmoured, mounted arm to cling to the belief that there was a future for the horse in combat.

One of the longest, most sustained advances of the war—300 miles (483 km) from Jaffa to Aleppo in thirty-six days depended much on armoured cars and motor-lorries and this occurred at the culminating stage of the Turkish campaign with peace in the offing.

The most far-reaching alteration in the balance of the world's land forces came about after the final German defeat, a defeat which was the result not of one striking set-back in the field but an accumulation of reverses and losses leading to retreats in which the fighting men's fortitude reverted to a mutinous unwillingness on the part of many to fight at all. Mutiny was, in part, a dividend of attrition (a dividend which had been paid by all of Germany's allies, by Russia and only narrowly avoided by the French when parts of their army rebelled in May 1917). But the totality of war also had its effect. Knowledge of deprivation among the civil populace sapped the soldiers' morale and a general war-weariness gave room for Communist agitators to introduce and spread the Communist virus which Germany herself had helped inject into Russia. However, the German soldier was also aware that he had been defeated by both superior technology and numbers, and felt it most strongly when evidence of a massive presence of American divisions began to appear in the autumn of 1918. The tank was the most emotive manifestation of Allied technical advantage but there was, in addition, a higher quality about every item of their opponents' equipment which dumbfounded the Germans. Deprived of vital raw materials by the Allied naval and economic blockade, German industry began to produce inferior, as well as insufficient, war material. Moreover, though the Allied armies which fought in 1917 were far better trained than the raw citizen armies of 1916, those of 1918 were the best trained—and the most wary—that had yet gone into action. They achieved results in offensive operations at a far lower cost in lives as the following table of British battle casualties per mile of territory gained shows:

Between July and November 1916   5,300
Between July and November 1917   8,200
Between July and November 1918   83

The largest armies the world had ever seen suffered the highest total losses ever recorded.
Not that there is an authoritative figure—only estimates of which one puts the total dead at 12,996,571. To these had to be added innumerable wounded and disabled. The losses of the principal combatants were approximately as follows:

	Enlistments	Dead	Wounded
British Empire	**9,496,170**	**947,023**	**2,121,906**
French Empire	**8,410,000**	**1,375,000**	**2,250,000**
Russia	**12,000,000**	**1,700,000**	**4,950,000**
Italy	**5,615,000**	**460,000**	**947,000**
U.S.A.	**4,355,000**	**115,660**	**205,690**
Germany	**13,400,000**	**1,808,545**	**4,247,143**
Austria-Hungary	**7,800,000**	**1,200,000**	**3,620,000**
Turkey	**2,850,000**	**325,000**	**400,000**

The rapid reduction of the armies to peacetime scales was, however, uneven by nationalities. France, for example, continued to maintain a large army as insurance against any subsequent German threat despite Germany being compelled by the Treaty of Versailles to reduce her army to 100,000. But while France retained a large force of heavy guns, bomber aircraft and tanks, Germany was forbidden to possess these so-called "offensive weapons". Yet Germany, with an army that was riddled by disaffection from 1919 until 1923, had to fight the threat of internal revolution. She was compelled to form special units as a substitute for a disrupted regular army—the Freikorps whose particles might be of platoon or divisional strength but whose officers and men were the professional soldiers who had learned their trade between 1914 and 1918. With uninhibited zeal and brutality they were to put down the equally brutal elements which rose up in the cities of Germany and which appeared, along with Russian Communist forces, in the Baltic States. It is to be emphasised that Russian Communist armies, while introducing nothing new in combat technique, undoubtedly reverted to the sort of uncontrolled violence and massacre such as epitomised the religious crusades and Asiatic invasions of the past. In self-defence the Freikorps became infected by these methods and carried them into central European practice where, for example, Polish troops of that reinstated nation fought with unparalleled ferocity and success to repel a Russian invasion in 1922.

The first period of world peace of a sort after ten years' almost continual war at last began in 1923. Every nation had more arms than it could handle. Wholesale scrapping took place though vast numbers of obsolescent guns, aeroplanes and tanks were kept for contingencies. Peoples who had suffered enough of war gave a mandate to governments dedicated to economy in armaments—those, indeed, which sought a measure of disarmament besides a revision of international law to make war more difficult to start and outlaw the blatantly horrific practices which had grown up. Yet there was

Richardson's Bluff, Palestine—mounted and dismounted assault by British hussars in 1918 against the Turks

The tanks and infantry in action under cover of a smoke-screen during the Battle of Cambrai, November 1917

Fascist infantry grenading a Russian-built Spanish Republican tank in 1936 during the Civil War

never a complete standstill in the evolution of military strategy or of new weapons.

The most fertile military minds of the time were those of the Italian, Giulio Douhet, and the Englishmen, Fuller and Lawrence.

> **Douhet**, in his book *Command of the Air*, 1921, along with **William Mitchell** of the U.S.A., promulgated a theory of future wars being won by air power, spreading terror with explosives and gas. But Mitchell never quite abandoned the position that land forces were essential and could draw healthy support from aircraft. These theories enthused the Italians and caused interest elsewhere, though no single nation whole-heartedly adopted the Douhet theory while all continued to allocate sizeable air forces to the support of armies. At the same time there was a distinct tendency to spend most money on aircraft with consequent stultification in new equipment for armies.
>
> **Fuller** advocated armoured armies, headed by the tank, to strike strategic blows, supported by air forces, at enemy heartlands. He also envisaged armoured striking forces being supported by a swarm of motorised guerillas, developing his most advanced ideas in his *Lectures on FSR III* published in 1933.
>
> **Lawrence** wrote penetrating studies of guerilla warfare culled from his experience with the Arabs. In *The Seven Pillars of Wisdom* he concisely defined the special conditions of guerilla warfare—dilating upon a need for guerillas to enjoy the support of the local populace; to practise the art of dispersion; to depend upon a dedicated élite since the mass of populace was unlikely to be reliable.

The essence of military thought after the First World War swung hard towards the virtue of élites, tending to reject the concept of mass as a figment of vivid memory of mass slaughter. Air, tank and guerilla enthusiasts were all, in their way, following this line. But in doing so they were, of course, demanding more machines to do man's work and thus withholding soldiers from exposure to fire. The trends in military technology, therefore, moved towards more powerful and efficient and lighter weapons carried by heavier machines.

> ● *Tank design*, however, adopted lighter, faster machines—for reasons of economy, though heavy, expensive types were produced in small numbers.
>
> ● *Guns and mortars* were made lighter and yet were extended in range while bomber aircraft were increasingly allocated the task previously undertaken by heavy artillery.
>
> ● *Special anti-tank guns* of light construction and low silhouette were designed and given sufficient power to penetrate the armour of every known tank. There was a large market in such weapons and a persistent traffic in industrial and weapon intelligence and espionage.
>
> ● *The first sub-machine-gun* was the Italian Villar Perosa, produced during the First World War to suit mountain warfare. The German Schmeisser MP 18 was manufactured in 1918 but never saw front-line service. These weapons, however, were to become common throughout the 1920s.
>
> ● *Light machine-guns* got lighter than the original Lewis by 2 or 3 lb (0·9 or 1·3 kg). The celebrated U.S. Browning automatic rifle of 1922 weighed only 19 lb (9 kg), the Czech ZB 30, from which was developed the British Bren, weighed 22 lb (10 kg). These guns were much more reliable than the Lewis which had a habit of contriving complicated stoppages in muddy and embarrassing battlefield circumstances.

The deepest experiments by armies after 1918 were in the field of mechanisation and communications. While the techniques of shooting both with artillery and small arms remained relatively constant, world-wide study was given to replacing the horse by the petrol engine as the essential means of motive power. It was generally conceded that, but for motor transport, the accumulation of enormous ammunition stocks to feed the vast artillery programmes of 1917 to 1918, would have been impossible. Gradually it was shown that motor-driven transport was cheaper than horse-drawn— the main inhibitions to its wholesale introduction by every army within a short period was the economic impossibility of replacing every vehicle with something new: neither the money nor the industrial output were available. By comparison with these problems the matters of fuel supply and the difficulty of overcoming the prejudice of those who regretted the obsolescence of the horse were exaggerated.

The first tactical experiment with an all-mechanised fighting force was conducted by the British Army on Salisbury Plain in 1927. A battalion of armoured cars and light tanks, another of fast medium tanks, a machine-gun battalion in cross-country carriers, motorised artillery and engineers, along with air support, demonstrated that they could outmanœuvre a conventional foot-and-horse-transported army. Watched by observers from all over the world, and enthusiastically reported by Captain B. H. Liddell Hart, whose ability to transmit ideas and formulate a coherent, modern military philosophy raised him high among the ranks of military thinkers, the experiment led the Russians, Americans, French and Germans to emulate the British system.

The first full-scale experiment with a complete tank formation controlled by radio took place on Salisbury Plain in 1931 and was made possible by the manufacture of the first voice radio set (the MB/MC) capable of being installed in a tank. This is just another instance of shortened time in the conversion of an invention to practical use, for **the first radio-telephone conversation** had taken place as recently as 1904. The period between 1910 and the 1930s was rich in radio research because of its recognised commercial application.

The first break in the "peace" which had begun in 1923 also came in 1931. Throughout the intervening years Britain and France had been engaged in interminable colonial wars, such as Lyautey had described. But in 1931 the Japanese invaded Manchuria. In response the Russians began to lay down large tank-production lines and in 1932 formed a mechanised corps composed of 500 assorted tanks and 200 armoured cars. In Italy, too, the Government of the Dictator Benito Mussolini began to build 200 light tanks. An arms race was on, joined in 1934 by Adolf Hitler's Germany with the recommencement of conscription and the laying down of an air force plus a tank force. Compelled to respond, the French and British began rearmament in 1935—the former giving prime attention to their land forces—building nearly 3,500 tanks by 1940 and creating a great new fortress system along her frontier with Germany. The British concentrated hardest upon their air force but, nevertheless, beginning the total mechanisation of their army even though the priority granted to tanks was lower than to artillery and infantry.

The first act of aggression by a Western power was instigated by Italy when, without declaration of war, she invaded Abyssinia in 1935. While her bombers dominated the

air and rained high explosive and poisonous gas upon ill-trained and
equipped tribal armies, her army mopped up irregular forces which tried
to fight in conventional style instead of reverting to guerilla tactics in
mountainous country ideally suited to that purpose. By terror the Italians
won. Economic sanctions by the League of Nations failed, largely because
an embargo on oil—the life-blood of the Italian air and mechanised
forces—was excluded. Though the campaign was a walk-over certain
important factors stood revealed. If the light Italian tanks were demonstrably highly vulnerable even to tribesmen, their ability to penetrate the
most broken, undeveloped terrain was remarkable in conjunction with
rapid road construction. At the same time air-delivered liquid gas was
exhibited merely as a terror weapon, useful only against the totally
unprepared.

*Italian light tanks in
action in Abyssinia in
1935*

The first use of Lewisite (another persistent liquid blister gas) was by the Japanese in 1938
against the Chinese in the second year of what the Japanese called the
"China Incident"—the series of incursions into China via Manchuria
and by amphibious landings which eventually were to seize a large slice
of the hinterland and the most important ports.

A far more sophisticated outbreak of war was that which began as a result of rebellion in Spain,
with **one of the first operational air lifts that took** 10,000 Fascist
troops from Morocco to Spain to begin the revolt. In the ensuing Civil
War not only was the full range of modern weapons (with the exception
of poison gas) used, but they were largely manipulated by those major
powers which were in ideological contention—the Communist Russians
supporting the Government side and the Fascist Germans and Italians
the Insurgents. Guerilla warfare was widespread, though patchy,
exemplified by raids launched against targets behind the lines: they
did little to bring a solution but helped maintain the ideological struggle
and increase the level of violence against the populace. Likewise terror
bombing of cities, while creating dramatic damage and striking horror
among foreign observers, did not cause the expected collapse of civilian
morale: on the contrary it stiffened the resistance of the garrison and

people of Madrid who held out under siege conditions for more than two years. Artillery and tanks were employed in much the same manner as they had been in 1918—as infantry-support weapons but never whole-heartedly in mass and for deep penetration in the mode suggested by Fuller and Liddell Hart: indeed, the idea became current that those who claimed there was no startling future for the tank as a weapon of decision were right.

As the Spanish Civil War ground ponderously towards its conclusion in March 1939 with a toll of about 120,000 killed in action, bombed to death or executed, the consensus of military opinion moved in favour of defensive operations on land—while granting that an offensive with absolutely overwhelming artillery, air and tank support might prevail against a thoroughly weakened opponent. In other words, nations faced with the prospect of war hoped that it would be the enemy who felt compelled to attack.

The most extensive single fortified systems the world had ever seen were constructed to face each other along the Franco-German frontier. The French Maginot Line, which was the most impressive along its 200 miles (320 km), was like a battleship set in concrete—a narrow barrier of deep, air-conditioned underground forts, sprouting guns in rotating, armoured turrets, shrouded in barbed wire, and bristling with machine-guns. The Maginot Line took more than ten years to build, whereas the German Siegfried Line, based upon interconnected pillboxes layered in depth, was begun in 1936 and was still incomplete in 1940. A far more flexible defensive zone within which the well-tried method of elastic defence could be practised, the Siegfried Line reached no further north than Aachen, while the Maginot Line stopped short of covering the approaches into France through the Ardennes. Both, therefore, were exposed to flanking attacks, via neutral countries.

The weapon system with the highest potential in 1939 was the German armoured force of élite troops. Whereas the French and British tended to commit their armoured forces either in direct support of infantry or as mechanised cavalry for reconnaissance, screening and pursuit of a broken enemy, the Germans, guided in the 1920s by General Hans von Seeckt, retained their faith in mobile warfare, by attacking weakness and avoiding strength, prosecuted by all-arms battle-groups in which the tank was the dominant element. Moreover the Germans were the keenest advocates of close support by bombers, above all dive-bombers, both in the immediate front line as heavy artillery and also for attack on enemy lines of communication. Strategic bombing they placed low in priority.

Typical of the main battle tanks in use in 1939 were the following:

Nation	Type	Armour (mm)	Weight (tons)	Gun (mm)	Speed (mile/h)(km/h)		Crew
German	PzKpfw IV	30	20	1 × 75	18	30	5
French	Somua S 35	55	20	1 × 47	25	40	3
British	Cruiser Mk IV	30	15	1 × 40	30	48	4
Russian	BT 7	22	14	1 × 45	33	53	3
Italian	M11/39	30	11	1 × 37	20	32	3

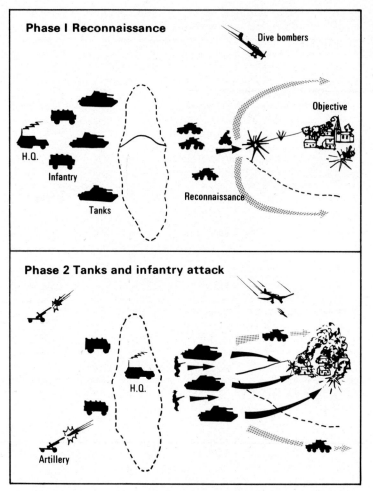

Phase I Reconnaissance

Dive bombers

Objective

H.Q.

Infantry

Tanks

Reconnaissance

Phase 2 Tanks and infantry attack

H.Q.

Artillery

The technique of all-arms assault in 1939—fire, movement, infiltration, elimination and pursuit

The first campaign in which the German "Panzer divisions" dominated was against Poland in September 1939. Although, out of the total German force of 55 divisions employed, only 10 had a tank component (and most of those light and vulnerable machines), it was these 10 divisions which spearheaded the attack and in a fortnight broke the Polish Army of 40 divisions.

The first great armoured battle of encirclement on the River Bzura came to an end on 15th September. The entire Polish Army of nearly 1,000,000 men was eliminated by the end of the month at a cost to the Germans of 40,000 casualties and 217 tanks. Yet of more than passing interest was the disquiet of the German commanders at the performance of their ordinary infantry divisions (most of whose artillery and transport were still horse-drawn) and the total inability of horsed cavalry to make any worthwhile contribution. Armour had come to dominate and the names of the tank enthusiasts made famous—above all that of General Heinz Guderian who was most responsible for shaping the force along British lines in the 1930s, strongly influenced by Seeckt and Fuller.

The first experiments in airborne warfare—the dropping of armed parachutists—had been attempted by the Italians in 1927. The idea of the parachute originates, in fact, with Leonardo da Vinci in 1514 and was first demonstrated in 1783 by Louis Lenormand in France. **The first really practical design** was demonstrated from an aeroplane in the U.S.A. by Captain Albert Berry in 1912. In 1918 **the first airborne operation was proposed** by Colonel William Mitchell—to drop men of the 1st U.S. Infantry Division behind the German lines and capture Metz. The Russians took the lead in development in 1934 by dropping 46 armed men and a light tank. In 1936 they publicly dropped 5,200 and at the same time developed an assault glider to carry 18 men. Japan, Poland and France also experimented with parachutists, but for the most part armies reckoned to deliver their airborne troops by a conventional aircraft landing. There were sound reasons for this. A parachutist weighs more than the normal infantryman because of the weight of his pack: therefore fewer can be carried. Moreover the parachutist is one of an élite who are not only very

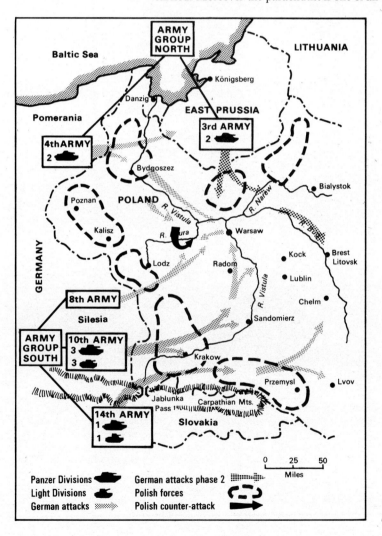

Panzer Divisions — German attacks phase 2

Light Divisions — Polish forces

German attacks — Polish counter-attack

The Battle of Poland, September 1939

expensive to train but also the very men who would almost all be selected as leaders in conventional units. Nevertheless the argument that parachute troops were worth while for special, spearhead actions in the vanguard of other airborne and land forces convinced the Germans in addition to the Russians.

The first operational use of airborne troops was probably by the Russians who dropped small parties during the winter war against Finland in 1939–40.

German parachutists land in Holland, May 1940

The first major strategic drop of parachutists was made by the Germans on 9th April 1940 ahead of their surprise invasions of Denmark and Norway. The German airborne force was typical of the élite, semi-technical forces of its day. Parachutists seized a zone or airfield where gliders or transport aircraft could land and disgorge reinforcements and heavier equipment. The success of any such operation depended upon the attackers being in possession of air superiority, its prolongation upon a quick link-up with ground forces. For, in 1940, neither tanks nor medium artillery could be lifted by air let alone with adequate ammunition.

German successes in 1940 owed their good start to spearhead air-borne operations. The firm bases seized for subsequent operations at Oslo and Stavanger in Norway virtually assured victory, nearly 10,000 men being landed within the space of a few hours and only the more scattered companies coming to serious harm. Holland was practically stunned by landings in the vicinity of The Hague, Dordrecht, Rotterdam and Moerdijk and upon neighbouring airfields. Despite fierce resistance these landings were mostly successful and fully consolidated when German columns broke through to reach them within three days.

The most striking airborne feat of all was the capture of the vital Belgian fort at Eben-Emael (said to be **the strongest in the world**), where it guarded the approaches to Liège. On the night of 10th May 1940, 85 glider troops seized its environs and 85 engineers landed right on top of the fort to begin its destruction with demolition charges. At dawn 300 parachutists landed as reinforcements and by midday on the 11th the fort was theirs along with 1,000 dumbfounded prisoners.

One of the swiftest, most complete and economic victories ever achieved by numerically inferior forces over a major power was won by the Germans in five weeks of May and June 1940 against the alliance of France, Britain, Belgium and Holland. Led by only eleven panzer divisions, whose total tank strength was 3,379 machines (mostly lightweight), the German Army of 2,350,000 (not all of which was deployed) defeated Allied armies with 4,170 tanks

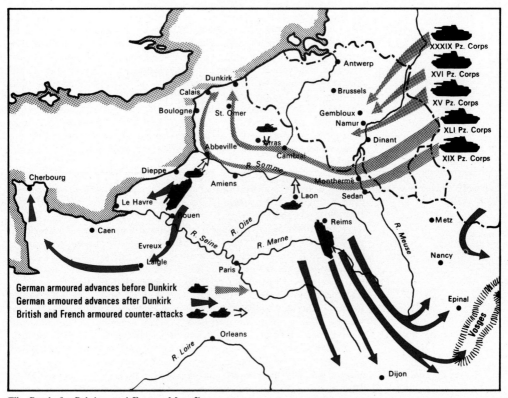

The Battle for Belgium and France, May–June 1940

(many of them technically superior to their opponents') and 2,862,000 men. Only in the air were the Germans greater in number and it was the effect of this weapon, combined with a seemingly irresistible armoured thrust, beating upon soldiers and peoples whose heart was never in the fight, which brought about the total rout of the Allied forces. French tanks, even those which were organised into special armoured formations, gave way with scarcely any retaliation. Only one French armoured division, under Brigadier Charles de Gaulle (France's principal and unheeded advocate of armoured warfare), made any impression along with a handful of British tanks which also fought well.

Some of the fastest and most sustained advances in history were achieved against opposition during the French campaign. Guderian's XIX Panzer Corps advanced 151 miles (243 km) from Sedan to the Channel coast in eight days at an average speed of 19 miles (30·5 km) per day of which 56 miles (90 km) were covered in one particular day alone. As the panzer divisions raced through Western Europe, they contrived something more than the greatest military envelopments of all times: they struck to the heart of government causing complete collapse in five major nations.

The most extensive maritime evacuation of an army occurred as the result of Allied armies becoming penned in Dunkirk at the end of May. Here the Germans encountered the old problem of breaching prepared defences and decided to resolve it by aerial bombardment instead of land assault. The reasons dictating this strategy were more significant than the failure to prevent the evacuation of over 330,000 men (mostly deprived of their equipment). Since the German tank force was looked upon more as a mobile arm than a direct assault force, and because it had suffered losses of 30 per cent in a fortnight's combat and still had the rest of France to conquer, it was withheld from an assault upon a defended perimeter in a close, built-up area which, experience told the Germans, would be appallingly costly in tanks. The air weapon, in the absence of a quick follow-up by land forces, could no more take ground than land forces without armoured support were able, inexpensively, to breach an entrenched position. Not only were tanks demonstrated as an essential element in land warfare but the necessity for co-operation between various weapon systems was again underlined.

The only major seaborne invasion projected by the Germans came close upon the heels of the French collapse and was planned against Britain whose army had been virtually disarmed at Dunkirk. The project was abandoned because the German Air Force was incapable of gaining air supremacy and, with it, the essential ability to freely land men from air and sea and establish the beach-head that would be a mandatory prerequisite of subsequent operations. Despite the addition of modern weapons the ancient demands of strategic, tactical and logistic orthodoxy remained inviolate. Indeed, those who regarded armoured forces as "unorthodox" were as far off track as anybody who may have levelled the same accusation against the Hussite waggon forts of 1420. Armoured forces merely represented an up-to-date combination of protection, mobility and striking power. But, through their extensive radio networks, they also provided battle information and executive services of greater speed and capacity than ever before. The pace of war was thus further compressed in time: events followed each other with dazzling complexity as management of strategy and tactics was geared to the new methods of communication.

One of the toughest fighting animals of the 20th Century—the German infantryman of 1942 armed with a 9 mm Schmeisser sub-machine gun and with a stick grenade at his belt. That other basic implement of the infantryman—an entrenching tool— also hangs from his belt, but the gas mask container probably does not contain the mask since gas warfare was not threatened

Russian tanks and infantry in the attack

The only new weapon to introduce a fresh dimension to land warfare, therefore, was air-portable troops. From 1940 onwards no army dared leave its rearward areas unguarded for fear of interference from large-scale landings or by small raiding parties. Instead of armies being left free to concentrate their strength at the front they had to learn to spread themselves over vast areas and yet retain the ability to concentrate swiftly either against danger or to create a threat of its own. Mechanisation and more comprehensive communications made this feasible, but the overriding requirement was for commanders and staff who were mentally adjusted, trained and organised to implement all the new facilities which suddenly crowded to their aid. Partly the French Army collapsed because its command system was unequal to the speed of events generated by a superior German Command. Wireless made it possible to vary the process whereby commanders controlled remotely from the centre of a web set deep in the Army's rear. Personal command by leaders who could actually observe the action from an armoured command post or from the air was now possible from the forefront of the battle.

The most potent threat of the air weapon was its capability to land a host of guerilla parties, deep in rear of battle fronts, who could provoke entire populations to insurrection against an invader. As invaders the Germans were able to make only small-scale if effective, use of these measures since they could not rely upon more than minority support in the countries they attacked. Their every aggressive move was prefaced by so-called "fifth column" activity and intervention by special forces such as those which had seized Fort Eben-Emael. **(The term "fifth column" was first used** by the Spanish insurgent General Emilio Mola when referring to Fascist dissidents within Madrid.) But, once in occupation of a country, increasing German effort had to be diverted to suppressing the cells of resistance which began to appear when the shock of occupation began to wear off and as German measures began to stir up resentment among the indigenous, defeated populace. It was an old story.

The first move towards creating what also came to be known as a "fourth arm" was taken by the British Prime Minister, Mr. Winston Churchill, when, in July 1940, he instructed Mr. Hugh Dalton to establish the Special Operations Executive and "set Europe on fire" by subversive warfare. Churchill seems to have had in mind something akin to Fuller's concept of a counter-invasion of Europe by a mass of twenty armoured divisions which would be supported by a swarm of indigenous guerillas trained and equipped by experts flown in from England. S.O.E. was to operate in every country that fell under German occupation. But the immense air and sea lifts required for sufficient men and material, the famine of trained operatives and weapons at a time when Britain was alone in the war and almost defenceless, and the counter-claims of the other three Services—besides an undeniable lack of enthusiasm among the people of the occupied countries to commit a form of *hari-kiri*—meant that progress with subversive warfare had to be awfully slow. Yet, throughout the war in steadily increasing volume and violence, guerilla forces in Europe grew. At the same time theatres of active operation spread until they covered almost the entire globe.

The most savage anti-guerilla forces of the war were drawn from the various agencies of the German Schutz-Staffeln (S.S.) which began existence as personal body-guard to Hitler and eventually grew to become the principal political and military organisation within the State. Apart from infiltrating every organ of government, intelligence and police the S.S. raised specially selected fighting units to take their place at the front alongside the Army and to lead the war against guerillas in the rear. Careful indoctrination in the Nazi code and a studied justification of the most ruthless methods of combat (which frequently eschewed the taking of prisoners) converted the S.S. into a force which for prowess, savagery and bestiality can be compared with the Mongol élite, the Russian Oprichniki of Ivan the Terrible and the Turkish Janissaries. Like all politico-military élites, however, they did as much harm as good. By absorbing the cream of German manpower, and resisting the induction of foreign blood, 'they helped deprive the Army of essential leaders at a time when the Army, to increase and maintain its strength at the expanding battle-fronts, had to suffer dilution by recruiting lower-grade men and a mass of foreign nationals—exactly the process which had led to the collapse of every army in history which had become overstretched.

The essential demands of mechanised warfare centred upon possession or denial of raw material and industrial resources. For example, the Germans invaded Norway as insurance against the British cutting in first to deny them Swedish iron ore. When Britain, with the connivance of the U.S.A., cut off Germany from seaborne supplies, Germany, joined in June 1940 by Italy and by Japan in December 1941, moved inland to find ways to circumvent the sea blockade. At the same time the Axis tried to prevent the movement of Allied seaborne supplies. The invasion of Russia in June 1941 was, in no small part, an ideological move in the religious war between Nazism and Communism, but Hitler was also clear about his vital need for Russian raw materials, particularly cereals and oil. Likewise his occupation of the Balkans, in a lightning campaign in April 1941, though aimed at securing the German right flank prior to the invasion of Russia and at preventing British aircraft flying from airfields within range of the Rumanian oil-fields at Ploesti, was of benefit in that useful deposits of bauxite (for the production of aluminium) and other ores came into German possession. Only by land warfare could the occupation of territory be accomplished: air attacks merely destroyed, antagonised populations and could never secure specific localities. When the Japanese Army invaded South-East Asia it was reacting against slow strangulation of vital war materials by the U.S.A. and Britain—endeavouring to seize oilfields, rubber and additional ricelands in order to feed the nation's hungry war economy with its ambitious demands for nationalistic expansion.

The two most ambitious invasions of the entire Second World War took place in 1941.

● *Germany*, filled with confidence in the prowess of her army—probably one of the finest élite forces the world has ever seen—sent troops into North Africa to bolster a failing Italian ally whose armies had been routed by the British; armies into the Balkans to mop up Yugoslavia and Greece; an airborne force of 22,500 men against the island of Crete, of whom no less than 30 per cent, including 4,000 paratroopers, became casualties; and invaded Russia with about 156 divisions in the greatest mechanised attack so far attempted. Yet nowhere was absolute success on the 1940 scale achieved. Though the British were pushed back in Cyrenaica they were fighting more strongly and victoriously than ever in the vicinity of Tobruk (which endured a siege of seven months without benefit of air cover) at the end of the year. Though the Balkans fell under German domination, the taking of Crete proved so expensive that Hitler wrote off airborne armies

Erwin Rommel—German Commander in North Africa

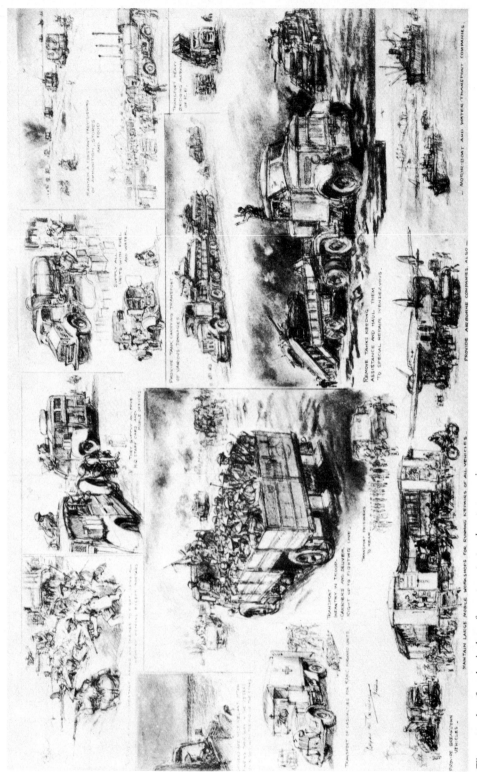

The corpuscles of mechanised warfare—transport and recovery services

Desert battle near Tobruk

as a failure, while the growth of guerilla forces in Yugoslavia, under Tito and other leaders, began what was to become **the greatest guerilla fight** of the whole war. And although German forces swept through Russia to the gates of Moscow, Leningrad and the Caucasus, causing the loss, in immense encirclements, of at least 20,000 Russian tanks plus enormous quantities of guns and uncountable men, the Russians held out. Then they threw the Germans back in battles which took little account of the weather and included some of the fiercest fighting in the deepest winter's cold ever recorded. At times the temperatures fell to -32 °F (-35.5 °C) and vehicles became frozen solid in what shortly before had been deep mud.

● *Japan*, eager to expand, was compelled by geography to execute a maritime campaign. Nevertheless it was her army which, in the final analysis, had to take and hold the key points—Hong Kong, the strategically placed outlying Pacific islands, the Philippines, Malaya and Singapore, Burma, the Dutch East Indies and New Guinea. The most remarkable aspect of the Japanese success in winning control over an area measuring 3,000 by 3,500 miles (3,836 by 4,636 km) in less than six months was the manner in which men who were adjusted to mountain and city

German air landing in Crete

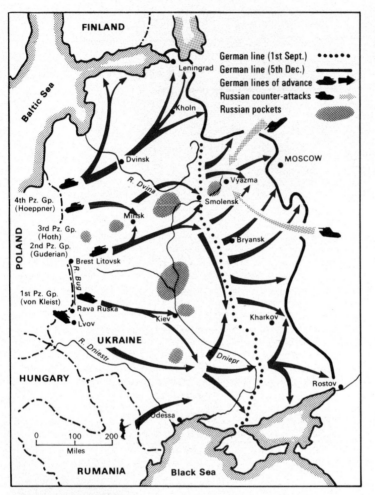

The German invasion of Russia in 1941 and the Russian counter-stroke at Moscow

General Yamashita

life were trained to fight so efficiently in the jungle. For example, the Army of 100,000 men, under General Tomoyuki Yamashita, which had the task of taking Malaya and Singapore from an almost equal number of British, was given an intensive jungle-warfare training course lasting only a few weeks before being launched to the invasion: their opponents had no such thorough training. And the 50,000 Japanese under General Masaharu Homma, who took on 130,000 Americans and Filipinos in the Philippines, were seasoned troops from years of war in China and Man-churia. In the air, too, the Japanese were in command since their initial attacks caught their opponents by complete surprise and largely destroyed their aircraft on the ground. Yet in equipment the Japanese were by no means superior—their tanks, in fact, were not nearly so good as those of the Allies, nor were they employed in concentrated fashion. Simply the Japanese produced them where they were most required and won their victories with better tactics, techniques and sheer dedication to battle in tight obedience to a strict military code. They were the latest in succession to those well-disciplined and trained men of the past who overcame ill-prepared foes.

(top) Russian cavalry the last of the breed

(above) Russian armoured train and tractor-towed artillery

Russian infantry in the assault

The Russian and Far East campaigns drew the main guide-lines for future combat.

● *The gun versus armour race*. In France the Germans had been depressed by the inability of their 37 mm anti-tank guns (all they had, that is, except for the dual-purpose 88 mm anti-aircraft gun) to penetrate the thick armour of Allied tanks. In Russia they met in the KV 1 and T 34 tanks, fighting machines whose 76 mm guns could penetrate their own tanks' 30 mm armour while remaining impervious to German shot— tanks, moreover, which were mechanically more reliable and with a better cross-country performance. To match Russian tank performance the Germans were forced into a crash industrial programme of up-gunning and up-armouring their tanks while setting in motion the construction of an entirely new generation of much heavier and more expensive models. The standard size for an effective anti-tank gun had to be raised to at least 75 mm with armour thicknesses to 80 mm or more by 1943. Speeds, however, remained at about 20 mile/h (32 km/h) which, in battlefield conditions (bearing in mind that most tanks fired their guns when stationary and that a good shot would usually hit a fast-moving target), was the optimum—as it remains to this day.

A Japanese tank in action with infantry support

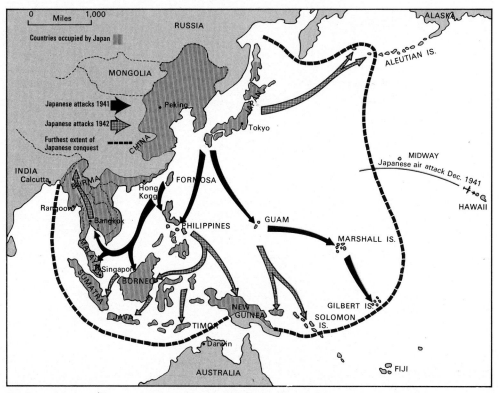

The Japanese expansion

● *Amphibious operations.* As the Germans and Japanese had mostly ejected their opponents (with the exception of the Russians) from the principal land masses where decisive battle could be joined, it was inescapable for the Allies to make provision for extensive sea and airborne invasions against the periphery of Hitler's Europe and the Japanese Pacific possessions. Though the implementation of widespread continental conquest, demanded by European geography, produced a different pattern of warfare to the type needed to conquer key island bases in the Pacific, the essential steps in each initial assault become almost standard practice.

The first major American amphibious assault began on 7th August, 1942 at Tulagi and Guadalcanal and represented a tribute to the U.S.A.'s remarkable recovery after a run of serious defeats. Everything stood against success by the 1st Marine Division. Many of the men were under-trained, the landing craft and their crews were, respectively, unreliable and unknowing, the dive-bombers allocated to support the landing were inexperienced and the Navy suffered from inadequate charts. Nevertheless, surprise was achieved against the Japanese garrisons so that, behind a somewhat unco-ordinated and ill-aimed barrage of naval shells and bombs, the assault won a bridgehead into which reinforcements and supplies were poured. The unpractised logistic organisation also invoked additional hazards, though none were fatal. However, the Japanese reaction was fanatical. Recovering from their initial set-back they held every position with ferocity and poured in reinforcements by sea despite all efforts of the U.S. Navy to prevent it. At Guadalcanal, however, the U.S. Marines and Army took the true measure of the Japanese soldier in attack and defence and found him among the most formidable fighting animals of the world.

More than any other army the Japanese Army meticulously obeyed orders telling it to die rather than surrender. In consequence its losses were stupendous since, as fast as men were killed on land by an opponent whose technical superiority was beginning to overbear, it brought in more by sea, even though the transports were heavily hit by U.S. air and sea attacks. The essence of the battle for any beach-head was a race between the build-up by both sides of men, equipment and supplies. This race the Americans won at Guadalcanal—as they were eventually to win in every succeeding amphibious invasion in the Pacific because their navy and air forces won absolute control in their own elements. However, with regard to Guadalcanal the moment came, in February 1943, when the Japanese High Command could no longer justify sending men and ships to their graves; they withdrew. But, at isolated islands such as Makin, in November 1943, where there could be no retreat, the entire Japanese garrison of 250 had to be eliminated; and at Tarawa, in a fiercely contested assault by the U.S. Marines against a beach-head covered by pill-boxes and bunkers, all but 100 of the garrison of 4,700 were killed. Nevertheless, at Tarawa, where the landing could not be supported by tanks because a coral reef prevented their coming ashore, the infantry were obliged to wade. It cost over 3,000 American casualties of whom 985 were killed—sometimes rated, in the ratio of casualties to troops engaged, **the most costly victory in American history.**

The turning-point of the war arrived at the end of 1942—and not just because at this moment the high tide of German and Japanese invasion was reached at Stalingrad, in the Caucasus, at El Alamein close to the strategic prize of the Suez Canal, in Burma, New Guinea and at the island of Midway. By the end of 1942 nearly every major nation (with the paradoxical exception of Germany) had tapped the full flood of conscription and industrial output. While the Allied land forces—the largest armies the world has ever seen supported by the most powerful weapons ever massed and supplied by logistic resources of imponderable size and complexity—were moving towards a thousand points of contact, the German, Italian and Japanese forces were failing from exhaustion and were deprived of the essential materials which alone assured their viability in battle. Against a mass of material, courageous manpower on its own lacked the stamina to prolong resistance indefinitely.

The most inhibiting factor in the conduct of land operations, excepting that of the combatants' morale and fighting ability (which were fundamental), was logistics. If a nation possessed enough space, and could maintain its will to fight a moment had to come when deep penetration by enemy forces had to stop short of complete conquest due to logistic failure. **The first time the British suffered from this** was in North Africa, during the Beda Fomm campaign, in the winter of 1940–41 when, having totally destroyed an Italian army of 230,000 and taken 845 guns and 380 tanks at a loss to themselves of less than 2,000 casualties, they were unable to complete the capture of Tripolitania because they were denied sufficient transport. As a result the Germans were given the opportunity to reinforce the Italians with their celebrated Afrika Korps, under General Erwin Rommel, who soon made a riposte to drive the British back to the Egyptian frontier.

*End of the war for
German infantry in Russia*

The first German experiences of being halted for logistic failure was suffered by Rommel when he failed to take Tobruk and had to revert to the defensive for shortage of fuel. In Russia, too, that July, the Germans were to discover that, after an advance of about 400 miles (640 km) or six weeks' constant battle, mechanised forces simply had to be rested for repairs and to allow the logistic organisation to restock. It was a lesson which they and all their contemporaries were to relearn in almost every succeeding campaign throughout the war. Air supply was certainly not a complete answer, merely a temporary expedient on desperate occasions.

The first decisive defeat of the German Army occurred at Stalingrad, in the winter of 1942–43, partly as the result of a strategic error by Hitler in committing so much effort to a relatively unimportant objective, partly because the Russians fought well within a narrow perimeter, and largely because the Germans could not spare sufficient strength or logistic resources to overcome the Russians. When the Russians counter-attacked on 19th November and clasped an armoured embrace round the Germans in the city and its environs, the German Air Force proved quite incapable of flying in sufficient supplies to provide for 200,000 men and their thousands of vehicles and guns. Meanwhile the Russian besiegers, who were located far closer to their bases of land supply than the Germans, were able to fend off such attempts at relief that were made. The German Sixth Army finally surrendered on 31st January 1943 and brought an epoch to its end.

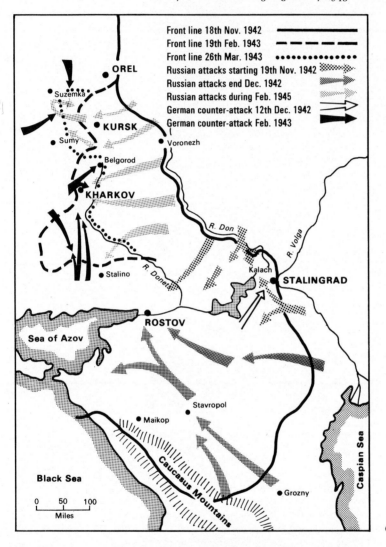

Front line 18th Nov. 1942
Front line 19th Feb. 1943
Front line 26th Mar. 1943
Russian attacks starting 19th Nov. 1942
Russian attacks end Dec. 1942
Russian attacks during Feb. 1945
German counter-attack 12th Dec. 1942
German counter-attack Feb. 1943

OREL
Suzemka
KURSK
Sumy
Belgorod
Voronezh
KHARKOV
R. Don
R. Volga
Stalino
R. Donets
Kalach
STALINGRAD
ROSTOV
Sea of Azov
Stavropol
Maikop
Caucasus Mountains
Black Sea
0   50   100
Miles
Caspian Sea
Grozny

The campaign in the Caucasus and at Stalingrad

The first great defeat of a German army by the Western Allies was consummated in Tunisia early in May 1943, at the end of nearly three years' ding-dong fighting in the desert. Throughout 1941 and 1942 the Germans and Italians had grappled with the British along the coastal strip between El Agheila and El Alamein. The logistic situation was always crucial since literally everything, except sand for sandbags and air in tyres, had to be transported to the front. Come the slightest transport failure or capture by the enemy of important stocks of food, fuel, munitions or water and a whole army might be brought to its knees within a matter of hours. This was also one of the few campaigns fought without inhibition by the presence of sizeable

The high-water mark of the German offensive— Thala in Tunisia—February 1943

civilian populations (the other was in the Arctic of north Scandinavia in the approaches to Murmansk). Because it was staged largely on firm terrain with long ranges of vision and very little cover, armoured vehicles and artillery predominated while infantry played a distinctly minor role, except on those rare occasions when they were able to entrench within a relatively small perimeter (such as Tobruk and the Egyptian frontier area) or on a narrow front, such as at El Alamein with the sea on one flank and an impenetrable marsh on the other. Under circumscribed conditions in-fantry could survive behind deep minefields (which made both infantry and tank attacks costly unless the mines were laboriously cleared beforehand) supported by concentrated artillery fire and tank forces—a reversion, in effect, to the conditions of 1918. But armoured forces, too, were quite incapable of operating independently, even in the desert. When confronted by anti-tank artillery it became too costly to charge: therefore combined assaults with artillery support were essential. But while the Germans were adept at making their guns work tactically in conjunction with tanks (and frequently used a tank gambit to lure British tanks on to a line of their own anti-tank guns) the British were slow to adopt a flexible policy and organisation that was adaptable to all kinds of situation. They scattered their artillery in location and abandoned the concentration of artillery fire such as had held good since the Siege of Constantinople in 1453.

The first time the British fully reverted to an orthodox policy of artillery concentration was during the opening rounds of their defensive battle under General Sir Claude Auchinleck to hold the Alamein position in July 1942.

The first operational use of a sophisticated system of centralised artillery control, in which

wireless provided the vital over-all communication coverage, had to wait until 23rd October however, when a new method, devised in England, was adopted by the British under General Sir Bernard Montgomery in his break-out battle from El Alamein. A senior artillery commander was appointed at every level of infantry or armoured formation command, his task to co-ordinate the fire of that formation's guns with those of adjacent formations and superimpose any medium and heavy guns brought into the area. A relatively simple drill was eventually devised at the instigation of Brigadier Sidney Kirkham, helped by the technical expertise of Colonel Jack Parham. Though individual field artillery regiments continued to

Montgomery

support battalions and regiments to which they were affiliated within a division, it was made possible for a single forward observation officer to aim the fire of an entire division within a matter of three or four minutes. He could do so by the simplest and shortest of orders on the radio, leaving the calculations to be worked out in a central command post and sent direct to the guns by wireless or telephone. So simple did the system of correction of fire become, after the first rounds had been directed against a map grid reference, that the only orders required were, for example: "Go north-east 400" to shift a concentration 400 yd (364 m) in that direction. Even mere infantry and tank officers were able to cut in on the artillery wireless net and supply these corrections.

The value of British artillery methods, which were far in advance of any other in 1943, were repeatedly demonstrated throughout the remainder of the North African campaign, proving as applicable in the mountainous terrain of Tunisia as in the flat desert of El Alamein. One can appreciate the value of the system by reference to a few figures. A regiment of twenty-four 25-pdr guns firing three rounds per minute could dump 1,600 lb (720 kg) of high explosive on any target within an area of 30 mile² (48 km²) inside a 90-degree arc of the gun position—and could do it, what is more, by day or night, in clear visibility or in fog.

● *The Germans*, who never achieved anything so efficient as this, continued to rely heavily upon dive-bombers, even as their air superiority was being eroded, and were thus at a steadily worsening disadvantage throughout the war. Nevertheless, in their two-month-long deliberate assault upon the Russians, besieged in Sevastopol in the summer of 1942, they employed 670 guns (the biggest with a calibre of 800 mm) and 720 mortars in addition to bombing and strafing from 600 aircraft and direct fire from 450 tanks—so it can hardly be said that they abandoned concentration of fire.

● *The Russians*, too, were great advocates of concentrated artillery fire prior to an assault, though their methods lacked the flexibility achieved by the British system, being comparable with British practice in 1916. In the same manner as the British organised their assault artillery into Army Groups Royal Artillery (A.G.R.As.) the Russians formed artillery divisions, 200 pieces strong, comprising everything from mortars and 76 mm to 152 mm guns, and shifted them from front to front, as the need arose, to achieve a crushing superiority of fire. In their initial breakthrough battle at the start of the envelopment of the Germans at Stalingrad no less than 3,500 guns and mortars were deployed on narrow frontages of attack— and these figures were as nothing to what would be achieved later when the Red Army reached its full strength in the full tide of new production in 1943 and 1944.

● *The Americans*, on the other hand, were quick to copy the British, first learning the art in action on the battlefield of Thala from Parham when their guns came to support the British who were under heavy pressure from Rommel's tanks in the culminating phase of the Battle of Kasserine.

The first major occasion upon which both American and Canadian troops went into action in Europe was during the amphibious raid against the heavily fortified port of Dieppe. Fifty officers and men of a U.S. Ranger battalion landed with British Commandos, who came ashore on 19th August on the flanks of the central assault by the 1st Canadian Infantry Division supported by twenty-eight Churchill tanks. Though this amphibious attack was a failure, in which all the tanks that landed were lost and there were 4,384 casualties, of whom 3,379 were Canadian, the lessons learnt were of importance in formulating the techniques which would be required in launching a sustained assault across the Channel.

Hand-to-hand combat. Gurkhas against Germans in Italy, 1944

American leaders—Patton, Eisenhower and Bradley

The first major assault by U.S. troops in the West took place along the North African coast between Casablanca and Algiers on 8th November 1942. A vast naval force was deployed in support of an operation in which British troops were kept in a minority during the assault for fear their presence would unduly antagonise the French, whose possessions were being violated. In the event the French resisted the Americans with asperity and only laid down their arms when diplomatic moves brought fighting to an end. Nevertheless this U.S. Army, among it their 1st Infantry and 1st Armoured Divisions, acquitted itself well and if, in the following winter, they were to learn hard and costly lessons against the far more experienced Germans in Tunisia, it was to the credit of the American military system that it could recognise failings and take instant advice and measures to put things right.

To conduct the battles for North Africa in the final phase in spring 1943, were appointed the Allied commanders who were to accomplish **the final victories over Germany and Italy in the West**. From Egypt came the British Generals Sir Harold Alexander and Montgomery; from the U.S.A. Generals Dwight Eisenhower, Mark Clark, George Patton and Omar Bradley—all of whom would rise to supreme or the highest command. Nor were their opponents tyros: the German Supreme Commander was Field-Marshal Albert Kesselring, a soldier turned airman who again was in charge of land forces—and, inevitably, Rommel. When finally the Allies cleared North Africa it was to scoop up something in the region of 150,000 Germans as part of a total of about 620,000 German-Italian troops who had been lost in that theatre of war since 1940. Set against that figure were 220,000 British, 20,000 French and 18,500 Americans. Coming so soon after the débâcle at Stalingrad this Allied victory assured the final defeat of Germany, since it also deprived Germany's armies of the best-trained officers and men upon whom fresh armies might have been founded.

Perhaps the greatest commander to dominate any battle-front, and the one with control over the largest army in the world, was Russia's Marshal Georgi Zhukov. Zhukov, who had been a non-commissioned officer in the Tsarist Russian Army, first made his name in high command when he defeated the Japanese at the Battle of Khalkhin River in Manchuria in August 1939. In June 1941, when the Germans invaded Russia, he was Chief of Staff in Moscow, but from then on it became Stalin's habit to employ him where the crisis was most serious. Hence it was Zhukov who commanded the defence of Moscow in 1941, covering a 400-mile (640 km) frontage with eleven armies until the Germans were finally thrown back. And Zhukov who, with over 1,000,000 men, 13,550 guns and 900 tanks, was in charge of the south-west front bearing the brunt of the German attack upon Stalingrad until he overwhelmed them at the end of 1942. It was Zhukov, too, who, as Deputy Supreme Commander, co-ordinated operations before Kursk in the summer of 1943 when the last German offensive was launched and blunted. Zhukov won a reputation for consuming, driving energy and absolute ruthlessness in imprinting his personality and wishes upon the ranks of the Red Army. He had to overcome the inefficiency of the Red Army, which had been wrecked by the defeats of 1941 and 1942, and at the same time cope with Stalin's premonitory intervention in military affairs when matters were desperate. These difficulties he was to survive and lead the Red Army in its final campaigns of the war against failing German resistance.

The last major German offensive on the East Front also caused the largest-ever clash between armoured forces in July 1943. With the main efforts concentrated against the flanks of a great Russian salient, over 6,000 tanks, 30,000 guns and 2,200,000 men came into collision on a frontage of 200 miles (320 km). Prior to the assault a widespread guerilla campaign had been waged by the Russians from the forests to cut the German railway lines and reduce their build-up. To this the Germans, under Field-Marshal Eric von Manstein, had responded with extensive anti-guerilla operations involving many divisions. Yet when finally the German assault exhausted itself, after eleven days' intensive fighting, the Russians still had nineteen armies, two of them heavy with tanks, to throw into a vast

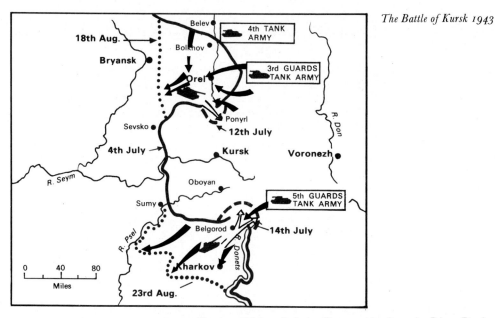

The Battle of Kursk 1943

counter-offensive which rolled the Germans back to the River Dneiper. Battles such as these defy description in detail since, amid almost boundless territories, they generated a hundred incidents, involving thousands of men, such as might have been rated major engagements in the previous century. Supreme command, though sometimes asserted by a Zhukov or a Manstein coming to visit a front-line division or watch part of the battle from a key observation post, remained a matter of remote calculation and risk based upon information that was never fully accurate and rarely sufficient. Thus the ultimate point of decision was to be found near the bottom of the scale of command where orders were given within sight of the battle. This is merely a matter of perspective in time and space and not so appalling in practice when it is recalled that a single armoured division of 1943 possessed infinitely more striking power than, say, the largest of eighteenth-century armies.

The truly appalling facet of the war on the East Front was the wholesale involvement of the civil population in almost every aspect of the land battle. Not only were un-equipped civilians herded into the ranks of partisan armies and forced to endure dreadful privations and cruelty by both the Germans and Russians, but they became immersed in every battle since nearly all were fought for principal cities and towns which stood at centres of communication. Since evacuation for humane reasons was almost always overlooked they had no option but to endure front-line conditions.

The longest siege of the campaign, and one of the most destructive and unsuccessful of its kind on record, began at Leningrad on 31st August 1941 and lasted until 27th January 1944. It is estimated that between 1,300,000 and 1,500,000 defenders died in addition to the many German assailants. Bombardment was almost ceaseless at some point or other of the perimeter. Rations were for ever down to starvation level and an endemic fuel short-age in winter made survival a truly formidable feat. Yet again, however, the massive defensive strength of an urban area, defended by a determined bunch of combatants, proved too much even for experienced besiegers: in the final analysis, a complex such as that was better sealed off than expensively assaulted.

The most serious difficulties inflicted upon the Germans emanated from Hitler who, in his capacity of C.-in-C., grew into the habit of applying detailed command of the front from a command post far in rear. At the root of his strategy was a pathological mistrust of his generals and a seeming inability to concede ground. Hence there were many occasions when German formations might well have evaded encirclement and fought all the more effectively if they had been granted full freedom of movement. It was not as if the Russian armies were capable of faster or more sustained advances than the Germans had been. Though their best formations might move 10 or even 20 miles (16 to 20 km) in one day, the average rate over a distance of 105 miles (169 km) was rarely in excess of 6·5 miles (10·4 km) compared with 16·5 miles (26·4 km) by the Germans in 1941. In this, too, they were very much dependent upon the U.S.A. for supplies of lorries of which Russian industry did not produce nearly enough to support such vast tank armies as theirs. Nevertheless, as an example of Russian success by encirclement, can be quoted the surrounding of two German armies at Korsun in February 1944, the failure of the Germans to relieve them due to blizzard conditions, the eventual loss of 100,000 men with most of their equipment—and no marked complementary slow-down of the inexorable westward advance of the Russians.

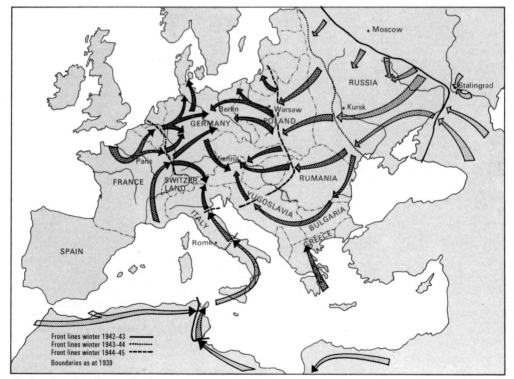

The invasion of the German Reich

The fight for the bridge at Arnhem

Street fighting

The most obvious conclusion to be drawn by the Germans in the winter of 1944 was that they had lost the war but, such was the grasp of a totalitarian system upon its subjects, that the will of one man—Hitler's—could keep them fighting even without hope. Despite miraculous efforts by German industry to raise weapon production to record levels—in 1944 they produced 17,800 armoured vehicles of different types and 56,000 pieces of artillery compared respectively with 11,800 and 14,400 in 1943—the noose of Allied invasion closing in from all directions, tightened. Apart from the contraction of the Russian front, guerilla forces in the Balkans were making large parts of the country untenable to German forces while, from Sicily into Italy, the Anglo-American amphibious invasion of summer 1943 crept up the peninsula towards Rome and knocked Italy out of the war in September. Aerial bombardment of German cities, though it failed to break civil morale (as Douhet had forecast it would) or even seriously hold back the expansion of production, was throwing an extra load upon the nation's resources which could only subtract from the land battle. Enormous numbers of sophisticated anti-aircraft units had to be created, absorbing valuable manpower and diverting the best technological brains in that direction instead of in aid of the front-line troops by the improvement of new tanks and guns to deal with the threat of Allied tank production which, in 1944, rose to an astonishing total of 51,000 tanks.

It is one of the paradoxes of the mechanical epoch that, while armies swallowed by far the largest share of available manpower, **the effort apportioned to research and development of weapons for land warfare fell far below that allocated to the other methods of warmaking on sea and in the air**. Thus, with the exception of tanks and anti-tank guns, which were recognised, along with air power and navies, as decisive weapons, the armies which went to war in 1944 were little better equipped, qualitatively, than they had been in 1939. Of machine-guns, for example, only the Germans introduced into service a strikingly advanced new machine-gun—the MG 42 with its rate of fire at 1,200 rounds per minute. **It first appeared in North Africa** in 1942. The philosophy of mass—mechanically inclined—therefore predominated upon land even if so much of 1944's mass was to be found in the rearward areas engaged logistically upon keeping relatively few soldiers in action in the front line. For an Allied infantry division going to attack the Germans in Western Europe in 1944 it required 42,000 men to maintain a mere 5,000 combat soldiers.

One of the more interesting developments in the projection of massed firepower originated in renewed interest in rocket projectiles. In the 1920s the Germans had turned to rockets as a possible substitute for the heavy artillery they were forbidden to possess. Considerable international interest was aroused and nearly all the industrial nations began to dabble in this form of missile propulsion. The British investigated them mainly from the standpoint of anti-aircraft and anti-tank weapons, only later developing them as a long-range supplement to mortars, to throw an instant "carpet" of high explosive upon the enemy from ranges up to 7,900 yd (7,189 m) as opposed to the slower delivery at 2,500 yd (2,275 m) by the normal 81 mm mortar. **First in the field with a production-type rocket projector** were the Russians in the winter of 1942 with their Katyusha—a set of sixteen rockets with 48 lb (21·8 kg) warheads carried on the back of a lorry and capable of engaging targets up to 6,500 yd (5,915 m). The Germans followed with their *Nebelwerfer* with its range of 7,300 yd (6,643 m). In the land warfare of 1944 rockets were never rated as serious competitors to artillery since, like Congreve's originals, they lacked sufficient accuracy: as a cheap means of producing heavy demoralising fire, however, rocket batteries were always attractive throughout the Second World War, and were far more responsive to the calls of front-line soldiers for high-explosive delivery than aircraft which always took time to brief and were liable, because of difficulties in accurate target description and identification by the airmen, to hit the wrong objective—be it friend or foe.

A Russian rocket battery

The largest amphibious assault in history was delivered by the Western Allies against the German fortress line (the Atlantic Wall) in Normandy on 6th June 1944. Not only had it on call some 6,000 armoured vehicles plus inexhaustible reserves but the heaviest-ever delivery of high explosive from aircraft, naval guns, artillery, rockets and mortars. The weight of metal thrown is incalculable, but it came from over 3,500 heavy bombers, striking in depth at the Germans, to rocket batteries (firing 1,000 lb (450 kg) of explosive per second for a minute each) and field artillery firing from the decks of landing-craft as they approached the shore. Moreover **the first-ever use of swimming tanks** made it possible for direct gunfire to be directed against German pillboxes from the water's edge even before the first infantry landed.

The Normandy landing provoked a classic example of the argument among the Germans between the protagonists of a mobile strategy and those who preferred to fight from fixed positions. Both Field-Marshals Gerd von Rundstedt and Rommel, who commanded the German forces in the West, had won their reputations as masters of the mobile battle. But prior to the invasion only Rundstedt adhered to the original concept as a viable proposition. He regarded the Atlantic Wall as an ephemeral hindrance and put his trust in intervention by massed panzer divisions against the Allied penetrations. Rommel, unlike Rundstedt whose last combat experience had been on the East Front in 1941, had deep and bitter experience of the effect of massed Allied air attacks in North Africa and Italy. He believed that the ordered movement of large land formations through country that was under constant air attack would be almost impossible. The supply lines would be cut to ribbons—indeed were recognisably in a parlous state before a single invader stepped ashore. So Rommel elected for an intractable defence of the shore-line and spent enormous effort strengthening the fortifications along a relatively narrow belt facing the Channel and North Sea. At the same time he tried, against Rundstedt's wishes, to locate the panzer divisions close to the coast, ready to intervene instantly in the battle without necessarily employing their combined strength in time and place.

The British, more than the Americans, appreciated that the initial assault would resemble a siege-type action. So, in addition to swimming tanks, they produced a collection of specialised armoured vehicles to act in combination and clear gaps through minefields, wire and obstacles. Thus they hoped to penetrate the defences quickly, with men under armour in the lead, ready to deal with German tank attacks before they could be fully developed. The Allies exploited air transport to the full, landing three parachute divisions to secure the flanks of the invasion area as well as deep raiding parties to add zest to the local guerilla movements which, prior to the landings, joined with the air forces in devastating the French and Belgian railway system. Thus the Allies, under the supreme command of Eisenhower but the tactical control of Montgomery, were bent upon creating the conditions of mobile warfare while the Germans tended to freeze into a form of positional defence. Grossly outnumbered, as they were, the Germans could but stick to this plan until, within six weeks, they reached breaking-point.

The biggest encirclements ever achieved by the Western Allies evolved as a result of their destruction of the stiff German cordon in Normandy. Moving at speeds which averaged up to 20 miles (32 km) per day over seven days, in the case of the First U.S. Army, and an exceptional 66 miles (106 km) per day for three days, in the case of the British Second Army, they caught about 60,000 near Falaise; 100,000 along the Seine; 200,000 in fortified ports from the Bay of Biscay to Dunkirk; about 15,000 in the approaches to Antwerp; 25,000 at Mons; and about 80,000 in southern France from an invasion launched in the region of Toulon. Along with these came a vast haul of tanks, guns and other equipment.

The most imaginative airborne operation ever mounted was intended to help extend the Allied advance through Belgium and Holland into Germany. Between Eindhoven and Arnhem, starting on 17th September, two United States' and one British division plus a Polish parachute brigade were brought in by 1,545 transport aircraft and 479 gliders protected by 1,000 fighter aircraft and supported by 1,500 bombers. For all that—due to logistical problems, difficulties with the land force striking northward to link with the airborne troops and the fierceness of German resistance guarding the frontier of their own country—the final objectives remained untaken and about 10,000 troops were lost.

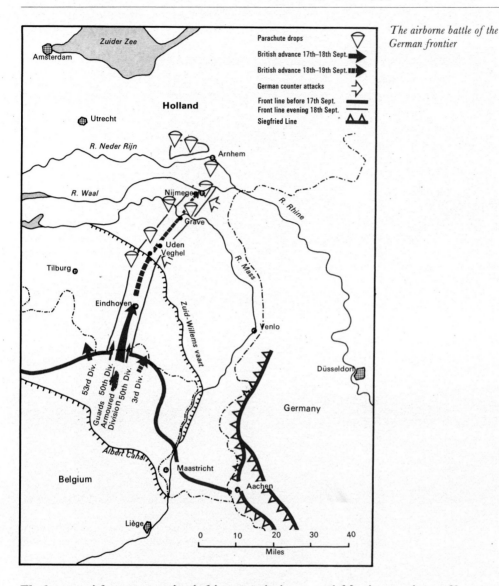

The airborne battle of the German frontier

The largest airborne operation in history took place on 24th March 1945 when 21,680 men were landed on the east bank of the River Rhine from 1,696 aircraft and 1,348 gliders. This drop represented a method of loosening enemy resistance and increasing the rate of the bridgehead's expansion. It fell just ahead of troops crossing the river in one of the largest river-crossing operations in history, and was the overture to the final advances into western Germany which coincided with the final Russian drives into eastern Germany and the capture of Berlin.

In the closing months of the war new weapons for land warfare began to appear in response to a demand which, though constant throughout the war, had often been held back by policies which put greater emphasis on quantity instead of quality.

German MG 34 team in action in Russia 1941

An American tank burns and infantry take cover in ruts during the advance on Germany

● *Tanks.* Weight, protection and striking power had redoubled since 1939, as this table of typical types shows, though the Western Allies still sacrificed armour for speed:

Nation	Type	Armour (mm)	Weight (tons)	Gun (mm)	Speed (mile/h)	(km/h)	Crew
German	Tiger II	150	68	88	23	38	5
Russian	JS II	160	46	122	22	43	4
British	Comet	101	32	77	29	47	5
U.S.A.	Pershing	102	41	90	30	48	5

● *Artillery.* Apart from anti-tank guns, whose increase in calibre and size matched that of tank weapons, there was little improvement in performance during the war. Indeed the main concern at all times was to make guns more mobile, either by mounting them on self-propelled chassis (of which there was a proliferation), or by reducing weight of the carriage to facilitate air-portability and manhandling. The U.S. 75 mm pack howitzer, for example, weighed only 1,340 lb (610 kg) (compared with 1·5 tons for the U.S. 75 mm gun) and furthermore could be easily broken down into component parts for ease of transportation. The most important measure to reduce weight was the introduction of recoilless systems in which the forces of discharge were absorbed by applying a counter-explosive force. **This was first done successfully** by an American called Davis in 1910, and used in the armament of British aircraft in the First World War. More sophisticated systems were examined by the Germans and Russians in the 1930s and in due course, too, the Americans and British became interested again. None of them however, entered service until after the war. **The most important addition to artillery potential** was in connection with war-heads. In 1880 an American called Monroe had discovered that explosives brought face to face with a steel plate produced a cutting effect, In 1938 the Swiss demonstrated a "shaped charge" which could cut a hole through thick armour. By 1942 nearly every nation was in possession of some sort of "hollow-charge shell" as an anti-tank device, the Germans taking it up most whole-heartedly of all in the unrequited hope that the tank might be made obsolete overnight. **The first proposals for a "radio proximity"** fuse were made by British scientists in 1940 and developed in 1941. As a weapon in land warfare this enabled air bursts to be aimed against troops in the open or trenches without the need to hand-set complex, mechanical fuses. For the most part, however, this sort of fuse was used in an anti-aircraft role to deal with pilotless bombs and Japanese aircraft flown by suicide pilots.

● *Mines.* The conventional metallic anti-tank and anti-personnel mines with which most armies began the war were still in service at the end, but by then the Germans, in particular, had added many much more efficient designs which were hard to locate and neutralise. Wooden, glass and bakelite bodies thwarted electric detectors while ingenious anti-lifting devices were incorporated to imperil manual neutralisation. The most efficient method of assault sweeping of mines was by the "flailing" tanks invented by the British.

● *Navigation and mapping.* Improvements in the accuracy of maps came from aerial survey and was of vital importance to the implementation of accurate artillery fire. In 1940 radio homing devices were introduced to guide aircraft towards clandestine landing- and dropping-zones in the enemy rear. These were later developed and augmented by radio beams so that land forces could be guided, in a somewhat rudimentary way, about the battlefield in conditions of poor visibility or darkness.

● *Night-fighting.* Prior to 1939 there had been experiments with searchlights to illuminate the battlefield and the British had begun a highly expensive project to mount a 13,000,000 candle-power searchlight on a tank as an aid to movement, shooting and (it was erroneously thought) to blind enemy gunners (it was never used aggressively in action). Mostly night attacks were timed to coincide with periods of moonlight. In North Africa, however, the British were **probably the first, in 1943, to enhance night movement by reflecting searchlight beams from clouds** and using tracer ammunition, fired on fixed lines towards the enemy, as boundary markers or axes of advance. Research into seeing without being seen, with the use of infra-red light, was carried out by several nations and it was the Germans who first produced, in 1944, an infra-red lighting device for use on a tank and a much smaller one as a sighting attachment to a rifle. Range of operation was limited by the power of the lamp, while the source of light was also visible, of course, to anybody having an optical detector.

● *Engineering equipment.* The increased mobility and pace of land operations placed heavy demands upon engineers who were under constant pressure not only to help demolish enemy fortifications, lay mines and blow up bridges and vital installations to deny them to the enemy in a retreat, but also were engaged on mundane construction of command posts and, chiefly, roads, railways and bridges. An immense range of powered tools were acquired by engineers of which earth-moving equipment—notably the ubiquitous bulldozer tractor—was among the largest single item and cranes among the most important. **The most famous type of bridge** was the British design by Mr. Donald Bailey who, in 1940, designed a simplified structure of small manhandled parts which could be put together at great speed on site and, by multiples of components, develop a bridge which could support loads up to 70 tons. The Bailey bridge was used by all Allied armies and remains a basic design to this day.

Bridging the River Moselle under cover of a smoke-screen

● *Transport.* As early as 1920 most armies appreciated the need for cross-country vehicles to supply tank forces. A good deal of work was put into designing half-track vehicles and lorries with all their four, six, or eight wheels driven. **The first operational half-track vehicles** were designed by the Frenchman Kegresse as early as 1917 and his products were to find extensive application in Russia, France, Britain, Germany and the U.S.A.

● *Chemical weapons.* Though gas was unused during the Second World War, because everybody feared the retribution which might result, vast stocks were maintained by both sides and new chemical weapons developed. The Germans discovered Tabun, shortly before the war, **the first of the nerve gases** which attack the enzyme cholinesterase. Nerve gases are far more deadly than any of a choking liquid nature and, if brought in contact with the eye, for example, kill in ten minutes. By 1945 the Germans had stocked more than 7,000 tons of nerve gas—sufficient to kill a population thirty times the size of Paris. Nerve gases have never been used, but their mere existence causes a diversion of military effort in the form of additional training and extra equipment. Flame, on the other hand, was extensively used by all the combatants, the most devastating devices being employed by the British using gelled petroleum as fuel—a substance known as "napalm" by the Americans. Barbarous as the flame weapon appeared to be, particularly if scattered indiscriminately from aircraft, it often had in the hands of ground forces, aimed at a specific target, the effect of causing the enemy to surrender rather than fight on.

Siege warfare in the 1940s with spearhead armies, flame throwing tanks and infantry assaulting across a minefield and ditch

Apart from life-takers the Second World War brought to the fore **an enormous proliferation of life-saving drugs and methods**. The most famous were the antibiotics which stemmed from the original observations by Alexander Fleming (who did not realize their potential) in 1928. Under urgent development, at the commencement of the war, penicillin was produced in such large quantities that thousands of wounded were saved and mankind as a whole enormously benefited. In response to the impulse to alleviate suffering and reduce mortality, great strides were made in, for example, skin grafting to heal burns and disfigurements, anti-tetanus injections, the storage and transfusion of blood for the wounded and the control of malaria. But for the war it is unlikely that the money for research into these costly processes would have been made available so quickly and in such quantity.

SECTION VIII
The Paradoxical Epoch, 1944 to the Present Day

The largest land campaigns of the Far East war, which absorbed most soldiers, took place on the mainland of China and in Burma. In China in 1944 the Japanese employed 820,000 men for their last offensives aimed against the Nationalist forces of General Chiang Kai-shek who were then located in southern and south-east China. They also committed 100,000 in Burma to fight the British, under General Sir William Slim, on the frontier of India. The controlling factors in both theatres of war were air power and logistics. The Japanese could neither hope to quell the whole of China nor India, but by land operations directed against airfields, they might neutralise their enemies' offensive designs. By further over-extending their lines of communication, however, at a time when they had almost forfeited air superiority was, for the Japanese, to court disaster. In the open plains and in jungle—above all upon their ports and communication centres—an enormous weight of bombing fell and eventually sapped the vitality of their armies at the front. Nevertheless it was shown that air power alone would not stop an army. It was mainly Chinese, British and American soldiers on the ground who put an end to the Japanese advance, before turning themselves to the attack. When the British and Americans riposted in north Burma in September it was to strike an enemy who was exhausted by fighting and wasted by disease: the collapse of Japanese communications and the failure of their administration, above all in dietary and anti-malarial measures, brought immense losses while the British and Americans were kept fit by a plentiful supply of food and daily doses of mepacrine. By May 1945 the better part of Burma had been recaptured and the Japanese were also in retreat from over-extended positions in China.

    It was the chief fault of Japanese strategy that, by 1944, they had become universally over-extended. Isolated garrisons dotted all about the Pacific area and deep into New Guinea were doomed to piecemeal destruction from immobility because their naval and air forces were defeated.

The number of soldiers used by the Americans and Australians in land operations was never very high—the largest force they ever deployed was the 200,000 men under General Douglas MacArthur, sent to tackle 350,000 Japanese holding the Philippines under General Yamashita in October 1944. Usually individual islands were stormed by a single division after a thoroughly devastating naval and air bombardment. Everywhere the Japanese fought on until totally wiped out. From the time the Japanese fleet was mostly sunk at the Battle of Leyte Gulf neither reinforcement nor withdrawal could be contemplated. It took two months' fighting—bunker by bunker—to clear the main Japanese defences on Leyte Island at a cost of 15,584 American casualties and some 70,000 Japanese. When Japan surrendered in August 1945, the battle for the remaining islands of the Philippines, which was still going on, had caused 192,000 Japanese dead but a mere 9,700 wounded—possibly **the highest ratio of killed in any major campaign** since the sixteenth century. American deaths were very low, the ratio being one to every twenty-four Japanese. These remarkable statistics—setting aside the suicidal Japanese battle philosophy—symbolised the good generalship of MacArthur and his subordinate commanders and the fighting spirit of the soldiers. Emphasis was also placed on the immense superiority in firepower enjoyed by the Americans, whose policy it was to drench everything with explosive or flame rather than waste a single life.

Gurkhas and tanks in Burma

U.S. tanks and infantry fighting the Japanese at Bourgainville in 1944

The longest bombardment ever recorded lasted for seventy-two days against the 23,000 Japanese holding the island of Iwo Jima—a base required by the Americans to support their air attacks against Japan. Nevertheless, from the three marine divisions which landed on 19th February, 6,891 died and another 18,000 were wounded to set against 21,000 Japanese dead (only 212 surrendered). Here, as on nearly every other island which had been heavily fortified with pillbox, minefield, bunker and wire defence, it was demonstrated, as it had been throughout the First World War, that a determined enemy could not be dislodged by missile fire alone. At the last he had to be rooted out at point of gun or buried where he fought. The intensity of the fighting of Iwo Jima produced some interesting combat statistics—figures recording a peak of 2,400 American casualties on the first day, when their bombardment was at its height—a rate which declined as tanks came ashore: it then took twenty-five days to subdue an island 6 miles (10 km) long by 2 miles (3 km) wide: among the casualties there were 2,650 men suffering from combat fatigue; 12,600 pints of blood were given to the wounded.

Probably the most celebrated soldier produced by the U.S. Army in the Second World War was General Douglas MacArthur. Closely associated with the Philippines and the Far East from early youth he was to see service, too, in Mexico and in France before 1918. An engineer officer by training he aspired to both command and staff, was several times decorated in action and eventually became Chief of Staff of the U.S. Army in 1930. In 1935 he became military adviser to the Philippine Commonwealth, charged with the task of creating a Philippine Army, but in 1941, as the Japanese threat drew near, he became commander of all the U.S. armies in the Far East, including that of the Philippines. From the moment the Japanese struck on 7th December and landed troops in the Philippines, MacArthur was central to the war in the Pacific—conducting the stalwart defence of Bataan, New Guinea and the south-west Pacific; and then beginning the gradual counter-offensive in 1942 which recoiled through New Guinea to the Philippines and the Ryukyu Islands on the warpath to Japan. MacArthur's fortunes in a war against islands depended very largely upon naval support, and so it was unfortunate that he did not enjoy the best of relations with the admirals and tended to set up in rivalry to the central Pacific island-jumping operations by Admiral Nimitz, the commander of the Pacific Ocean area. Nevertheless MacArthur possessed the attributes of a great commander in his ruthless determination to achieve an aim—even at the risk of upsetting higher authority. Like every commander in the field, in a day when first-class radio communications made it possible for a political C.-in-C. to intervene rapidly from several thousand miles distance, he had problems with his chief—in this case the President of the United States.

MacArthur

Okinawa—U.S. Marines come ashore in amphibious vehicles and pour inland on foot and on tracks

The culminating actions in the Second World War were denied to land forces. Though it was Eisenhower, through his chief of staff, who accepted the German surrender in May 1945 and MacArthur who received that of the Japanese upon the deck of a U.S. Navy battleship in August, the decisive event blossomed over Hiroshima on 6th August when **the first atomic bomb** was dropped. With a destructive power equal to 20,000 tons of conventional explosive, that caused immense blast and fire effects, the bomb represented to all who first beheld it an irresistible weapon. And when it was announced that the explosion released an unknown hazard—lethal alpha and gamma radiations—people realised that a new era had begun not only in war but also for prime existence. Destruction which might have taken multitudes of people days or weeks to accomplish in the past could now be wrought by a handful of men in a few seconds.

The nuclear bomb

The most expensive war in life and property was the Second World War. No exact total will ever be known and so the casualty figures below are merely estimates which give but a notion of the final military outlay.*

Nation	Enlistments (million)	Dead	Wounded	Civilian dead	Cost ($) (billion)
British Empire, etc.	6·2	397,762	475,000	65,000	150
U.S.A.	14·9	292,000	571,822	—	350
France	6·0	210,671	400,000	108,000	100
U.S.S.R.	20·0	7,500,000	14,012,000	15,000,000	200
China	10·0	500,000	1,700,000	1,000,000	?
Germany	12·5	2,850,000	7,250,000	500,000	300
Italy	4·5	77,500	120,000	100,000	50
Japan	7·4	1,506,000	500,000	300,000	100

* Extracted mostly from *The Encyclopedia of Military History* by Dupuy and Dupuy. As stated there, many of these figures are approximations or estimates.

The overriding paradox of the post-war years arose out of a manifest demonstration and threat of unlimited power inherent in the so-called ultimate weapons—the atomic bomb and its successor, in 1951, the hydrogen bomb (with its capacity to devastate 150 mile^2 (240 km^2))—and the actual implementation of so-called "limited" and guerilla wars with their attendant violence and massacres. The concept of "limited war" grew throughout the 1950s in response to a realisation that nuclear stalemate would be reached when all the major powers possessed their own atomic weapons. The concept of "nuclear deterrence" evolved universally as the result of a public, international debate. Indeed, so widespread were the discussions that it was study groups, as opposed to brilliant individuals, who produced their answers to the delicately involved problems of martial response and counter-response in a world where the pace of complex ideas and inventions moved faster than a single brain could encompass. Government-sponsored research was directed at great expense both into advanced weaponry and deep consideration of the political and military reflexes which might be created by the advent of new weapons and ideas.

The most extensive campaigns on land subsequent to 1945 were those conducted by the Chinese Communists under Mao Tse-tung. Since 1921, when the Chinese Communist Party was formed, it had been involved in constant struggle against war-lords, the Nationalists under Chiang Kai-shek, and foreigners such as British, Americans, the French and the Japanese. In 1927 the Communists began the reign of terrorism which developed into a guerilla movement. In the way of all such movements, when permitted to grow unchecked, armies arose which challenged the authority of the central Government. This, in China, was the apotheosis of the revolutionary kind of war advocated by Marx and Engels. By 1930 Chiang, advised by the German, von Seeckt, was engaged in intensive anti-Communist extermination campaigns. The system of cordon and search, which was to become the standard tactic of all anti-guerilla wars in Europe, was employed and with all the more effect because the Communists tried to fight a positional war. Vast numbers were killed and by October 1934, when they were in dire straits, Mao was compelled to revert to guerilla tactics and to a total withdrawal from the south-east into the inaccessible region of Shensi to the north.

The longest march by any purely foot army was accomplished in thirteen months by the Communist First Army under Chu Teh. It covered 6,000 miles (8,600 km), fighting part of the way, but leaving parties behind to establish cells around which new underground Communist organisations could be established throughout the country against the advancing Nationalists. Out of 200,000 Communists who began the march it is said that 100,000 were missing by the end, though many of these could well have fallen out by desertion. A guerilla army thrives only on success, and in retreat is prone to disaffection. Yet Mao held his people together throughout the Japanese invasion and, with Russian assistance and captured Japanese weapons, was ready in 1945 to reassert pressure against the Nationalists who were in possession of formidable American aid. Civil war raged from 1946 until 1949, a thoroughly conventional struggle between orthodox armies. Processes of old were repeated. Mao's armies, imbued with an idealistic solidarity such as the Chinese had rarely acquired before, swept aside Nationalist forces which were torn by internal strife. Like a tidal wave the Communists drove through the country from end to end until, in 1949, only the sea preserved from invasion all that remained of Chiang Kai-shek's empire—the island of Formosa.

Infantry searching for guerillas in Malaya during the 1950s. Note the light-weight, short-range carbines in use

Perhaps the most frequently quoted thoughts of practical modern commanders and military philosophers have been those of Mao Tse-tung. *On Guerilla Warfare* of 1937 is possibly the most authoritative military book since it was produced at the height of the guerilla struggle as a manual of instruction. Like all great military leaders Mao was a firm disciplinarian, one who dismissed those who broke the regulations and who, like the great eastern conquerors of old, showed little regard for life—though claiming that people and not weapons decide wars. Mao illuminated the paradox of mass destruction when, in 1957, he estimated that 900,000,000 people might die if nuclear warfare broke out, saying: "Of course it is most terrible. But if half of humanity were destroyed the other half would remain but imperialism would be destroyed entirely and there would only be Socialism in all the world." Lacking the atomic weapon until 1964 Mao has left nobody in any doubt that the Red China of his creation has inherited the predatory zeal of the earlier dynasties. Apart from fermenting revolution throughout the Far East, his armies moved into Tibet and intervened in Korea in 1950. Furthermore it is imputed (by the Russians) that under Mao's regime no less than 26,300,000 Chinese were massacred between 1949 and 1965—the most devastating slaughter in history which stemmed from a constant state of land war atmosphere throughout China based upon Mao's thesis that war and politics are inseparable.

What, on paper, appear to be far-reaching improvements in the laws of war were formulated by the Geneva Convention of 1949 in the aftermath of the various international trials which had sentenced German and Japanese leaders for war crimes. The defeated (alone) of those who had violatèd previous laws in connection with the treatment of prisoners, hostages and civilians were executed. Yet in effect the 1949 Convention dealt only marginally with the conduct of hostilities and tended to hope' rather than rule that weapons of mass destruction should not be used—the hope being based upon a feeling that the sheer deterrence of threatened mass destruction was sufficient. Little of this applied to the actual conduct of limited wars and guerilla encounters which thrived in abundance from the moment the Japanese sued for peace in August 1945.

The driving forces behind most post-1945 wars were Communism and Nationalism—often merged into a single conflict with all sorts of economic and local pressures that were deliberately exploited by propaganda. The empires which had been created by the European powers in their hey-day of the previous century began to crumble because their originators neither had the resources nor, in cases, the will to persevere in interminable combat.

The first major withdrawal of a European power from a large part of empire was by the British from India in 1947. The basic racial and religious disputes between Hindus and Møslems could no longer be contained by land forces which were stretched to the limit and, in the case of indigenous Indian troops, involved in the dispute between races. The practice of riot control by minimum force had small affect on crowds inflamed by fear and hatred. Fighting took place at close quarters in the confines of cities and villages at high cost in life—23,000 casualties in one four-month period of 1946, for example. After the British departed in 1947 it is estimated that about 200,000 people out of a population of 400,000,000 were killed (compared, for example, with 1,500,000 million who died in the Bengal famine of 1943). Thus the British avoided involvement in a head-on land war in India, such as flared in Kashmir between India and the newly created state of Pakistan.

The first post-war guerilla campaign fought by the French began in 1946 against the Communist Viet Minh in Indo-China. The poorly trained and inadequately equipped French were confronted by a well-trained enemy on Maoist lines armed with a good assortment of American and Japanese weapons. The Viet Minh lived in the villages and jungle, constructed well-fortified camps and infiltrated their attacks along the lines of communication towards the main centres of population held by the French. Though the French, under Marshal De Lattre de Tassigny, endeavoured to placate the Viet Minh with political concessions (while implementing a firm military counter-offensive) they could never totally eliminate an opponent who was resolute, ruthless and highly mobile. After De Lattre died in 1952 the French, with aid from the U.S.A., challenged the Viet Minh to battle at Dien Bien Phu—flamboyantly flying in 15,000 men to occupy a confined perimeter that was some 220 miles (352 km) distant from Hanoi. But while the French could only fly in 28 guns and a handful of light tanks (that had to be assembled on the spot) General Giap was able to concentrate a vastly superior Viet Minh army with over 200 guns and rocket-launchers. In the end it cost Giap 25,000 men, but only 73 French escaped and France was compelled to withdraw from the war and concede North Vietnam to the Viet Minh.

The last days of Dutch rule in Indonesia came in 1949 after their airborne forces had won local victories in 1948 over Nationalist troops. Here the inability of the Dutch to persevere was caused by financial difficulty made more acute by an order of the United Nations Security Council that was enforced by diplomatic pressure from the U.S.A. Both the Indo-China and Indonesia campaigns thus indicated that, within a modern society, external pressures bit hard upon nations which respected the rule of law. On the other hand long wars by people who cared not for law, covertly supported by the law-abiding people, were feasible. The so-called "limited wars" have underlined this tendency: those sponsored by the super-powers of the U.S.A., Russia and China have been long-lasting. Yet when a small nation has resorted to arms, without big-power aid, they have either been compelled to desist by the super-powers or, if victorious, have accomplished their aims so swiftly that outside intervention in time was impossible.

U.S. Marine rocket battery in action in Korea

The first limited war conducted by a super-power was waged in Korea from 1950 until 1953. On 25th June the Communist North Koreans, armed with Russian weapons, attempted a lightning overrunning of the ill-armed South before anybody could intervene. Some 240 North Korean tanks made swift inroads into the South and swept aside the first U.S. troops sent to bar their way.

In his last battle as Supreme Commander of U.S. forces in the Far East General MacArthur imposed a naval and air blockade on North Korea and, using the immense facilities of U.S. sea and air transport, established a strong defensive perimeter round the port of Pusan in the south-east corner of the country. From here, joined by British troops, he mounted a counter-offensive when the last North Korean attacks had exhausted themselves. Air power played an extensive part in the defensive battle with air-dropped napalm doing considerable damage to enemy tanks and supply vehicles.

The highly imaginative U.S. sea and airborne landing at Inchon, on 15th September, completely turned the tables upon the North Koreans. By striking at the root of their communications, when all their troops were committed to a drawn battle in the South, MacArthur threw the North into confusion. The Pusan bridgehead, too, was breached by a U.S. offensive and what remained of the invaders thrown back upon the frontier of Manchuria. This was as complete a land victory as could have been hoped for in mountainous terrain where men can escape more easily than upon the plains. Over 125,000 North Korean prisoners were taken in addition to the thousands who fell in battle. Yet nothing so complete could be hoped for from MacArthur's subsequent advance into North Korea, for not only did he then begin to butt against direct opposition in a hostile country but Chinese Communist forces were drawn into the conflict across the Yalu River. As a result the United Nations forces found themselves opposed by greatly numerically superior forces whose skilful tactics of infiltration by night, through the mountains, were superior to daylight operations directed almost solely along the roads in the valleys. Under these conditions air attacks did little to check Chinese battlefield movements even though they seriously hampered their tenuous supply lines. It was not until the United Nations adopted the technique of siege warfare in an almost continuous line of hilltop entrenched defences stretching the width of the Korean Peninsula, that the Chinese (whose logistics were primitive) were held in check—and caused terrible losses whenever they rose in massed attacks. However, siege conditions prevailed

U.S. tanks in the artillery role at night in Korea

only because President Truman of the United States of America decided (against the will of MacArthur whom he sacked) that further escalation of the war by air and possibly atomic attack against Manchuria and China were unacceptable political risks, particularly in the knowledge that the Russians had developed their own atomic bomb. A vital political point had been made. Eventually, from the condition of stalemate, an armistice was arranged in July 1953 with both sides roughly back where they had been in 1950.

The most important technical innovation of the Korean War was the helicopter. Although the first man-carrying helicopter, designed by Paul Cornu in France, made its first vertical ascent in 1907 (the first suggestions for the breed having been made by da Vinci in the sixteenth century) it was not until 1941 that Igor Sikorsky produced in the U.S.A., the first, practical single-rotor machine. In Korea the early small types were mostly used for re-supply of troops in difficult forward positions, evacuation of wounded and for personal command and control. One U.S. officer claimed that with a helicopter he could command over a 25-mile (40 km) frontage.

The longest limited campaign fought by a British army dragged on from 1948 until 1960 against Communist guerillas (mostly of the indigenous Chinese) who sought to seize government of the Malay Peninsula. Working on the Maoist theory that guerillas could win even if unsupported by outside help, the Communists tried to terrorise the populace into giving aid. The British replied with a mixture of political concessions (which eventually led to outright Malayan sovereignty) and a military campaign, with 45,000 men against 12,000, based upon control of food supplies and route centres in an essentially jungle environment. The guerillas operated from jungle camps located a few hundred yards from the roadsides. The British (the pick of whom were well-trained professional soldiers), having discovered the enemy location, ambushed trails and attacked the camps. Sometimes they were supplied by air, but usually they lived in the jungle with the same skill as their opponents. This was an infantry battle in which artillery, armour and air played only minor though noisy roles. It took six years to break the back of the Communist forces and another six before all but a few frontier bands were eliminated. It cost the Communists 10,500 men and their enemies about 5,000. It set the pattern for a series of successful anti-guerilla operations in which the British have come, from bitter experience, to be supreme—in Palestine, East Africa, Cyprus, Borneo and Northern Ireland, to name but the most prominent theatres of operation.

The most extensive anti-guerilla operations waged by the French were carried out in North Africa after 1947—wars against Nationalists in Tunisia, Algeria and Morocco which France was unable to quell despite the killing of at least 70,000 guerillas for the loss of 10,000 of their own men. To increase tactical pace and mobility the French used large helicopters as troop transports to increase their mobility in mountainous and desert terrain. Yet they could not suppress determined guerillas before internal and external political and military pressures proved too strong for a succession of unstable French governments. In 1964 the last French withdrew from Morocco, having already been persuaded to leave Tunisia and Algeria in 1962. Victory for the guerillas was the product of psychological stamina, their ability to relay a measure of aggression mixed with survival while manipulating political opinion against the French. The French lost because they could not win quickly enough for political realism.

Helicopter delivery in Vietnam

Israeli combat team in Syria, 1967

The largest armoured battles in the style of the Second World War have been fought since 1956 in the Middle East and along the Indo-Pakistan frontier.

● *Israel*, which was a nation born out of guerilla warfare against the British, found herself from inception as a State, in 1948, embroiled at war with her Arab neighbours—a condition in which, formally, she has remained ever since. From the outset the Israelis employed improvised forces, armed with the weapons of the Second World War, against better-equipped Arab forces. The Israelis, almost totally lacking in tanks and

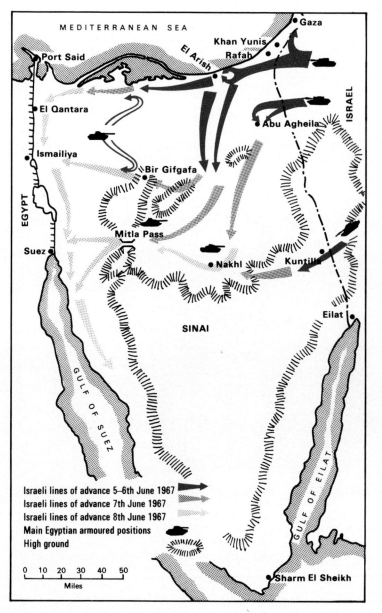

Israeli lines of advance 5–6th June 1967
Israeli lines of advance 7th June 1967
Israeli lines of advance 8th June 1967
Main Egyptian armoured positions
High ground

0 10 20 30 40 50
Miles

The Six-Day War in Sinai, 1967

with little artillery, preserved and expanded their frontiers by sheer combat spirit and determination against inefficient opposition. United Nations intervention gave Israel breathing-space in which to organise an army based upon offensive characteristics—offensive because, with so little territory to spare, she could not afford to fight on her own soil. The Israelis began to acquire a formidable air force and efficient mechanised divisions in which tanks were relegated to an infantry-support role. **However, in this army's first major campaign** against the Egyptian Army in Sinai in 1956, it was tanks supported by artillery, infantry and air power which cut through the Egyptian Army, causing 10,000 casualties and capturing 125 Egyptian tanks for only 150 Israeli killed. From that moment Israel concentrated upon building a tank-preponderant army— one which, in June 1967, utterly defeated the combined armies of Egypt, Syria and Jordan in six days' fighting, completing their work so swiftly that the intervention of outside political pressures came too late to alter the decision.

● *Indo-Pakistan.* The war which broke out in Kashmir and the Punjab in August 1956 was also predominantly between tanks and guns. Neither side could totally dominate the other, with the result that a series of head-on and indecisive clashes developed without leading to strategic gain. Inevitably the impact of external pressures—above all the application of sanctions by the U.S.A. to the supply of new equipment, fuel and finance— brought a quick end to the fighting.

An Indian Army recoilless gun detachment advances into East Pakistan in 1972

The most important war from the point of view of advanced technology took place in Vietnam. The struggle which died down when the French withdrew in 1954 began, once more, to gain in violence when the North Vietnamese Communists initiated small-scale guerilla attacks against the South Vietnamese in 1956. At that time the South Vietnamese Army was only under initial training by the French and the United States. Therefore, the well-trained so-called Viet Cong were able to make steady headway in taking over all but the highly populated zones, and in 1959 virtually challenged the South Vietnamese for control of the entire nation.

The first direct U.S. aid, as opposed to advice, training and supply, came in December 1961 when helicopter units were introduced as mobile support for the South Vietnamese—the crux of the American appreciation being that guerilla war could be won by technology, and the Vietnamese were technically retarded. The escalation of the war (sometimes, it seemed, without political constraints or aims) became closely geared to the attritional might of American technology and industrial power against a somewhat impoverished opponent. Nearly 500,000 U.S. servicemen were at one time engaged in the land battles, their qualities as soldiers impaired because the vast majority were short-term conscripts whose tour of duty at the battle-front rarely exceeded a year. Against a silent, highly professional fighting animal like the Viet Cong and North Vietnamese regular, the individual American, noisily grinding into battle, could only achieve superiority by expensive material means. Nevertheless, when the Viet Cong came out into the open with the Tet offensive against the South Vietnamese cities in 1968, they were smashed and have yet to recover from the defeat. Likewise the all-out North Vietnamese Army offensive in 1972, although it benefited from tank support and superb long-range artillery fire from the new Russian 130 mm guns, was beaten by an air offensive, which disrupted supplies, and a failure to co-ordinate attacks in both the strategic and tactical aspects.

A South Vietnamese gunner dives for cover against mortar fire and an exploding ammunition truck

The highlights of organisation of land forces during the Cold War period under the threat of total nuclear war have been the competitive demands for highly specialised and trained massed, conscript armies for employment in large battles for position. Insurgency has come face to face with soldiers using a proliferation of machines which tend to reduce the number of front-line combat personnel. Yet, in the Western-orientated North Atlantic Treaty Organisation, only Britain has done away with conscription and relies upon a small regular army to meet her commitments, backed by reserves for call-up in case of a major outbreak. The Communist nations all depend upon mass conscripted armies despite the wastage through turnover and inadequate training in a technological age. It is a sign of the times (if only an echo from history) that the U.S. Army is abandoning conscription and hoping to recruit sufficient, educated men by offering financial inducements which will match the status of the soldier to that of the civilian. Money alone, however, will not purchase combat determination.

The most significant changes in the relation between the demands of the battlefield and technology is the arrival of a moment at which the soldier no longer has to wait for a random invention to enhance his armoury, but can call for what he needs in the knowledge that modern science may well be able to satisfy his wants – at a price.

Advances in battlefield technology cover practically the entire military field from command, through combat techniques to support and logistics. The most significant changes have been related to automation and miniaturisation in addition to increased destruction. Tanks of nearly 50 tons still stalk the battlefield and have been used in Vietnam despite the difficulties of moving them through jungle and paddy. But tanks, guns and aircraft have been made to respond more sensitively to small devices.

● *Detectors and sensors.* Though the development of infra-red detectors for night viewing continued after 1945, with the Russians taking a lead, recognition of the insecurity of an "active" light source, which could itself be detected, led to a search for so-called "passive night-fighting aids". Three kinds have emerged—the image intensifier and low light television (which make use of natural illumination to be found at night to give clear vision without the aid of a vulnerable searchlight), and the thermal imaging device which detects the target by scanning the contrasts in heat given off by its various surfaces. From the latter emerges a picture on a screen. The subtlety of the last named being that no light source of any sort is required.

Sensors, too, are of several kinds. There are radar sensors which detect movement by the "Doppler effect", and seismic sensors which pick up vibrations caused by a body or machine on the move. There are heat sensors, too, which detect a body in close proximity, while "sniffers", which suck in air and analyse its ammonia properties, give notice of human presence. Harness all these methods for finding the enemy into a consolidated "surveillance plan", centred upon one place which contains all the necessary receiving and transmitting communication devices, and it becomes almost impossible to move without being detected or heard. Land warfare then enters into the realms of automation.

● *Communications.* Between the two world wars radio communication became more sophisticated and mobile as sets which transmitted on the higher frequency bands were developed for commercial use. Very high frequency speech radio was coming into common use by armies in 1945—above all in the U.S. Army. Operating was also made much simpler and with this simplification came greater reliability. Whereas the smallest infantry sets were unreliable and difficult to tune in 1943, by 1960 infantry communications in the V.H.F. range were far better than had been possible with tank and artillery high-frequency radio in 1945. In 1946 the first radio relay system was produced in the U.S.A. enabling long-distance radio-telephone conversations. **Junction transistors, which were first described** in 1948 by Professor William Shockley, introduced new standards of reliability and miniaturisation into all sorts of electronic communication devices. All these techniques, when exploited by voice and telegraph or teleprinter systems to establish more reliable, easily erected networks within a zone of combat, enabled leaders to make loud and clear contact with almost any corner of their command, eliminating the remoteness which had been endemic with earlier systems. The development of satellite communications in the early 1960s made it possible to extend intimate communications to a world-wide basis, while the invention of complex encoding and decoding machines reduced the time wasted by the demands of security.

● *Memory-stored computers*, **of which the first was run** at Cambridge University in 1949, gave an enormous boost to data processing throughout the 1950s and had immediate military applications on land. They could store, collate and help display the vast accumulations of information gathered from enemy sources as well as about the state of friendly forces. They could give automatic control over the switching of signals so that an almost instant dialling system, via radio, could be established during mobile operations. Artillery fire, missile guidance and tank gunnery could all draw on these devices as the means to consolidate every piece of information available—such as target movement, meteorology and weapon performance—so that extremely accurate fire could be aimed in a fraction of the time required by the old manual systems. For example the U.S. Army vehicle-mounted, compact Tacfire systems can produce an artillery mission for one fire unit, which once took 60 seconds, in 10 seconds, and for 35 targets by 10 fire units in 700 seconds, compared with the 7,200 seconds of old.

● *Rocket missiles*—guided or free flight—a technology in which the Germans were pre-eminent in the 1930s, leading up to the use of such weapons in the air war, were in increasing use at the end of the Second World War. Afterwards, so far as land forces were concerned, free-flight rockets provided a useful vehicle for carrying low-yield atomic warheads to their battlefield targets. The first of these to come into service in 1955 was the U.S.A.'s Honest John with a range of 23 miles (36·8 km). But for pin-point accuracy against a tank, for example, the method, first suggested by the Germans, and developed after 1945 by the French, was a rocket manually guided to its target by an operator passing signals down a thin wire that was paid out behind the missile in flight: the first of these to enter service was the French SS 10 with a range of 1,750 yd (1,600 m). Anti-tank missiles have since been developed to fly to ranges of 4,360 yd (4,000 m) and are incorporating semi-automatic guidance systems which permit the operator merely to lay his sights on the target to enable the missile to follow that line. **The most sophisticated missiles** are those which home accurately on to a target either by tracking infra-red emissions from the target or by following a radio or laser beam aimed at the target. The U.S.A.'s SMART guided bombs home on to infra-red emissions reflected from a laser aimed at the target or can be guided to the target by reference to pictures transmitted from a television camera in the bomb's nose. This is the world of electronic warfare in which, as counter, a whole range of detector and spoofing devices are also fully active.

● *Vertical take-off aircraft.* **The first armed helicopters** were French Alouettes armed with SS 10 guided missiles, but **the first use of armed**

Honest John launching

The Swedish S tank, a sophisticated armoured fighting vehicle of unproven battlefield capability

helicopters in battle was by the U.S.A. in Vietnam. Initially, machine-guns were mounted to give suppressive fire to help other helicopters as they approached a landing-zone carrying infantry. Gradually, as enemy anti-helicopter fire increased, it had to be challenged by mounting batteries of machine-guns, grenade throwers, rocket-launchers and mini-cannon in pods on either side of the aircraft, in the first so-called "gunships". Gunships escorted load carrying helicopters and also gave close support to ground troops (beside reconnaissance) as a more responsive and accurate method of applying airborne firepower than that supplied by conventional aircraft. Thus helicopter units became integral to ground forces and are usually manned by pilots who have a soldier's basic training.

● *Mines* are a more prevalent threat on the battlefield than ever because greatly improved methods of laying have been allied with decreases in size, higher and better-controlled sensitivity, improved anti-defusing devices and increased lethal power. Miniature camouflaged anti-personnel mines, which can be scattered from the air or by ground-to-ground rocket-dispensed containers, have the ability to arm themselves once they have landed and can amputate limbs with the deftest of ease. Claymore-type mines, which detonate and broadcast a hail of steel balls, can be triggered by attachment to the various kinds of sensors mentioned above. Anti-tank mines, which are designed to detonate under the belly of a tank, can cause total disruption of the vehicle instead of merely disabling it by breaking the track. In practice the deployment of vast numbers of indiscriminately laid mines (which are also capable of disarming themselves after a period) and controlled mines to activate what amounts to automatic ambushes, can deny whole tracts of country to enemy forces, with a resultant economy in outlay by the layers. Thus a small number of troops can quite easily dominate enemy country while hardly exposing themselves to retribution. In Vietnam areas, which at one time were freely used by Viet Cong, were almost totally denied to them and great numbers began to surrender from fear of automatic ambush. The process is somewhat more discriminate than the use of an atomic demolition mine!

● *Chemical and biological warfare.* Although poison gas is still largely taboo (its only use since 1938 seems to have been mustard gas and phosgene by the Egyptians against the Yemenis in 1966 and 1967) many chemical agents of a non-toxic nature are in constant use by ground forces. Irritant and nauseous gases are frequently used to control unruly crowds (as a preferable method to shooting them). The Viet Cong tried to cause infection, such as gangrene, in wounds, by impregnating spiked booby traps with excreta. In efforts to deny food to guerilla forces, and also expose their jungle hiding-places, the widespread use of herbicides and defoliants to kill crops and strip leaves from trees has been practised—with awful effectiveness but only marginal results. The Viet Cong has also been successful in introducing their opponents to "hard" drugs, thus sapping their will to fight. There is no guarantee that a ban on biological weapons, signed by the principal powers in 1972, will prevent this sort of warfare any more than anti-nuclear treaties will outlaw the atom bomb.

● *Propaganda.* **The Vietnamese war was the first** to be fought under full coverage by the world's television news media. In consequence entire populations were exposed to the sight of men in action and a good deal of what that means in terms of horror. The shock effect was considerable and led to significant anti-war movements which persuaded the combatants most exposed to it—those of the U.S.A. and Australia—to attempt a withdrawal from the contest before a decision had been reached.

On the other hand the use of this method can also escalate fighting by inducing such revulsion that revenge is called for—as, for example, has tended sometimes to be the case in Northern Ireland.

Battlefield surveillance in Northern Ireland with a ZB 298 radar

It is an irrefutable fact that during the twenty-five-year war in Vietnam, **a far higher tonnage of explosive has been expended than in the First and Second World Wars**, greater material outlay made and an unheard-of level of automation reached. This outpouring of resources failed to eliminate a guerilla army which fought with dedicated perseverance, but it did defeat conventional forces. Gross casualty figures are not available but it is fairly certain that civilian losses far exceed those of the military. It is to be concluded that, faced with the efficient organisation of a modern police state, the termination of an ideological war can only be achieved by the occupation and surveillance of every acre of important territory—an almost impossible task. To engineer a conclusive act of war, the fighting man with weapon in hand—the arbiter of land warfare—has to win absolutely in combat. History shows that only when further resistance is demonstrably futile can lasting political measures based upon reasonableness and moderation be applied in order to eradicate the foundations of insurgency.

Land warfare is almost certain, therefore, to remain a feature of everyday existence. Reflection shows that the human basic considerations of several thousand years have hardly changed at all. The employment of the populace harnessed to sophisticated technology has merely and progressively compressed the time-scale under the urging of people whose fundamental outlook remains predatory.

SECTION IX
Appendices

Appendix 1

WAR OF THE FUTURE

The advent of the atom bomb and the full range of modern technology which has accompanied it into the armouries of the nations, drives the prophets of war to the depths of depression. As I. F. Clarke remarks in *Voices Prophesying War*: "There is now nothing left that the imagination can do with the shape of the total-war-to-come except describe the end of civilisation." From the literary angle this is apt. Yet, since the holocaust of Hiroshima, the world has managed to survive for twenty-eight years in a condition of almost constant tension and, for the better part of that period, under the threat of what is icily described as "nuclear plenty". Though war is a permanent spectre it has stopped short by a hair's breadth of the nuclear kind, a trend to which we simply must pin our faith if the prophets of doom are to be disillusioned.

Military prophets are compelled to anchor their projections of future war either to a mild variation of present-day methods, caused by the multiplying impact of practical inventions, or must take flights of fantasy in imagining the results of advances in technology which are well beyond current technical feasibility. The apostles of fantasy foretell (perhaps in the escapist mood) galactic wars which have scant connection with land warfare on our own planet. But, as history shows, it is those realists who restrict their imagery to a twenty-year span (however bold they are to scan that far) who are most likely to land somewhere near the centre of truth's target. For no matter how feasible a complex and crucial invention may seem, it may take ten years or more to develop it to the state of practical reliability —and only then if sufficient and often gigantic funds are made available to the project. But armies today come low in the order of priority for new weapons since it is air forces and navies who cream off the most money. Hence the land campaigns of the next decade or so are likely to be dominated by those inventions which have already been announced—the ones, which, with improved reliability and modification, have been described in Section VIII above.

As Shelford Bidwell has written: "Military prophets are a discredited lot. Most of their time is spent in salvaging their reputations by counting their hits and ignoring their misses." Nevertheless there seems little reason to doubt that land combat will remain the basic act of war (regardless of the claims of those who persist in pressing the dictum that air power in isolation brings a decision) and, therefore, something similar to the pattern of the past couple of decades will be repeated in the next two. **Low-intensity guerilla warfare** will persist interspersed by periods of **medium- to high-intensity non-nuclear war**. In their shaping of these patterns tactical and technological artists may paint fresh variations, but these will merely give extra impulse to the cycle of evolving history. Low- and medium-level warfare, therefore, lodge firmly within our imaginations because we see them in action today. The final disaster—**nuclear total war**—enters such wide realms of conjecture that the imagination boggles. Let us now consider each type in order of escalation.

Low-intensity guerilla warfare. Assuming that the prime requirements of a viable guerilla organisation are met—the possession of a convincing cause, support from an indigenous populace and material aid from an external agency—success for the guerillas will continue to depend upon seizing and holding the initiative by the careful selection of appropriate targets to attack, and the timed escalation of military measures in cadence with political advances. Guerillas' weapons have not changed very much this century—propaganda, explosives and small arms are their basic simple tools with small rockets making a gradual, if clumsy, appearance. Only by subtlety of initiative does the guerilla maintain an advantage. It is anti-guerilla forces which now have the edge with their ability to tap the enemy's communications, to detect clandestine movements and to penetrate that favourite hiding-place of the guerilla—cover of darkness. It is likely, now that the guerilla is being subject to deadly harassment by technical devices, that in the future he will be very hard put to maintain a worthwhile military presence. Even if he attempts to introduce technical devices to match those of the professional anti-guerilla forces it is likely that he will be outmatched unless all-out backing is forthcoming from some adjacent and friendly power—in which case the struggle is thrust a stage nearer limited war. Perhaps, therefore, we may witness within the next decade a decline in martial guerilla activity and a reversion by insurrectionists to the methods of the late nineteenth century—a proliferation of subversion by assassination, such as got nobody anywhere, or the realisation of solutions by negotiations that fall short of violence.

Medium- and high-intensity non-nuclear war may take place anywhere within the spectrum between an escalating guerilla confrontation and the outbreak of a nuclear exchange. Whereas guerilla war is mainly the concern of land forces, helped by logistic air support, medium-level war can involve the full range of airborne weapons (short of nuclear), perhaps a naval commitment and certainly an unleashing of immense destruction. The dimensions of calculated destruction may well draw the essential distinction between wars of the past and those of the future. Improving accuracy of weapon delivery implies, in theory, an ability to hit pin-point targets without the side-effects of area destruction. A tank or a bridge can be hit by a single guided bomb and therefore obviate the demolition of the surrounding countryside as might have been unavoidable in the past. On the other hand the appearance of massed, highly mobile armoured cross-country vehicles capable of approaching their objectives along almost any route in company with fleets of vertical-take-off aircraft, widen the scope of

A street in An Loc. In the foreground is a T 54, the first North Vietnamese tank to be destroyed in the town in 1972

combat almost to infinity. With numbers is associated the philosophy of saturation which accompanies the proliferation of mines and small yet extremely powerful, easily concealed, indirect-fire guided missiles which add enormously to the power of the defence. Somewhere about 1980 a point will be reached when it will no longer be possible for battle-field movement to take place without an opponent being instantly aware of it and without an almost immediate and whole destructive engagement. In essence, the advantage of surprise may be almost impossible to acquire by the methods of the past and the defensive will again become supreme.

One therefore envisages armies of the future seeking to acquire surprise by extending their range of electronic coverage, coincident with the development of weapons which can be located in depth, yet with an almost instant ability to concentrate their fire and presence deep within the enemy hinterland. In other words, creating an ability to strike instantly and accurately without resort to a redeployment such as the enemy must detect before it becomes effective. Operational methods, however, are liable to be orthodox in principle. Intensive attacks by aircraft and missiles will blanket the enemy air bases and weapon sites. Conventional artillery of longer range, more rapid delivery and far greater accuracy than in the past will direct short concentrations of fire against pin-point targets to achieve what is known as "first-salvo effectiveness". The old systems of ranging by single shots will be eliminated because the gunners will be provided with much more accurate meteorological data as well as improved positioning from survey and up-to-the-minute information about enemy targets. Electronic counter-measures, preferably of a unique kind, will be employed to baffle the foe.

A series of airborne or indigenous guerilla *coups de main* will be projected against vital enemy communication systems. Satellite sensors and transmitters in inner space also will be attacked by guided missiles. Highly mobile, armoured land forces will advance to seize territory which is so vital to the enemy that he cannot permit its loss to go unchallenged. The aim of both sides will be to establish a dominating defensive posture and thus goad an opponent into the open to expose him to destruction, under a devastating firepower, launched by guns and rockets. Aircraft, elevated platforms, reconnaissance drones and armed helicopters will seek out enemy targets in depth and themselves become targets for short-range guided missiles launched from the forward edge of the battle zone. These well-concealed guided-weapon launchers would themselves become targets for helicopters and conventional artillery fire. The occasions upon which a man could expose himself in unarmoured nakedness on the open battlefield might dwindle to almost none. While there would be moments of hand-to-hand combat in enclosed, urban areas, close country and wood-land, the trend of battle would be towards automated remoteness of control by a small hierarchy of commanders and technicians from within heavily guarded, deeply emplaced command posts into which would be fed the complex tentacles of intelligence and communication systems.

In theory, therefore, the commander of the future will hardly need to leave his command post so comprehensive should be the information available to him, so extensive his means to disseminate orders. However, this is to overlook the commander's principal responsibility of fostering the soldier's morale. Both the highest technician and the lowliest rifleman will seek confidence in the higher leadership—and all the more so in an age when advanced educational standards have taught people to question major issues before committing themselves in support. So the commander always will have need to make contact with his subordinates and become known to those beneath him. Moreover, viable armies will not get any smaller in number, for though fewer men may actually control the machines, the sheer magnitude of the demands for holding ground to protect control centres, plus the enormous losses which may be inflicted, create as large a demand as ever for combat soldiers spread throughout a vastly enlarged combat zone. Fewer men there might be in the forward zones, but the reserves to replace enormous wastage will have to be as great as ever—and become even greater as machines are destroyed or break down.

Hence conflict of policy will arise between the demand for a small élite of technical soldiers, for use in peacetime guerilla operations and as the core of action in limited war, and the requirement for a mass of individuals to perform the traditional functions of guard and occupation duties. Thus an age-old pattern is projected into the foreseeable future—the need for an élite surrounded by a massed conscripted army or militia.

The perils of escalation above limited war are all too obvious. Unless a quick solution is reached of the battle's own volition or from a halt imposed by diplomatic pressure or economic sanctions, a condition can be reached in which one side or the other is driven to use nuclear or chemical and biological weapons. The causes of escalation may be complex and vary between fear of imminent defeat or sheer desperation at an apparent inability to overcome a stern defence—a form of frustration as the spectre of attrition looms up to inflict heavy losses for no strategic gain. The trouble may stem from insufficient information and time upon which to base a rational solution—military or political. But, if one or other of the protagonists possesses nuclear weapons, and decides wrongly, the next stage of escalation will take place.

Total war. Although it is possible that an outbreak of total war might occur with an instant airborne exchange of thermonuclear weapons upon the hinterlands of the major powers, it is equally likely that the release by a minor power of a single, low-yield tactical weapon upon a remote battlefield could act as the trigger. Under these conditions the elaborate constraints imposed by the existing system of international parley among the major powers might collapse in a matter of hours—if not minutes.

Whichever way total war begins the result must be the elimination of civilisation as it is known—but not necessarily a termination of conflict. Survivors there will be and none more belligerent than soldiers who, along with their weapons, have hidden in the best-protected underground shelters or behind the shield of armoured vehicles. Though it is probable that disciplined armies will turn to the rescue of the civil populace in the event of a nuclear holocaust, it is also fairly certain that combat will continue to be prosecuted—if at a reduced tempo. Combat units would be used to defend frontiers and vital positions in a struggle between dispersed and emaciated armies. Soon the last atomic shell would be expended, gradually fuel would run out, inevitably the machines would atrophy from lack of spares, and insidiously men's health would decline from radiation, chemical warfare, malnutrition and disease. Formal battles for position would be replaced by intermittent guerilla struggles as the contenders staked out claims for future influence. War-lords would appear. There seems no positive reason to assert that the "ultimate" catastrophe would convince men of the need to sink their enmity in the cause of universal salvation. It seems more likely, in fact, that the breakdown of society would be reflected in a reversion to primitive warfare such as was described in the opening pages of this book.

Appendix 2

TABLE OF IMPORTANT RECORDED CAMPAIGNS WITH THEIR CRUCIAL LAND BATTLES

This table aims to assemble important campaigns and battles in chronological order as a reference for those who wish quickly to relate events to time. It is not intended to be comprehensive since this would be absolutely impossible within the space of a few pages, even if every campaign and battle which had been fought was recorded in history—which is far from the case. The guide-lines for selection are the political significance of the campaigns and the tactical and technological importance of each battle in relation to the shaping of a campaign, or the development and introduction into service of some new and important matter of technology. A few battles of low emotive value have been included while, as a general rule, minor civil wars and guerilla struggles which fall short of formal combat have been excluded. Read in conjunction with the Select Bibliography and, of course, the main body of this book itself and it is hoped that a useful guide is provided for the reader who wishes to delve deeper into any particular period of the history of land warfare.

Period	Major combatants	Main localities	Major associated battles and sieges
BC			
1800	Hyksos	Middle East	Numerous but none recorded
1766–1123	Shangs	Eastern China	Indications of several but unspecific
1469–1294	Egypt v. Hyksos	Middle East	Megiddo, 1469; Kadesh, 1294
1116–616	Assyria v. all-comers	Middle East	Numerous but none specifically recorded
1122–256	Chous	Eastern China	Numerous but none specifically recorded
616–612	Media v. Assyria	Mesopotamia	Harran, 616; Nineveh, 612
600–530	Persians v. Medes	Middle East and India	Pteria, 547; Thymbra, 546; Babylon, 538
500–323	Greece v. Persia	Greece and Middle East to India	Marathon, 490; Thermopylae, 480; Plataea, 480; Cunaxa, 401; Granicus, 334; Issus, 333; Arbela, 331; Hydaspes, 326
400–146	Carthage v. Syracuse and Rome	Central Mediterranean	Syracuse, 398 etc.; Utica, 238; Trebia, 218; Lake Trasimene, 217; Cannae, 216; Metaurus, 207; Zama, 202; Carthage, 146
221–201	Ch'ins v. Hans and Hsiung-nus	Central and East China	Numerous and of a civil war nature
202–221	Hans v. Ch'ins and Hsiung-nus	Most of present-day China	Defeat of Hsiung-nus, 119
215–150	Rome v. Greece	Central Mediterranean	Cynoscephalae, 197; Pydna, 168
50–30	Roman Civil War	Central and East Mediterranean	Massilia, 49; Dyrrhachium, 48; Pharsalus, 48; Alexandria, 48; Nile, 47; Zela, 47; Thapsus, 46; Munda, 45; Philippi, 42; Actium, 31
AD			
1–400	Barbarians v. Rome	Europe and Middle East	Teutoberger Wald, 9; Philippopolis, 250; Nish, 269; Turin, 312; 1st Adrianople, 323; Argentorate, 357; 2nd Adrianople, 378

Period	Major combatants	Main localities	Major associated battles and sieges

AD

374–490	Huns (Hsiung-nus) v. Rome and other Barbarians	Europe and Middle East	Tanais River, 373; Nish and Sofia, 443; Utus and Thermopylae, 447; Chalons, 451
401–629	Barbarians v. Rome and Byzantium	Europe and Middle East	Pollentia, 402; Rome, 410 and 455; Tricameron, 533; Rome 537; Taginae, 552; Melanthius, 559
629–814	Moslems v. Byzantium and Franks	Europe and Middle East	Muta, 629; Ajnadain, 634; Yarmuk, 636; Babylon, 640; Constantinople, 717; Tours, 732; Lyon, 739; Barcelona, 800; Crasus, 805
815–1000	Moslems v. Byzantium	Middle East and Europe	Dasymon, 838; Samosata, 873; Tarentum, 880; Anchialus, 917; Pankalia, 979
800–1189	Norsemen v. Western European peoples	Western Europe	Britain, 802; Ireland, 807; Frisia, 809; Edington, 878; Paris, 885; Tempsford, 918; Civitella, 1053; Hastings, 1066; Durazzo, 1082; Brindisi, 1156; the Strymon, 1185
1048–1453	Moslem Turks v. Byzantium and Crusaders	Western Europe and Middle East	Manzikert, 1071, the Orontes, 1098; Jerusalem and Ascalon, 1099; Philomalion, 1116; Acre, 1189–91; Arsouf, 1191; Constantinople, 1204; Fariskur, 1250; Bursa, 1317; Constantinople, 1391–99; Varna, 1444; Constantinople, 1453
1190–1405	Mongols v. China, Europe and Middle East	Asia, Eastern Europe and Middle East.	Irtysh, 1208; Chin Empire, 1211–15; Persia, 1218–24; Russia, 1222–23; Yellow River, 1226; Pien Liang, 1233; Kiev, 1240; Cracow, Liegnitz and Sajo River, 1241; Kosedagh, 1243; Japan, 1274–81; Marj-as-Suffar, 1303; Kerulen River, 1388
1295–1457	English v. Scots and French	France, Scotland and England	Dunbar, 1296; Falkirk, 1298; Bannockburn, 1314; Halidon Hill, 1333; Crécy, 1346; Calais, 1354; Poitiers, 1356; Agincourt, 1415; Orléans and Patay, 1429; Formigny, 1450; Castillon, 1453
1381–1405	Tartars v. Mongols, Russians, Persians, Indians and Turks	Central Asia, Middle East and India	Persia, 1381–87; Syr-Darya, 1389; Kandurcha, 1391; Terek, 1395; Panipat, 1398; Aleppo, 1400; Baghdad, 1401
1419–34	Hussites v. Catholics	Bohemia	Prague, 1419; Kutna Hora, 1421; Horid, 1423; Lipany, 1434
1481–92	Spain v. Moslems	Spain	Granada, 1488–91
1495–1559	Spain v. France (Swiss involved on both sides)	Spain, France and Italy	Montpensier, 1496; Cerignola, 1503; Ravenna, 1512; Novara, 1513; Marignano, 1515; Pavia, 1525; Ceresole, 1544; Calais, 1558
1499–1598	Turks v. all neighbours	Middle East and Europe	Chaldiran, 1515; Ridanieh, 1517; Belgrade, 1521; Rhodes, 1522; Mohacs, 1526; Vienna, 1529, Valpo, 1537; Malta, 1565; Famagusta, 1570; Sissek, 1593; Kerestes, 1596

Period	Major combatants	Main localities	Major associated battles and sieges
AD			
1562–1648	European religious wars between Catholics and Protestants	Most of Europe	Dreux, 1562; Jarnac and Moncontour, 1569; Leyden, 1573; Gembloux, 1578; Coutras, 1587; Ivry, 1590; Tournhout, 1597; Nieuport, 1600; Ostend, 1601–4; Sablat, 1619; Fleurus, 1622; Dessau and Lutter, 1626; La Rochelle, 1627; 1st Breitenfeld, 1631; Alte Veste and Leipzig, 1632; Nordlingen, 1634; Breda, 1637; Rheinfelden, 1638; 2nd Breitenfeld, 1642; Rocroi, 1643; Freiburg, 1644; Mergentheim, 1645; Lens, 1648
1601–1700	Russia, Poland, Sweden, Turkey and Austria-Hungary	Eastern Europe	Kircholm, 1604; Balkhov, 1608; Klushino and Moscow, 1610; Cecora, 1620; Smolensk, 1633; Riga, 1656; Konotop, 1659; Raab River, 1664; Vienna, 1683
1635–59	France v. Spain	Western Europe	See religious wars above, until 1648; Dunes, 1658
1640–51	British Civil War	United Kingdom	Edgehill, 1642; York, Marston Moor, Tippermuir and Newbury, 1644; Kilsyth and Philiphaugh, Leicester and Naseby, 1645; Preston, 1648; Rathmines and Irish sieges, 1649; Dunbar, 1650; Worcester, 1651
1648–53	French Civil War	France	Champ Blanc, 1650; St. Antoine, 1652
1667–1714	France v. Holland, Britain and Habsburg Spanish adherents	Western Europe	Maestricht, 1673; Senef, Sinsheim, Enzheim and Turckheim, 1674; Messina, 1676; Chiari, 1701; Liège, 1702; Blenheim, 1704; Gibraltar, 1705; Ramillies and Turin, 1706; Almanza and Toulouse, 1707; Oudenarde and Lille, 1708; Mons and Malplaquet, 1709; Denain, 1712; Barcelona, 1714
1700–39	Russia, Sweden, Poland, Denmark and Turkey, with French involvement	Northern and Eastern Europe	Narva, 1700; Kliszow, 1702; Franstadt, 1706; Holowczyn, 1708; Poltava, 1709; Moldavia, 1711; Toningen, 1713; Parma, 1734; Bitonto, 1735; Nish, 1737; Kroszka, 1738; Khotin, 1739
1709–47	Persia v. Afghanistan, Turkey, Russia and India	Middle East, India and Afghanistan	Kandahar, 1711; Herat, 1719; Gulnabad, 1722; Zarghan, 1730; Hamadan, 1731; Karkuk and Leilan, 1732; Baghavand, 1735; Karnal, 1739; Kars, 1745
1740–63	Prussia (with allies) v. Austria (with allies)	Central Europe and Scotland	Mollwitz, 1741; Chotusitz, 1742; Dettingen, 1743; Amberg, Fontenoy, Hohenfriedberg, Sohr, Kesselsdorf and Prestonpans, 1745; Culloden, 1746; Lobositz, 1756; Prague, Rossbach and Leuthen, 1757; Zorndorf and Hochkirk, 1758; Minden and Kunersdorf, 1759; Warburg, Liegnitz and Torgau, 1760; Burkesdorf and Freiburg, 1762
1754–63	Britain v. France	North America and India	Monongahela, 1755; Fort William Henry and Plassey, 1757; Fort Ticonderoga, 1758; Plains of Abraham, 1759

Period	Major combatants	Main localities	Major associated battles and sieges
AD			
1775–83	Britain v. Americans with France and Spain.	North America	Lexington, Boston and Bunker Hill, 1775; Long Island, White Plains and Trenton, 1776; Princeton, Ticonderoga, Saratoga and Brandywine, 1777; Monmouth, 1778; Savannah, 1779; Camden and King's Mountain, 1780; Cowpens and Yorktown, 1781
1792–1815	France v. all neighbours	Europe and Middle East	Valmy and Jemappes, 1792; Wattignies and Toulon, 1793; Fleurus, 1794; Quiberon, 1795; Friedberg, Wurzburg, Momenotte, Lodi, Mantua and Arcola, 1796; Rivoli, Lahn, 1797; Pyramids and Acre, 1798; Stockbach, Cassano, Trebbia, Aboukir, Novi, Castricum, Zurich and Genoa, 1799; Marengo and Hohenlinden, 1800; Aboukir, 1801; Ulm and Austerlitz, 1805; Jena-Auerstadt, 1806; Eylau, Danzig and Friedland, 1807; Saragossa, Baylen and Vimiero, 1808; Corunna, Abensberg, Landeshut, Eggmuhl, Ratisbon, Aspern-Essling, Wagram, Talavera and Ocana, 1809; Cadiz, Bussaco and Torres Vedras, 1810; Fuentes de Onoro and Albuera, 1811; Ciudad Rodrigo, Badajoz, Salamanca, Smolensk, Borodino, Krasnoi, Burgos and Beresina, 1812; Lutzen, Bautzen, Vittoria, Sorauren, Dresden, Kulm, Leipzig and Hanau, 1813; Orthez, Laon, Rheims, Paris and Toulouse, 1814; Ligny, Quatre-Bras and Waterloo, 1815
1812–15	Britain v. U.S.A.	North America	Detroit and Queenston, 1812; Fort George, Detroit, and Chrysler's Farm, 1813; Chippewa, Lundy's Lane, Bladensburg, Plattsburg and Baltimore, 1814; New Orleans, 1815
1818–61	U.S.A. v. American Indians, Spain and Mexico	North America	Florida, 1818; Alamo and San Jacinto, 1836; Monterrey, 1846; Buena Vista, Churubusco, Molino del Rey, and Chapultepec, 1847; numerous Indian encounters throughout the period
1848–49	National revolts	Europe	Paris, Schleswig-Holstein, Berlin, Milan, Custoza and Vienna, 1848; Rome, Novara, Venice, Kapolna and Temesvar, 1849
1853–56	Britain, France and Turkey v. Russia	Baltic and Black Sea areas	Oltenitza, 1853; Alma, Balaclava and Inkerman, 1854; Sevastopol and the Traktir, 1855
1857–58	Britain v. Indians	India	Cawnpore, Delhi and Lucknow, 1857; Gwalior, 1858
1859	France v. Austria	Piedmont	Palestro, Magenta and Solferino, 1859

Period	Major combatants	Main localities	Major associated battles and sieges
AD			
1861–65	U.S. Federals v. Confederates	North America	1st Bull Run, 1861; Winchester, Yorktown, Shiloh, Fair Oaks, Seven Days, 2nd Bull Run, Antietam, Corinth, Prairie Grove, Fredericksburg and Murfreesboro, 1862; Chancellorsville, Vicksburg, Gettysburg, Chickamauga, Chattanooga, Lookout Mountain and Missionary Ridge, 1863; Wilderness, Spotsylvania, Cold Harbor, Petersburg, Tupelo, Kenesaw Mountain, Atlanta and Nashville, 1864; Bentonville, Fort Stedman, Selma, Dinwiddie Court-house, Petersburg and Appomattox, 1865
1864–71	Prussia v. Denmark, Austria and France	Europe	Dybbol, 1864; Langensalza and Sadowa, 1866; Weissenburg, Fröschwiller, Spicheren, Mars-la-Tour, Gravelotte-St. Privat, Metz, Sedan, Paris and Orleans, 1870; St. Quentin, Le Mans, Strasbourg and Belfort, 1871
1881–1902	Britain v. Boers	South Africa	Laing's Neck and Majuba Hill, 1881; Krugersdorp, 1896; Modder River, Stromberg, Magersfontein and Colenso, 1899; Kimberley, Paardeberg, Ladysmith and Mafeking, 1900
1876–1913	Turkey v. Serbia, Russia, Bulgaria, Italy and Greece	South-east Europe and North Africa	Djunis, 1876; Plevna and Aladja Dagh, 1877; Senova, 1878; Tripoli, 1911; Derna, Monastir, Lule Burgas, Istanbul and Salonika, 1912; Yannina, Adrianople and Struma Valley, 1913.
1904–5	Japan v. Russia	Korea and Manchuria	Port Arthur, Yalu River, Telissu, Moteinlung River, Liaoyang and Sha-Ho, 1904; Sandepu and Mukden, 1905
1914–16	Germany, Austria-Hungary, Bulgaria and Turkey v. France, Belgium, Russia, Britain, Serbia, Italy, Rumania, Japan and Portugal	West and south Europe	*West and southern fronts:* Battle of Frontiers; Liège, Mons, Le Cateau, Guise, 1st Serbia, Marne, Aisne, Antwerp, 1st Arras, 1st Ypres; 2nd Serbia, 1914; Neuve Chapelle, 2nd Ypres, 1st Vimy Ridge, Isonzo, Champagne, 2nd Vimy and Loos, Serbia, 1915; Salonika, Verdun, Isonzo, Trentino, Somme, Florina and Ancre, 1916
		East Europe and Middle East	*East Front:* Tannenberg, Lemberg, 1st and 2nd Warsaw, Lodz and Sarikamish, 1914; Qrna, Suez, Masuria, Przemsyl, Gallipoli, Gorlice, Warsaw, Sulva Bay, Kut and Ctesiphon, 1915; Erzerum, Kut, Lake Narotch, Galicia, Arges River, Bucharest, 1916
1917–18	Germany, Austria-Hungary, Bulgaria and Turkey v. France, Russia, Britain, Belgium, Italy, Rumania, Greece, Japan, Portugal, China and U.S.A.	West, east and south Europe	*West and southern fronts:* Arras, Chemin des Dames, Messines, 3rd Ypres, Isonzo, Riga, Caporetto, Piave and Cambrai, 1917; Picardy, Flanders, Chemin des Dames, 2nd Marne, Ourcq, Amiens, Albert, Drocourt-Quéant, the Varda, St. Mihiel, Meuse-Argonne, Hindenburg Line and Vittorio Veneto, 1918

Period	Major combatants	Main localities	Major associated battles and sieges

AD

1917–19 continued | | | *East Front:* 2nd Kut, Baghdad, 1st and 2nd Gaza, Galicia, Riga, 3rd Gaza and Ramadi, 1917; Baku, Megiddo, 1918

1917–22	Russian Civil War (with intervention by many other nations)	Russia, Baltic States and Poland	Kiev, Denikin offensive and Caucasus, 1919; Wrangel offensive, 1920; a plethora of guerilla actions over the length and breadth of the area
1919	Afghanistan v. Britain	North-West Frontier of India	Bagh, Khyber Pass and Kabul, 1919
1920	Russia v. Poland	Poland	Kiev and Warsaw, 1920
1920–22	Turkey v. Greece	South-east Europe and Asia Minor	Inonu and Sakkaria, 1921; Bursa and Smyrna, 1922
1925–49	Chinese Imbroglio (with interventions by European nations, Japan and U.S.A.)	China	Wuch'ang, 1926; Shanghai, Canton and Lungtang, 1927; Tsinan, 1928; anti-Communist campaigns 1930–37, 1st Shanghai, 1932; 2nd Shanghai and Pinghsinkuan, 1937; Taierchwang, Chengchow and Canton, 1938; Hainan and Changteh, 1943; Hengyang and Japanese "rice offensive", 1944; Japanese anti-air base offensives, Russian invasion of Manchuria and Communist offensives, 1945; Mukden and River Sungari, 1946; Yenan River, Sungari, Szeping and Liaosi Corridor, 1947; Shensi, Yellow River, Mukden and Hwai Hai, 1948; Peking, Yangtze River and Sian, 1949
1935–36	Italy v. Abyssinia	Abyssinia	Adowa and Hara, 1935; Addis Ababa, 1936
1936–39	Spanish Civil War (with Russian v. German-Italian intervention)	Spain	Esquivas and Madrid, 1936; Guadalajara, Bilbao, Aragon and Teruel, 1937; Ebro and Catalonia, 1938; Barcelona, Madrid and Valencia, 1939
1938–39	Japan v. Russia	Manchuria, Korea and and Siberia	Changkufeng Hill, 1938; Khalkin River, 1939
1939–Dec. 1941	Germany, Italy, Finland, Hungary Rumania and Bulgaria v. Poland, Britain, France, Norway, Belgium, Holland, Greece, Yugoslavia and Russia	Europe, North Africa and Middle East	Battle of Polish Frontiers, River Bzura, Warsaw and Finland, 1939; Suoussalmi, Mannerheim Line, Oslo, Narvik, Trondheim, north Holland, Eban-Emael, Gembloux, Sedan, Arras, Abbeville, Dunkirk, Somme, 1st Cyrenaica, Somaliland and Koritza, 1940; Beda Fomm, Somaliland, Eritrea, Abyssinia, 2nd Cyrenaica, Tobruk, Yugoslavia, Greece, Crete, invasion of Russia, Minsk, Smolensk, Kiev, Leningrad, Moscow, Rostov and 3rd Cyrenaica, 1941

Period	Major combatants	Main localities	Major associated battles and sieges
AD			
1941–45	Germany and Allies v. British, Russia and Allies with U.S.A.	Europe, North Africa	4th Cyrenaica, Russian counter-offensive, Kersh, Sevastopol, Gazala, Tobruk, Voronezh, Don River, 1st Alamein, Caucasus, Stalingrad, Alam Halfa, 2nd Alamein, Casablanca, Oran, Algiers, and Medjerda Valley, 1942; Kasserine, drive to the Don, Kharkov, Mareth Line, Akarit, Tunis, Bizerta, Kursk, Sicily, Salerno, Smolensk, Kiev and Volturno River, 1943; Leningrad, Anzio, Korsun, Cassino, Rome, Normandy, Mannerheim Line, Belorussia, Falaise, drives through France and Belgium, Warsaw, drive through Baltic States, drive into the Balkans and Hungary, Arnhem, Gothic Line and Ardennes, 1944; Rhineland, Danube Valley, Oder River, Rhine crossings, conquest of Italy and Germany, 1945
1941–45	Japan v. U.S.A., Britain and Holland, China and Russia	Pacific, Indian Ocean and East Asia	Hong Kong, Wake Island, Bataan and Malaya, 1941; Singapore, Sittang River, Toungoo, Lashio, Mandalay, Corregidor, Java, New Guinea, Madagascar, Guadalcanal and 1st Arakan, 1942, New Guinea, New Britain, Solomon Islands and Tarawa, 1943; Arakan, Marshall Islands, Hollandia, Japanese offensive in China, Indian-Burma frontier, Myitkyrina, Marianas, Leyte and Chindwin River 1944, Luzon, Meiktila, Iwo Jima, Okinawa, Corregidor and Rangoon, 1945
1946–73	France and anti-Communists with U.S.A. v Communists and North Vietnamese	South-East Asia	Hue, 1947; Fort Caobang, 1950; Dien Bien Phu, 1953; Direct U.S. military involvement 1961–72, Tet offensive, 1967; Cambodia 1970
1946–49	Greek Civil War	Greece	Border war, 1946; Konitsa and Mount Grammos, 1948
1947–72	India v. Pakistan	India, Pakistan and Kashmir	Kashmir war 1947; Punjab and Kashmir, 1967; Punjab, Kashmir and East Pakistan, 1972
1948–	Israel v. Arab States (with interventions by Britain and France)	Middle East	Jerusalem, Tel Aviv and Nazareth, 1948, Sinai and Suez, 1956; Sinai, Syria and Jordan, 1967
1950–53	North Korea and China v. United Nations	Korea	Taejon, Pusan Bridgehead, Inchon, Kunu-ri and Chosin Reservoir, 1950; Seoul and spring offensives, 1951

Appendix 3

MILITARY ENGINEERING

Engineers were the first specially trained soldiers to be found in the order of battle. Their date of origin is unknown but it is definite that they were, at first, very few in proportion to the size of armies though of fundamental importance to the survival of soldiers at war. Probably **the first tasks** allocated to military engineers were the construction of simple fortifications such as barricades and walls. Thus **the first members of an élite** were the most skilled tradesmen of their day—the carpenters, masons and metal-workers whose knowledge of materials was unique in society.

The construction of chariots, siege-engines, bridges and river-crossing devices was the responsibility of military engineers. Indeed, as armies began to acquire more complex weapons and also came to depend heavily upon walled forts in defence, as opposed to earthworks, it became the engineers' prime task to direct the unskilled or semi-skilled labour forces. Hittites, Egyptians, Assyrians and Persians possessed fine engineers. Alexander's army included a corps of engineers who directed his infantrymen and civil labourers in cutting and transporting timber from which ballistae and catapults were constructed adjacent to the battlefield. The Romans employed a similar system and spread their knowledge throughout the world of their conquests. Until the advent of artillery, military engineers were the only technically trained soldiers to be found in any army—and were recognised as such by higher pay and better treatment. In the English Army of 1346, engineers were paid 6*d*. a day or more compared with 3*d*. for the invaluable foot-archers.

The greatest monuments to the skill of pre-artillery military engineers, are the stone-built residential castles to be found throughout the world—from the towers of the Great Wall of China to the medieval forts of Europe. These forts gradually assumed a fairly standard pattern. The diagram shows one of the most comprehensive layouts along with the names given to each essential part.

The advent of artillery compelled the military engineer to share duties with a new generation of technicians—the gunners or artillerists. Nevertheless artillerists, whose activities doomed vertical walled castles, provoked engineers into devising an entirely new generation of specialised fortified works such as would resist the latest methods of destruction. Evolution was dominated by the organisation and thoughts of the most distinguished military engineer ever—Vauban. Not only did Vauban raise the art of fortification and siege warfare to a science but he also created in France, in 1690, the **first modern corps of engineers,** giving it officer status and a formal training in his methods. Copies of Vauban's star-shaped master-works are to be found throughout the world, particularly in Europe. As can be seen from the diagram on page 76, he introduced a totally new system and a fresh terminology. But though sieges became more difficult to prosecute they were far from irresistible. Engineers, along with artillerymen, were to the forefront in siege operations, modifying the methods of tunnelling and battering until the breaching system described on page 75 evolved. Thus engineers became integrated with assault infantry, even though, in some armies (particularly the German), there was resistance to suggestions that they might be classified as more than technicians—a word implying low caste among fighting men.

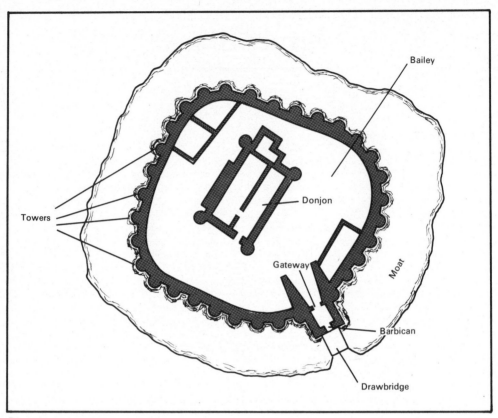

Plan of a Norman fort

It was inevitable that engineers should operate nearly every new device (except artillery) which entered service: as map-making improved they became engaged in survey; when the telegraph was introduced, engineers laid cable and operated the system; in many armies they were given the job of operating balloons and then the first flying machines. It was military engineers who founded the signal, air and tank corps in many armies. The handling of gas, in the first instance, also fell to engineer troops, except when projection was by the artillery, and in some armies remains an engineer responsibility to this day.

In peacetime, engineer corps found employment in a variety of works —from a military angle largely concerned with the design and preparation of fortifications but also in a civil capacity of road-making, land drainage and the like. The vast expansion and increase in the dimensions of forts after 1860 naturally threw a heavy load upon engineer corps. The greater complexity of the new-style armoured defences of the 1890s, the gigantic forts of the First World War and then the ultimate colossi, as represented by the Maginot Line of the 1930s, threw redoubled demands upon the ingenuity and resource of engineers, not only in the art of construction but in the knack of persuading governments to expend vast sums of money on such projects. Military engineers became influential members of a technological society as being among the most diverse of technicians; whose services were in demand from all walks of life; their graduates rose high in civil employment with monotonous and well-merited regularity. At the same time the military engineer became realistically pampered in battle and sometimes forbidden to expose himself to undue combat risks because his skills were in short supply.

Forts of the Maginot kind, of course, forfeited their value in the French débâcle of 1940, but this did not mean that military engineers became redundant overnight; quite the reverse, in fact. For mechanised war created a colossal demand for all sorts of engineering works in support of the new mobility—the construction of roads and base installations, the removal or crossing of obstacles and the laying or clearing of mines and demolitions being but a few of the tasks imposed. It is to be noted, however, that although large numbers of engineers were employed (nearly 300,000 in 1918 and 700,000 in 1945) in the U.S. Army—the proportion in the U.S. Army to other troops fell from 12 per cent in the First World War to 8 per cent in the Second—figures which reflected the increased use of mechanical tools and plant in place of muscle power. This is a continuing trend. The engineering works carried out by the U.S. Army engineers in Vietnam have been distinguished by the massive use of plant to build installations—above all roads and airfields—at great pace with a relatively low labour outlay.

In the final analysis no military force gets far without its engineers who were first among educated soldiers and remain to this day among the élite of every well-founded army.

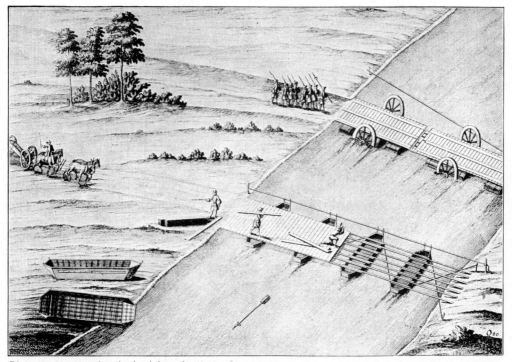

River-crossing operations in the eighteenth century

Select Bibliography

The bibliography of books about war is so enormous as to be uncountable and therefore cannot possibly be published in entirety even if it were desirable to do so. I have made reference to a great many books besides original material and have visited several of the battlegrounds described. For guide-lines reference has frequently been made to three admirable encyclopedias—*Encyclopedia Britannica*, Singer's *History of Technology* and the Dupuy's *Encyclopedia of Military History*. In addition reference has been made to relevant articles in *History Today*. The list below is selected with a view to advancing the reader's awareness and to introduce them to key works on the subject without delving among the plethora of regimental histories, special campaign accounts and personal narratives which lie, of course, at the core of war's story. Nor are official histories recorded; most nations produce their own and all merit examination.

Andrzejewski, S. *Military Organisation and Society* (1954).

Anon *The Reign of George VI* (1763).

Anon *The Invasion of England* (1803).

Arrianus (tr. de Sélincourt). *The Life of Alexander the Great* (170).

Bidwell, S. *Gunners at War* (1970).

Blackett, P. *Studies of War, Nuclear and Conventional* (1962).

Bloch, I. *The Future of War: Is War now Impossible?* (1898).

Bonnal, H. *Sadowa* (1907).

Bradley, J. *Allied Intervention in Russia, 1917–20* (1968).

Burne, A. *The Crécy War* (1955).

Caesar, Julius. *Commentaries* (50 BC).

Catton, B. *Centennial History of the (U.S.) Civil War* (3 vols. 1965).

Carlyle, T. (ed. A. Hughes). *History of Frederick II of Prussia* (1916).

Chandler, D. *The Campaigns of Napoleon* (1966).

Chandler, D. *The Battlefields of Europe* (2 vols. 1965).

Chesney, G. *The Battle of Dorking* (1871).

Churchill, W. S. *The World Crisis* (6 vols. 1932).

Churchill, W. S. *The Second World War* (6 vols. 1948–53).

Churchill, W. S. *Marlborough, His Life and Times.* (1933).

Clausewitz, K. von. *On War* (1835).

Clark, A. *Barbarossa, the Russian-German Conflict 1941–45* (1965).

Clarke, I. F. *Voices Prophesying War 1763–1984* (1966).

Cruttwell, C. *A History of the Great War* (1934).

Dayan, M. *Diary of the Sinai Campaign* (1967).

De La Gorce, P. M. *The French Army* (1963).

Delbrück, H. *Geschichte der Kriegskunst* (1920).

Dixon, C. and Heilbrunn, O. *Communist Guerilla Warfare* (1954).

Douhet, G. *Command of the Air* (1921).

Earle, E. *Makers of Modern Strategy* (1943).

Eggenberger, D. *A Dictionary of Battles* (1967).

Einhard (tr. L. Thorpe). *The Life of Charlemagne* (1970).

Eisenhower, D. *Crusade in Europe* (1948).

Featherstone, D. *The Bowmen of England* (1967).

Fortescue, J. *A History of the British Army* (1899).

Frederick the Great (tr. Phillips). *Military Instructions for the Generals* (1747).

Fuller, J. F. C. *The Decisive Battles of the Western World* (3 vols. 1956).

Fuller, J. F. C. *Memoirs of an Unconventional Soldier* (1936).

Fuller, J. F. C. *Lectures on FSR III* (1932).

Garthoff, R. *Soviet Military Doctrine* (1953).

Gibbon, E. *Decline and Fall of the Roman Empire* (1776).

Goerlitz, W. *History of the German General Staff 1857–1945* (1953).

Grousset, R. *Conqueror of the World. The Life of Genghis Khan* (1966).

Guderian, H. *Panzer Leader* (1952).

Guibert, J. *Essai général de tactique* (1772).

Guibert, J. *Défense du système de guerre moderne* (1779).

Hackett, J. *The Profession of Arms* (1962).

Halder, F. *Hitler as War Lord* (1950).

Heilbrunn, O. *Partisan Warfare* (1962).

Herodotus (tr. Cavander). *The Struggle for Greece* (430 BC).

Heymann, F. *John Zizka and the Hussite Revolution* (1955).

Hodson, H. V. *The Great Divide. Britain-India-Pakistan* (1969).

Hoffman, M. *The War of Lost Opportunities* (1925).

Howard, M. *The Franco-Prussian War* (1962).
Jackson, W. G. F. *Attack in the West* (1953).
Jomini, A. *Précis de l'art de la guerre* (2 vols., 1838).
Kahn, D. *The Codebreakers* (1966).
Kitson, F. *Low-level Operations* (1972).
Lawrence, T. *The Seven Pillars of Wisdom* (1926).
Lewin, R. *Rommel* (1968).
Liddell Hart, B. *The Decisive Wars of History* (1929).
Liddell Hart, B. *A History of the World War 1914–1918* (1930).
Liddell Hart, B. *The Tanks* (2 vols., 1959).
Los Alamos. *The Effect of Atomic Weapons* (1950).
Ludendorff, E. *Memories* (1920).
Luttwak, E. *A Dictionary of Modern War* (1971).
MacArthur, D. *Reminiscences* (1964).
MacDonald, C. *The Mighty Endeavour* (1969).
Machiavelli, N. *On The Art of War* (1520).
Mackintosh, M. *Juggernaut* (1967).
Macksey, K. *Guinness Book of Tank Facts and Feats* (1972).
Mao Tse-tung. *On Guerilla Warfare* (1937).
Marko, A. *Ungarisches Soldatentum, 895-1914* (1951).
Marshall, G. *War Reports* (1947).
Marshall, S. *Men against Fire* (1947).
Marx, K. *Capital*
Montgomery, B. *The Art of War* (1969).
Napoleon (tr. T. Phillips). *Maxims* (1827).
Nef, J. *War and Human Progress* (1950).
Ogorkiewicz, R. *Armour* (1960).
Oman, C. *A History of the Art of War in the Middle Ages* (1924).
Oman, C. *A History of the Art of War in the Sixteenth Century* (1937).
Parker, H. *The Roman Legions* (1959).

Pergamon Press. *European Resistance Movements 1939–45* (1964).
Phillips, T. *The Roots of Strategy* (1943).
Plutarch (tr. I. Scott-Kilvert). *The Rise and Fall of Athens* (1960).
Purnell's (ed. B. Pitt). *History of the First World War* (1969).
Purnell's (ed. B. Pitt). *History of the Second World War* (1966).
Rhodes James, R. *Gallipoli* (1965).
Safran, N. *From War to War: the Arab-Israeli confrontation 1948–1967* (1969).
Saunders, J. *The History of the Mongol Conquerors* (1971).
Saxe, M. de *My reveries upon the Art of War* (1757).
Seaton, A. *The Russo-German War 1941–1945* (1971).
Slessor, J. *Strategy for the West* (1954).
Slim, W. *Defeat into Victory* (1956).
Smith, A. *The Wealth of Nations* (1776).
Suetonius (tr. R. Graves). *The Twelve Caesars* (1957).
Sun Tzu (tr. T. Phillips). *The Art of War* (?500 BC).
Teveth, S. *The Tanks of Tammuz* (1968).
Toy, S. *A History of Fortification 300 BC–AD 1700* (1955).
Toynbee, A. *A Study of History (2 vols., 1957).*
Vegetius, F. (tr. J. Clarke). *De Re Militari* (?385).
Wavell, A. *The Palestine Campaign* (1929).
Wedgwood, C. V. *The Thirty Years War* (1938).
Wheeler-Bennett, J. *The Nemesis of power* (1953).
Wilkinson, F. *Antique Firearms* (1969).
Wilkinson, F. *Edged Weapons* (1970).
Wilkinson, F. (with M. Windrow). *The Universal Soldier* (1971).
Wilmot, C. *The Struggle for Europe* (1952).
Zhukov, G. (ed. H. Salisbury). *Marshal Zhukov's Great Battles* (1969).

Index

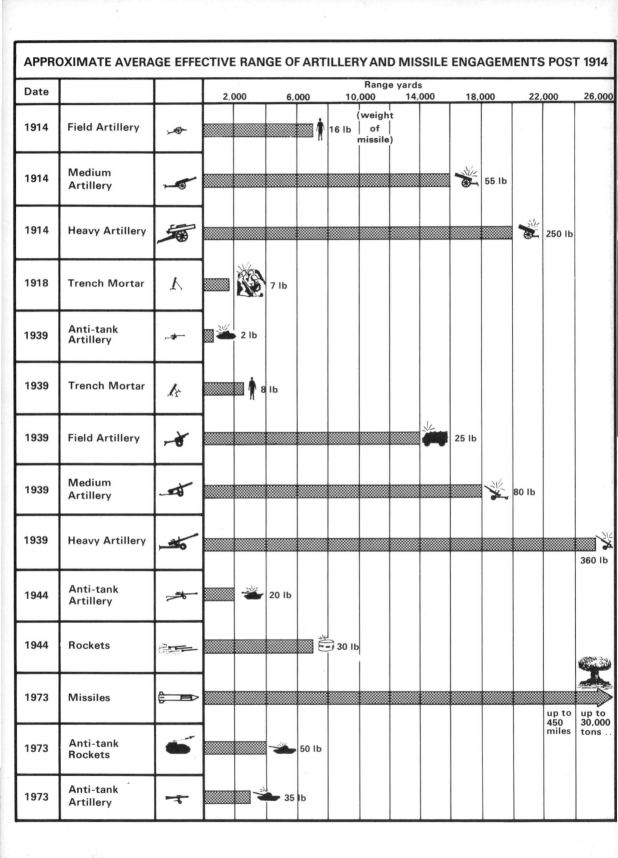

APPROXIMATE AVERAGE EFFECTIVE RANGE OF ARTILLERY AND MISSILE ENGAGEMENTS POST 1914

Date			Range yards					
			2,000	6,000	10,000	14,000	18,000	22,000	26,000
1914	Field Artillery		16 lb (weight of missile)					
1914	Medium Artillery		55 lb					
1914	Heavy Artillery		250 lb					
1918	Trench Mortar		7 lb					
1939	Anti-tank Artillery		2 lb					
1939	Trench Mortar		8 lb					
1939	Field Artillery		25 lb					
1939	Medium Artillery		80 lb					
1939	Heavy Artillery		360 lb					
1944	Anti-tank Artillery		20 lb					
1944	Rockets		30 lb					
1973	Missiles		up to 450 miles / up to 30,000 tons					
1973	Anti-tank Rockets		50 lb					
1973	Anti-tank Artillery		35 lb					